SACRED EARTH,
SACRED STONES

SACRED EARTH, SACRED STONES

BRIAN LEIGH MOLYNEAUX

AND PIERS VITEBSKY

DUNCAN BAIRD PUBLISHERS

First published in the United Kingdom and Ireland in 2001 by
Duncan Baird Publishers
Sixth Floor, Castle House
75–76 Wells Street
London W1T 3QH

Conceived, created and designed by Duncan Baird Publishers.

Copyright © 2000 by Duncan Baird Publishers
Text copyright © 2000 by Duncan Baird Publishers, Piers Vitebsky
and Caroline Humphrey
For prelim captions and copyright of photographs see page 256,
which is to be regarded as an extension of this copyright.

Managing Editor: Christopher Westhorp
Designer: Clare Thorpe
Picture research: Emily Stone
Commissioned artwork: Line + Line, Jennifer Dent

British Library Cataloguing-in-Publication Data:
A catalogue record for this book is available from the
British Library

ISBN 1–903296–07–2

1 3 5 7 9 10 8 6 4 2

Typeset in Sabon and Apollo
Colour reproduction by Colourscan, Singapore
Printed in China by Imago

NOTE: The abbreviations BCE and CE are used throughout this book:
BCE Before the Common Era (the equivalent of BC)
CE Common Era (the equivalent of AD)

Contents

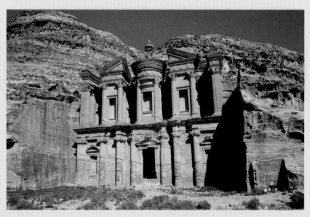

Introduction

Since prehistoric times humankind, in many cultural guises throughout the world, has had a dynamic relationship with the Earth as a living, nurturing body, a sacred source of vitality. Images and materials of the Earth have been used to make sense of life. The Aboriginal peoples of Australia have drawn the landscape into a complex system of interconnecting social and religious beliefs, informed by the idea of the Dreaming—the time beyond memory when ancestral beings roamed the land and formed its features. Elsewhere (in the Shinto beliefs of Japan, for example), rocks, trees, rivers, and other aspects of the natural world have been seen as deeply invested with spirit life, perhaps as a way to account for the teeming otherness of natural phenomena. Additionally, many belief systems accommodate a view of the Earth and its flora and fauna as material for the myth-making impulse, whose function may be interpreted as a means of coming to terms with the mysteries of birth, life, and death, and other fundamental human experiences.

For centuries humans have expressed their yearnings for the divine by practicing different religions and by developing sacred architecture, creating special spaces in which to make powerful and precious contact with the divine. We are accustomed to thinking of magnificent temples, cathedrals, and mosques that are built to last and clearly reflect human longings for eternity. But in nature permanence is often expressed through death and renewal, and in the human world an everlasting presence can also be established through the periodic destruction and

RIGHT *An archway of a ruined temple on Peru's Taquile Island in Lake Titicaca. It is believed that the creator god Viracocha emerged from this sacred lake, and that the Sun and Moon first cast their light from near here.*

reerection of temporary structures, such as wooden Shinto shrines at Ise in Japan (see pages 154–155), or certain Mesoamerican temples that seem to have been rebuilt after every fifty-two-year calendar cycle. However long they were intended to last, the erection of such buildings reflects a universal human concern. Furthermore, a building's sacredness lies not in any idea of permanence, but in the concentration of sacredness that it embodies or makes possible.

Since the rise of Newtonian science in the West, the balanced relationship between humankind and the natural world has come under threat. Global warming and deforestation are planetary causes célèbres. In a scientific context, the new conservationist picture of nature's infinite variety is encapsulated by the term "biodiversity." Yet alongside the scientific defense of the planet there is currently a broad movement of sympathy for the ancient wisdoms of a range of cultures, from the astronomical preoccupations of Mesoamerica to the shamanistic beliefs of the Amazon basin, Siberia, and the Arctic. In a sense this movement reverses the orthodox position of popular Western thinking with regard to science and the supernatural: science becomes the object of skepticism, while mysteries ("Earth mysteries," in the fashionable idiom) acquire new credibility. These tendencies have inspired a quest for understanding such enigmas as the prehistoric stone monuments of Britain, the Paleolithic cave paintings of southern France and northern Spain, and the medicine wheels of the Great Plains of North America.

No longer do we elevate inventiveness to quasi-divine status or celebrate technology as a benefit in itself. Increasingly we attach greater importance to a true sense of our place in the scheme of things, and this has recently become a theme of the new science, with its emphasis on time and cosmic origins, and the dizzying paradoxes of the Uncertainty Principle.

Technology has alienated many billions of people from the natural world by distancing them from basic resources: electricity reaches us through a wire, food comes to us packaged. Such separation has made it hard for people to appreciate the influence of nature on their lives. However, it has been argued that religions, just as much as science, have played a part in skewing the relationship between humankind and the natural world. The supposed displacement of an ancient, universal, and nurturing mother (nature) goddess by male sky gods (symbolized by Apollo's victory over the serpent Python at Delphi, the navel of the world) has been used as an argument in the feminist attack on patriarchal societies. An oft-repeated extension of this argument is that the most influential religions of the historical era have contributed to the process by focusing on a single, supreme sky god, separate from creation.

At a more secular level, the landscape is widely seen in the West as having a calming influence, correcting urban perspectives and adjusting our eyes to the long view. Walking, a simple and universal activity, reintroduces us to old rhythms and expectations far removed from those of the fast-paced modern world. Most of us find that we benefit from the experience in some way. A more profound and more challenging adjustment comes about when we look in a spirit of intelligent open-minded inquiry at the sacred meanings given to the landscape by various cultures now foreign to us in time or space. The mysteries of the Earth are transmitted in images, structures, texts, and oral traditions that enshrine a wealth of myths, rituals, and religious beliefs. Approaching these sources we feel our imagination open up under the influence of ideas that will always lie just beyond the reach of the intellect—profound ideas to which we are tempted to apply the term "truths" because they move us to champion their instinctual validity. Engaging with them, we feel ourselves invigorated and refreshed.

RIGHT *Reaching toward the skies, Al-Malwiyah, near Samarra in what is now Iraq, is a 9th-century minaret. It is based on the stepped tower of ancient Sumer known as a ziggurat, viewed as a ladder linking Heaven and Earth.*

Where Gods and Heroes Walked

Earlier peoples were closer, emotionally and spiritually, in most respects to their surroundings than the inhabitants of postindustrial societies are today. Mostly animists, they believed supernatural forces were present, hidden, all around them. Numinous powers, that existed for good and bad, resonated throughout the many features of the landscape.

This remains true of indigenous peoples in many places today. Even in western Europe the Roman writer Tacitus observed long ago of the tribes he encountered that they did not consider it respectful to create human images of gods and confine them in temples, but instead revered their hidden presence in woods and groves.

This natural yet sacred world also served as a stage for the great myths and epics of humankind's many diverse cultures, tales which reinforced a people's sense of identity and place. The sites of past heroic deeds could be pointed out to new generations, strengthening their bonds with, and sense of belonging to, their own familiar landscape.

RIGHT *The unusual basalt rocks at Giant's Causeway, County Antrim, northeastern Ireland, were said to have been built by Finn mac Cumhaill (or Fingal), the Celtic hero of gigantic stature, to serve as part of a crossing linking Ireland to Scotland.*

EARTH AND CREATION

Scientists explain the origin of our planet and the universe by referring to a massive explosion that tore through a featureless void many billions of years ago. According to the myths of the ancient storytellers, however, the existence of the Earth is a consequence of actions and motivations that are often distinctly human in character.

In many of the world's mythologies a primal goddess is cited as the source of creation. According to the poet Hesiod's *Theogony*, written in ancient Greece in the eighth century BCE, the Earth Mother, Gaia, was one of the five original elements—alongside Tartarus, the underworld; Erebus, the gloom of the underworld; Eros, the force of love; and Nyx, the power of darkness—to emerge from the enormous, shapeless darkness he called *chaos* ("a yawning void"). Nyx mated with Erebus and gave birth to Day and Aether, the pure upper atmosphere, as well as many of humankind's evils such as Doom and Death. Gaia was described as not only the physical body of Earth, but also its essence and power. Gaia, unpartnered, produced Uranus, the starry sky; the mountains; and Pontus, the personification of the sea. Gaia then lay with Uranus and Pontus to bring forth the twelve Titans, the first gods and goddesses.

Many centuries earlier in the Akkadian creation stories in the *Enuma Elish* (*c*.1750 BCE), Tiamat, the saltwater ocean, is represented as a primordial deity by a female dragon-like monster that must be vanquished before the ordered universe can come into existence. Tiamat's grandson Marduk kills her and uses her dismembered body to remake the world she had created in union with the freshwater god Apsu.

Creation is an immensely dramatic act. One myth might tell how the land was forced apart from the sky in a struggle between cosmic giants, such as the Polynesian story of how Tane pushed asunder his parents Rangi the sky god and Papa the Earth goddess. Another might describe how the land was dredged up from the depths of an immense ocean by an animal, as in the many "earthdiver" myths of the Native Americans.

After its initial appearance, the Earth's landscape is radically transformed by the introduction of mountains, chasms, and valleys in the next stage of the monumental task of creation. Among the West African Fon people, this form is said to have been provided by the writhing movements of the giant snake Aido-Hwedo, while the ancient Persian tales explain how ripples of evil irrupted into the cosmos, releasing dynamic, creative rhythms to shape things.

Most creation stories are the prelude to the introduction of human beings, who sometimes emerge from other worlds and sometimes are fashioned by divinities from the very substance of the Earth itself.

A World Created in Sand

In the Shootingway, an important curing ritual of the Navajo people of Arizona and New Mexico in the southwestern United States, the medicine man and those associated with the patient create a sacred sandpainting depicting the figures Father Sky and Mother Earth. Such complex images are in effect a re-creation of the world, designed to restore the patient's physical and spiritual harmony, or *hozho*. The traditional Navajo mud home, the hogan, is emptied of domestic objects and the floor is prepared. The space is consecrated and the task of creating the "painting" with sand, pollens, and powdered charcoal begins. The images represent creators, objects, and events at the beginning of time. The place where humans are said to have emerged is symbolized by a small bowl of water buried in the sand of Mother Earth. After the painting is finished, a thin line of corn pollen is run between the figures. The line represents the sacred route that is believed to be taken by all supernatural beings, and the patient's path to harmony.

ABOVE *Mists rise from a vast, wooded landscape. In prehistoric times the slow return of color and of definition to the world with every sunrise may have stimulated thoughts about the events of creation.*

Forming the Earth

The belief in a world created out of nothingness is found in many different cultures. According to the Hebrew Scriptures, Yahweh simply commanded Heaven and Earth to spring into existence. For the Zuni people of North America it was the great god Awonawilona who brooded on the heavens and made Sun and Earth out of his own essence. Some creators are said to remain active in earthly affairs, while others are believed to have receded into the remote and abstract realms from which they came.

The sexual union of male and female is often a metaphor for creation, as in the Egyptian myth of the sky goddess Nut and the Earth god Geb (see page 15), which is also related to the life-giving waters of the Nile River. Normally the Earth is female, no doubt reflecting the consonance between nature's fecundity and the fertility of women. In a creation myth from the Luiseño people of southern California nothing existed in the beginning except a brother and sister, one above and one below. The brother forced himself on his sister and eventually she gave birth to a quantity of earth and sand—the first solid ground.

Creation is often expressed in terms of a powerful and universal symbol of fertility, the egg. According to a number of Chinese and Japanese accounts, the egg yolk and the albumen that surrounds it represent the Earth floating in the cosmic waters of the heavens. However, the symbolic egg can also restrain the latent energy of creation until it is ready to burst forth. The old supreme god of Tahiti, Tangaroa, is said to have been born in this way, breaking out of his shell to begin his work.

Often creation results from sacrificial death. After separating Earth and sky the Chinese giant Pan Gu lies down and dies, exhausted. His body parts then become the features of the landscape and the skies:

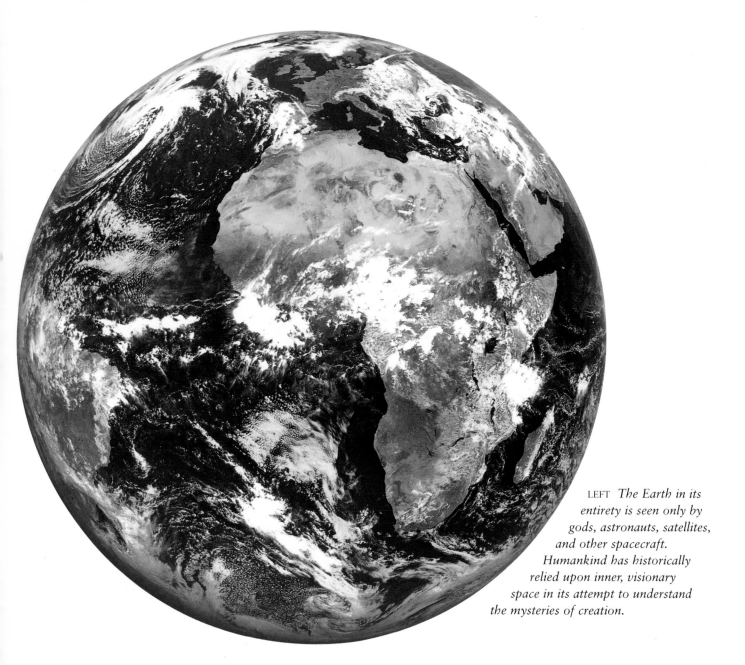

LEFT *The Earth in its entirety is seen only by gods, astronauts, satellites, and other spacecraft. Humankind has historically relied upon inner, visionary space in its attempt to understand the mysteries of creation.*

his tears made rivers, his voice thunder, his breath wind, his eyes formed the Sun and Moon, and his head, hands and feet made five sacred mountains. This elemental thinking also reflects a belief that humans contained the essence, the *prima materia*, of the universe, so that humankind is linked spiritually and physically both to living nature and to the heavens, source of wisdom and understanding. In this philosophy humankind reflects not rules the elements.

Earth, sky, and the cosmos

The skies are commonly viewed as an abode of divinities and cosmic forces that have a direct influence on humans. In ancient Judaic cosmology the firmament was a solid dome pierced by windows, above which was a dome of water and, beyond that, Heaven, the dwelling place of God. The ancient Babylonians also conceived of a three-layered realm of the heavens, and other cultures describe four, seven, or more levels. Parallel worlds, invisible from Earth, are often believed to exist in the skies.

North American Huron and Iroquois myths say that humankind was founded by Ataentsic, a woman who fell to Earth from the upper world through a hole in the sky. In a similar vein, one Navajo myth states that Sky-Reaching Rock, near Mount Taylor, once grew so high that it carried the hero Younger Brother through a sky-hole into the upper world.

According to many mythologies, sky and Earth were joined before being forced apart. The ancient Egyptians told how Shu, the god of air, and Tefenet, the goddess of moisture, copulated to produce the Earth god Geb and the sky goddess Nut. These deities embraced so tightly that there was no room for anything to exist between them. Nut became pregnant, but there was no space for the children to be born, until Shu separated them.

In several traditions the Earth and sky are said to be connected by a cosmic tree with its roots in the underworld and its branches in the skies (see pages 82–84). Some cultures believed that Earth and Heaven were once joined by a rope or bridge that was severed in ancient times owing to human transgression, divine anger, or both.

The sense that humans are subject to the powers of the heavens, the key principle of astrology, is expressed, too, in the baptism rites of many societies —for example, some African and Native American peoples still expose newborns to the Sun and Moon.

The Oracle of the Cosmos

The Baule people of the Ivory Coast sometimes use a "mouse oracle" to solve difficult problems. The oracle is a wooden vessel split into two sections connected by a hole: the upper part is called the sky, the lower part the Earth. The vessel is a model of the cosmos, reflecting the inseparable nature of the sky and Earth gods. The diviner uses a field mouse as a messenger, as the creature is believed to be close to *asye*, the Earth's sacred energy, which comes from the Earth spirit Asye. The mouse is placed in the top section of the box, whereupon it runs through the hole into the lower compartment; the diviner then arranges small bones in a pattern in the upper half, scatters rice to lure the mouse and covers the vessel. After the mouse has eaten the rice and disturbed the bones, the diviner reads the revelation contained in the new pattern formed inside the box.

RIGHT *A stone structure built by the people of the pre-Inca Aymara culture, c.1000–1476CE, at Sillustani, near Lake Titicaca, in what is now Bolivia. Little is known about Aymara religion but this may have been a sacred observatory used by priests of the cult of a sun god. More is understood about the succeeding Inca culture, which elaborated very detailed astronomical beliefs.*

The ancient mother

The belief that the traditional notion of "mother nature" is rooted in a long-forgotten prehistoric religion devoted to the worship of an all-powerful Earth goddess (the Ancient Mother or Great Mother) has attracted many adherents in the Western world

today. The concept appeals both to feminists, because of its inherent antipatriarchal implications, and to ecologists for its suggestion of due respect awarded to nature.

Some scholars have suggested that the first deity was indeed a goddess who was believed to have created the world from herself; that the early religions were dominated by worship of this supreme being; and, by extension, that early societies were therefore matriarchal. This hypothesis is based mainly on the evidence of pre-historic cave paintings, carvings, and the remains of pottery.

ABOVE *Images of spirit totems and the Dog Star, Sirius, were etched centuries ago into this rock near what is now Sante Fe, New Mexico. The night sky fascinated many ancient cultures and it can be deduced today from surviving constructions and imagery that observations, recordings, and measurements were made of the planets and stars many centuries ago. Sirius attracted particular interest because it is the brightest of all the stars seen from Earth and is also visible just before sunrise.*

The carvings, such as the so-called "Venus" discovered at Laussel in the Dordogne, France, and the numerous other "Venus" figurines (see below), suggest that the association between women and fertility, albeit a self-evident one, may actually have been celebrated in Paleolithic times. However, they do not provide conclusive evidence of the existence of an early belief system focused on the worship of an

Earth Mother, and any attempt to extrapolate, as some have done, a matriarchal model for the most ancient societies must remain speculation.

The female statuettes known as "Venus figurines" appeared across Europe during the Upper Paleolithic era (Old Stone Age, *c*.35,000–*c*.10,000BCE). Carved from stone, bone, and ivory or shaped from clay, many of them, such as the Venus of Willendorf, are naked, fleshy females with large pendulous breasts, big buttocks, and swollen bellies. This physique implies an association with fertility. Moreover, the statues have no feet: the legs taper to a point, suggesting that they could be stuck upright in soft earth and worshiped. Some experts argue that the figurines' unwieldy shape is intended subliminally to suggest that they would in fact be more comfortable sitting or lying down —thereby becoming joined to the body of the Earth.

Rather than goddesses, the figurines may have been emblems of identity used to cement social relationships among widely dispersed groups of mobile hunters in the late Paleolithic era. It is also possible that some of the figurines may be portraits of actual women. Certainly archaeologists have discovered hundreds of stone slabs that are inscribed

RIGHT *Found in sites from France to Siberia, the "Venus figurines" are obese in the same body areas. The exaggerated thighs and hips of this 6,000-year-old figure from Anatolia suggest that she may have been associated with fertility and reproduction.*

with drawings that date from the same era as the Venus figurines, and among them are some striking and highly individual representations.

As more settled agricultural societies developed in the later Neolithic (New Stone Age) period, spiritual concerns came to focus even more on the fertility of the Earth. In the 1960s, during excavations at the ancient Anatolian town of Çatal Hüyük, which flourished *c*.6500–*c*.5700BCE, an enthroned female figure apparently giving birth and flanked by leopards was found in a grain bin next to a shrine. Some experts saw her as evidence of a religion based upon the Ancient Mother, but others insisted she represented only a minor fertility goddess. She rests her hands, with apparent affection, on the leopards' heads, leading some to view her as a Mistress of Animals.

During the Bronze Age, at the time of the Minoan civilization centered on Crete (*c*.1400–*c*.1100BCE), palace shrines were built at Knossos, Gournia, Phaistos, and Mallia. Each was set in a similar landscape and appears to form part of a vast female figure: the palaces are close to a pair of mountains resembling breasts, and beneath a rounded hill that may represent a woman's belly. These settings are not proof that the Minoans worshiped a supreme goddess, but do suggest that they recognized a sacred female power within the living world.

OVERLEAF *Monument Valley in the heart of the Navajo territories of the Southwestern United States. This is sacred terrain in which the landscape and the people are intimately bound together through the complex interconnections of myth and religion.*

A romantic, soft-focused notion of Mother Earth was used in the nineteenth century to shore up the widespread cult of idealized femininity. An ironic parallel to this is the more recent strategy whereby women across the Western world have been turning to ancient Earth goddesses as a means of legitimizing female power. They have looked for inspiration to goddesses such as Cybele, Rome's Magna Mater, who can be terrifying and chaotic as well as nurturing, and Kali, the Hindu goddess, who is both fearsome and benevolent.

For many women the great Earth goddesses offer liberation precisely because they contain all aspects and all contradictions, just as nature itself is both creator and destroyer. Christianity, by contrast, is sometimes viewed as having polarized the cultural notion of femininity into the earthly, carnal temptress Eve and the irreproachable Virgin Mary, for whom birth is a process outside nature.

In many tribal societies the Earth goddess embodies the stages of birth, death, and rebirth—the endless cycle to which humankind must learn to be reconciled. The Earth goddess does not try to deny death by promising eternal life, but instead celebrates death as a part of the rhythm of nature.

The Ibo of Nigeria often portray Mother Earth holding a large knife, because she symbolizes both abundant vitality and its opposite; and in a myth of the North American Huron people the goddess Yatahéntshi was both the mother of humanity and the keeper of the dead.

In Çatal Hüyük several buildings have shrines with breast-like forms protruding from their walls. These strange, suggestive shapes have been molded around the skulls of scavengers such as vultures, foxes, and weasels, their sharp beaks and teeth acting as the nipples. It would seem that the people of Çatal Hüyük made a spiritual association between women and death.

The intense interest that the ancient Earth goddesses have attracted in modern times reflects a view of the world composed not of warring opposites but of continually unfolding processes. The sacred is widely regarded as being mysteriously inherent in nature, rather than transcending nature.

RIGHT *Artemis of Ephesus was a Mother goddess from Asia Minor, possibly influenced by the Anatolian figure of Cybele, who gave birth at Ephesus. A version of this statue, now lost, was housed in the temple built at Ephesus in 550BCE in honor of Artemis. The multiple animal forms and exposed, egg-like breasts serve to reinforce the impression of a woman of nature and fecundity.*

Races of clay

In some creation myths the first human being is said to have been fashioned from the mud, sand, or clay of Earth. The Tahitian creator Tangaroa is thought to have used the earth of Tahiti to conjure up Ti'i, the first man, who appeared, aptly for the first inhabitant of an island fringed by beaches, "clothed in sand."

ABOVE *The Ugaritic Mother goddess Astarte or Asherah*
(sometimes known as the "Lady Who Traverses the
Sea") and Greek Gaia of Earth suckling their
children, depicted in a bronze portal from San Zeno
Cathedral, Verona. In Hebrew, Asherah translated as
"grove," and she was often shown as the Tree of Life.

According to North America's Hopi, Spider Woman, the great weaver of the universe, spun the first people from the four colors of the earth—yellow, red, white, and black—and in so doing set the pattern for their society's ritual sandpaintings (see page 12).

The intrusion of routine work into creation myths shows how everyday experience can inform a society's spiritual beliefs. According to the ancient Egyptians, the ram-headed god Khnum molded human beings on a potter's wheel. In the belief that God fashions children in the womb, Rwandan women before retiring to sleep leave water ready so that God may use it to form the clay that humans are made of. In Babylon the potter's craft was seen as analogous to the shaping of life, and the words for rebirth were, "We are as fresh-baked pots."

Earth's raw materials, however, do not always prove suitable for the purposes of creation. According to the sixteenth-century *Popol Vuh*, the traditional history of the Quiché people of Guatemala, the grandmother of all creatures tried to form men from clay and dirt but, because they were soft and malleable and failed to make good servants, she destroyed them.

The ancient Mesopotamian goddess Mami was more successful when she mixed clay and spittle with the flesh and blood of a god to make the first seven men and seven women. Her choice of heterogeneous materials for the sacred act of creation demonstrates the importance of bringing together physical and spiritual essence. An important tool in Mami's task was an ordinary mud-brick, the use of which connected the origins of the people with the mud-brick of their dwellings, villages, and temples, and in the process highlighted the sacred nature of even the most routine tasks of life.

RIGHT *Fired from clay models to protect the emperor in the afterlife, the life-size warriors of the Terracotta Army were buried in pits to the east of the underground tomb of Shi Huangdi, China's First Emperor, near Xian. The tomb exactly modeled the ruler's earthly kingdom.*

SPIRIT PATHS AND LANDSCAPES

The history of the Earth, whether told by scientists or by shamans, is a tale of tumultuous change—one that has left its mark on the planet's surface. Many cultures have believed that in the far-distant past supernatural beings roamed the world, transforming it as they went. They wrought lakes, mountains, rock outcrops and seas, intentionally or unwittingly, and their homes and resting places, it is thought, may still be seen. Supposed traces of mythic human ancestors and heroes are similarly resonant, with a symbolism that can be important to a group's sense of identity.

For societies that possess a profound sense of the sacred, no terrain can be merely geophysical: there is

always some inherent, animated meaning. The section that follows explores various manifestations, in a range of cultures, of sacred vitality in the landscapes around us.

The mythic dimension

Myth interprets the present in terms of the past and is a way of explaining how phenomena in the world came to be as they are. The meanings behind the structure of a sacred building, as well as the rituals that take place within it, can also be explained through myth. If the order of the temple mirrors the order of the cosmos (see pages 116–127), it is through myth that we learn how this is so.

A sacred building can serve as a location for the re-enactment of mythical events and the affirmation of the truths they represent. In Vedic Hinduism the consecration of the sacrificial altar reenacts the creation myth. The clay in the foundation of the altar symbolizes the earth; the water with which it is mixed represents the primeval waters; and the side walls of the altar symbolize the atmosphere. In Christianity at Christmas and Easter, churches provide a setting for rituals that commemorate the birth, crucifixion, and resurrection of Christ, while the Last Supper is repeated daily in the rite of the eucharist.

In a similar way it may be possible that certain historical structures gave rise to explanations passed down in myth. For example, the stories about the Minotaur and the Labyrinth of Crete (see box above and page 42) may have been drawn from folk recollections of the royal Palace of Minos at Knossos, which is known to have existed. Excavations have

LEFT *The formation of landscape features, such as the dramatically contoured Hidden Canyon in the Utah desert, is attributed in many cultures to the actions of supernatural beings, often perceived as giants. Even in Europe, where myths of the landscape are not a major strand in the surviving tradition, many placenames refer to folkloric associations between prominent geological landmarks and mythical figures such as King Arthur.*

Dedalus and Cosmic Architecture

In Greek mythology the architect and inventor Dedalus designed and crafted the Labyrinth in which the bull-human monster the Minotaur was imprisoned. His employer, King Minos of Crete, was subsequently unwilling to allow the valuable Dedalus to leave the island and had all the exit routes guarded. Dedalus therefore made wings of wax and feathers for himself and his son, Icarus, which the pair used to escape by flying to freedom. As he soared above the Labyrinth, Dedalus was able to look down on the maze that baffled those who were still caught in it.

In this myth Dedalus escapes the limitations of the human condition and approaches the perspective of the gods. His son Icarus, despite his father's warnings, could not resist flying too high so his wings were melted by the Sun, causing him to plummet to his death; but Dedalus survived and returned to Earth, because instead of being dazzled by the revelation of the Labyrinth, he absorbed its lesson. By understanding the architecture of humankind, he also understood the architecture of the cosmos that it imitates.

revealed that the building had a groundplan of startling complexity: hundreds of rooms led off corridors and passageways around a central court, at a time when most mainland Greeks lived in simple two-room dwellings. It may well have been, then, that the palace struck visitors as a forbidding maze. Moreover, it was also a place where the dangerous sport of bull-leaping was practiced: skilled acrobats, and perhaps prisoners of war, attempted to seize the horns of a charging bull and somersault over its back. Add to this the palace's decorative motif of a double-headed ax or *labrys*, which suggests an explanation for the term "Labyrinth" (literally "House of the Ax"), and a convincing number of

ABOVE *A granary door in the Dogon village of Sangha has been carved with symbols and figures relating to tribal myth. These signs are intended to placate the spirit world that surrounds and influences everyday life.*

elements of fact are in place to provide context for the subsequent story about the Minotaur.

Unlike almost all other sacred architecture, the Labyrinth's lowest level has the greatest power. The archeological remains in Crete suggest the throne-room was like a sacred cavern. The palace seems to have had an upper solar section, consecrated to life, and a lower lunar area, dedicated to death, reflecting the idea that death and the afterlife were, in spiritual terms, more important than life. This echoed the Egyptian labyrinth, where beneath an accessible cult area lay a subterranean region for secret rites and tombs, entry to which was restricted to initiates.

Among the Dogon people of Mali the beliefs and myths of their culture are embodied within the structures of their domestic buildings. Each household's granary mirrors in its architecture the granary of the Master of Pure Earth who descended from the sky on the fourth day of creation. For the Dogon the granary represents a fertile female figure and the "belly of the world." In a further mythical correlation it is divided into eight internal spaces for storing the eight seeds that God gave to the eight ancestors, which correspond to the eight internal organs of the body. These myths are reaffirmed in rites and in the respect shown toward grain in daily life. As with the Vedic altar or the Christian church, the religious meaning embodied in the Dogon granary is conveyed through narratives, or myths, that can be understood on many levels. The sacred building provides a map or point of reference for such understandings, as well as a space within which to experience them.

Sometimes sites and myths converge. The migrating ancestors of Mesoamerica's Aztecs were told by their god Huitzilopochtli to search for an eagle sitting in a cactus and eating a snake: this was the sign that would identify the place where they should settle. They found the eagle on an island in Lake Texcoco, and there they built their capital city, Tenochtitlán.

In a similar way the building of a temple is so highly charged with significance that designs are often seen as originating from a divine source. In ancient Iraq (*c.*2100BCE), King Gudea of Lagash built a temple dedicated to the city's patron god Ningirsu after a dream: "Here was a man: his height equaled the sky, his weight equaled the Earth . . . He told me to build him a temple . . . " It later transpired that the figure

RIGHT *The Dogon people live in earth-built structures within cliff-face villages on a plateau in Mali, West Africa, called the Bandiagra Escarpment. The Dogon believe they were led to this sacred place in ancient times by an ancestral snake. The nature of their arrival helps to root them in their specific landscape and their distinct housing reflects deeply held myths and beliefs.*

who revealed the design of the temple to Gudea was, in fact, Ningirsu himself, and the king is often shown in statues of the period with the plan on his lap.

Songlines of the ancestors

According to the traditional belief of Aboriginal Australians, all things began with the *Altjeringa* or Dreaming (also called the Dreamtime), an epoch when ancestral creator spirit-beings lived on Earth. These spirits, said to have taken the forms of people, animals, plants, or inanimate objects, could change shape at will and their existence is revealed by the marks they left on the landscape.

The Aborigines believe that the Dreaming spirits, as they traveled across the Earth, created and named animals, rocks, trees, waterholes, and other natural features. They also deposited the spirits of unborn children and determined the forms of human society. A particular ancestral spirit is often associated with a group of sites, each of which serves as a landmark to denote the course of its travels. The routes of these spirits are called "Dreaming tracks" or "songlines."

At each site the ancestor is believed to have left either spiritual essence or physical remains such as footprints or body impressions. For example, the Yarralin people of the Victoria River Valley regard the spirit Walujapi as the Dreaming ancestor of the blackheaded python. Walujapi left a snakelike track along a cliff-face and the imprint of her buttocks when she sat down to camp. Both features are visible today.

Australia's landscape is crisscrossed with songlines, some of which are no more than a few miles long, while others extend for hundreds of miles through various types of terrain and pass through the lands of many different Aboriginal groups, who may speak different languages and subscribe to different traditions. For example, the Native Cat Dreaming

BELOW *For many peoples a feature of the landscape served as their place of origin. Some American cultures believe that the ancestors emerged through an opening in the ground. The subterranean* kivas *(chambers for sacred rituals) built by the Anasazi people, such as this one at Pueblo Bonito, New Mexico, reflect this belief in their design, which includes a symbolic hole in the floor.*

The Living Dreaming

When the Dreaming ended, all things were fixed —the forms of the landscape and its life, the organization of societies, and the guardianship of land. However, the Dreaming continues to play an important role in Aboriginal life. Anyone born near a sacred Dreaming site, for example, is seen as the incarnation of its associated being, and becomes the site's guardian. Aboriginal holy men, known as *karadjis* or "men of high degree," are believed to be in direct contact with the Dreaming and its spirit-beings. They sometimes wear feathers on their ankles to symbolize their ability to "fly" to the spirit realms, and are the only people who may create new dances, songs, and stories about the Dreaming.

Not long ago an anthropologist studying the Pintupi of the Western Desert witnessed the discovery by a group of men of an unusual multi-colored sedimentary rock on the bank of a creek. Elders were summoned to interpret the find, and one claimed that it was related to the Kangaroo Dreaming, in which two ancestral heroes speared a kangaroo several miles away from the creek. The elders agreed that the wounded kangaroo must have crawled along the creek to try to reach its own country, but the heroes caught up with it and gutted its carcass on this spot. The rock, therefore, was the entrails of the kangaroo.

the Gurindji language but each time they crossed into a different country they adopted the language of the people who would live there. Such songlines provide common ground among culturally disparate groups.

At the end of the Dreaming the spirit-beings either became the species they represented or retreated into the Earth. The landscape remained as they had created it. Their dwelling places and the sites of important Dreaming events came to be seen as sources of great power. Aborigines believe that the spiritual seed of every individual derives from a specific site created by beings of the Dreaming. Consequently each person's identity is intimately tied to the landscape.

As well as having a connection to the land, the Aboriginal people, in common with many other cultures, see the rhythm of human life and animal life as interlinked. When an Aborigine decorates himself and dances in imitation of an ancestral emu from the Dreaming or a shaman travels mystically in the form of a bear, the act symbolizes the social process of living as part of the Earth rather than as its master.

The role of animals in the life of the Earth is expressed in many origin myths. In Native American and other mythologies all was endless sea until an animal (such as a muskrat) dived to the bottom of the sea and returned with mud that became the Earth (see page 12). In Western traditions, however, the distinction made between humans and animals is influenced strongly by the Biblical emphasis on the superiority of humankind.

ancestors are said to have begun their journey at the sea and to have moved north into the Simpson Desert, traversing as they did so the lands of the Aranda, Unmatjera, Kaititja, Ilpara, Ngalia, and Kukatja. Each group tells part of the myth relating to those events that took place in its territory.

Among the Yarralin people the Pigeon Dreaming story tells how two pigeons, a brother and sister, followed the Victoria River from the edge of the desert to the coast. On the first leg of the journey they spoke

The sacred journey

The movement of peoples across the Earth plays a large part in the history of the human race, and it is

OVERLEAF *The rock formation known as Katatjuta or The Olgas lies in central Australia, some 25 miles (42 km) from the better-known Uluru or Ayers Rock. Katatjuta is sacred to female Aborigines and men are forbidden to visit the site. A waterhole here is said to be home to a giant snake, and the site's vast mounds are explained as food piles for gigantic mice women.*

unsurprising that epic journeys of migration, exploration, and conquest appear so often in stories. Such journeys, many of them probably rooted in real wanderings of the distant past, may serve to explain and to justify the occupation of a land by people who are still haunted by the sense that they were originally intruders. The migrations are often said to have been at the instigation of a divine or supernatural figure who guided and sustained the people and instructed them where to settle. One famous example is the story of the Exodus in the Hebrew Scriptures: Moses led the Israelites from servitude into a land expressly promised to them as a homeland by the god Yahweh.

The Exodus represented a process of communal spiritual renewal that laid the moral and religious

BELOW *King Arthur and his knights, in the 15th-century* Livre de Messire Lancelot du Lac. *The Grail the men sought was said to have been brought to Britain by the wandering follower of Jesus, Joseph of Arimathea.*

foundations of a settled society. The same can also be said of the Aztec migration story referred to earlier and recorded in a variety of sixteenth-century images and texts. Probably based on a historical movement that took place *c.*1150–*c.*1350BCE, the tale tells of the journey of the Mexica from the island of Aztlan in the northwest to the site of their future capital city, Tenochtitlán, in the Valley of Mexico. Along the way the Mexica people gain knowledge and experience that will help them in their future homeland.

The Mexica are guided by their supreme god, Huitzilopochtli, and at the first place at which they break their journey they build a temple in his honor and receive his instructions. During their next pause, at the birthplace of the god, they are taught how to conduct a sacred fire ceremony. As the journey progresses the Mexica acquire more of the sacred rituals, skills, and other cultural characteristics that distinguish them from other peoples: they learn how to control water resources when they build a dam across a river at Tula, and before reaching their destination they learn the arts of politics and warfare. They also change their name from Mexica to Aztec (People of Aztlan), emphasizing the extent to which the migration represents a new beginning.

The sacred wandering need not be undertaken by the people themselves in order for them to acquire its spiritual benefits. According to the Midéwiwin or Grand Medicine Society, a shamanic organization of the Ojibwa people who live around Lake Superior in North America, the spirit-being Bear brought the Ojibwa their curing rites to grant them health and long life. The Earth Spirit Shell and the Great Spirit in the sky ordered Bear to carry the sacred objects needed for the rites up through several layers of earth to the surface of the water (Lake Superior) and then through the lakes and rivers of Ojibwa territory toward Leech Lake in Minnesota. As Bear headed for the west end of Lake Superior he halted at several places to establish a Midéwiwin lodge attended by a guardian spirit. The sacred route leading from Lake Superior to Leech Lake is recorded in maps on

In Search of the Holy Grail

The quest for the Holy Grail was one of the most widespread themes of medieval European epic literature: versions of the story are recorded in almost all the countries of western and northern Europe. Rooted in Celtic myth and the powerful mysteries of early Christianity, the Grail legends explore the theme of spiritual transformation. The Grail itself was reputed to have the ability to confer everlasting life. According to one legend, it was the vessel used by Christ at the Last Supper, and in another the cup in which Joseph of Arimathea caught some of Christ's blood at the Crucifixion. Joseph is said to have journeyed abroad with the Grail, eventually carrying it to Britain and the legendary land of Avalon, sometimes identified with Glastonbury in Somerset.

According to medieval French sources, the search for the Grail was a spiritual quest undertaken by many of the legendary knights of King Arthur. Three knights—Galahad, Perceval (the Parsifal of German accounts), and Bors—found the Grail in a mysterious city across the sea. Only Galahad looked into the vessel, and he died from the ecstasy of his vision.

Today several esoteric movements use the Grail as a subject for meditation. They regard it as a symbol of the means of attaining inner spiritual perfection, rather like the alchemical philosopher's stone (see page 115).

scrolls of birchbark, which are used by a Midéwiwin shaman during curing rituals to illustrate his narrative of the sacred journey.

The wandering heroes
The heroic journey across an unknown landscape is encountered in a great number of myths and legends worldwide, from the Japanese epics of the heroes

Travels in Multiple Worlds

According to the origin myth of the Hopi people of Arizona, their ancestors rose through three lower worlds before emerging into this, the Fourth World. When they appeared their guardian spirit told them that they had to walk to the four ends of the Earth and return before they could settle in the center, their homeland. Each of the four clans into which the ancestors were divided was given a sacred tablet to guide it on its way. The four clans walked all over what is now North and South America, and their passing is marked to this day by ancient monuments and ruins. When members of the Snake Clan stopped in the Great Plains of North America they decided to leave a mark. Because there were no rocks on which to carve their clan symbol, they built a large earthen mound in the shape of a snake. Some Hopi today believe that the great Serpent Mound in Ohio (see pages 110–111) is the legendary mound of the Snake Clan.

Jimmu-tenno and Yamato-takeru to the Greco-Roman stories of Odysseus (Ulysses), Jason, and Aeneas. The journey usually involves an individual (often of princely status and accompanied by a band of followers) who ventures from the familiar home environment into the outside world, where he (rarely she) accomplishes great deeds and overcomes many difficulties before returning to general acclaim. For example, Homer's epic poem the *Odyssey* (*c*.750BCE) relates the journey of the hero-king Odysseus from the Trojan War back to his homeland of Ithaca. On the ten-year voyage he encounters many fabulous lands and monsters, but all his comrades perish.

The heroic journey has been interpreted as a metaphor for the process of individual spiritual development, in which the varied landscapes traversed by the heroic figure stand for different aspects of the human psyche, and physical trials represent tests of spiritual endeavor. The symbolism becomes more profound if the journey takes the form of a quest. The object of the quest is generally something extremely precious that may be said to represent the goal of spiritual enlightenment or self-knowledge. In the West, the most famous example of the heroic journey as spiritual quest is the search for the Holy Grail (see page 35).

The labyrinth or maze that a hero or heroine must sometimes penetrate (especially the original labyrinth on Crete in the Greek myth of the hero Theseus) is a complex symbol that has been said to represent the passage from the profane to the sacred, the journey through the trials of life to the center of enlightenment. In order to attain enlightenment one may have to overcome the dark side of one's own nature, represented by the monster that may live at the heart of the labyrinth (the Minotaur, for example, slain by Theseus). When the goal has been achieved, finding the way out of the labyrinth is easy: Theseus followed a golden thread given to him by the princess Ariadne.

The labyrinth or maze has also been interpreted as a mandala, an image of the cosmos used in the East to assist a meditator to find his or her own spiritual focal point or "center" (see also pages 120–123).

A recurrent figure in Celtic myth is the hero who voyages to the Otherworld, an ambivalent place of danger and festivity, whose inhabitants know neither age nor death. One Irish example, Mael Dúin, encounters ants as big as foals, horse-racing demons, and a magical silver net, part of which he lays on the altar of the holy city of Armagh when he returns.

The dragon's haunts

The dragon is one of the most potent symbols of the primordial energy that is the source of all power, both good and evil. In the West dragon symbolism has tended to emphasize the negative side of that energy, mainly as a result of the influence of Christianity, whereas Oriental mythology represents the dragon as a positive force, a symbol of human potential to combine the power of the elements to creative ends. This distinction is reflected in the way in which each tradition views the relationship between the dragon and the landscape.

In Western mythology the dragon's association with particular locations is often through its role as a guardian. The dragon is seen as a fearsome fire-breathing beast that guards treasure (spiritual knowledge) or a maiden (a symbol of purity), and is set up as an obstacle to be overcome by such saintly heroes as St. Michael and St. George.

In China the primal power of the dragon was said to be channeled through the landscape along paths of energy, or "dragonlines." These were regarded as very auspicious locations and used by members of the imperial family as burial sites. Detecting the way in which the flow of energy, both positive and negative, interacted with the landscape was developed into a highly sophisticated practice, geomancy, which is still used today.

The Chinese dragon is fierce but rarely malevolent: it represents the east, the Sun, and the bounty of the land. The four-clawed dragon, Mang, represents temporal power. The dragon named Long holds a fiery

BELOW *A water dragon from the wall of the Palace of Peaceful Longevity in Beijing's Forbidden City. Dragons epitomize the male principle (yang) and were held to be ancestors of the emperors.*

pearl in its claws, which may represent the Moon as a source of fertility, although for Daoists and Buddhists it is the "pearl that grants all desires" (wisdom and enlightenment).

As symbols of the dark powers of Earth, dragons —from the Greek *dracon* or "large serpent"—and serpents are close relatives and, in myth, often indistinguishable. In North America the rock art of the Algonquin people depicts serpents beside natural holes and crevices, perhaps as spiritual messengers to the underworld. In Algonquin myth the dark side of Earth energy is shown in the great underwater serpent spirit Mizhipichew, which can stir up the waters of lakes with its tail and must be appeased with offerings of tobacco.

In Australia giant serpent-beings identified with the rainbow bring forth life through the rains and yet are the dangerous guardians of waterholes, easily roused to anger if rituals to propitiate them are not followed correctly.

Pilgrimages

As we have seen, traveling across the landscape toward a certain destination appears in many traditions as a metaphor for the process of spiritual growth and the acquisition of knowledge. This is shown in its most literal sense in the act of pilgrimage, in which the physical and spiritual journey are simultaneous. The thousands of people who toil up the slopes of Mount Fuji in Japan, or painfully creep up the steps of a Catholic shrine on their knees, travel the same path of spiritual progress. In doing so they hope to develop a more complete self and a closer relationship with the divine. The pilgrim leaves the shelter of home and family in order to travel to a place where he or she can encounter some other, superior world, perhaps in the belief that the process will vouchsafe physical or spiritual healing, or divine assistance with personal problems or predicaments. In the ancient Greek world people covered hundreds of miles to seek counsel from the sacred oracle of Delphi, or to be cured at Epidaurus, at the shrine of Asklepios, the god of healing. Many Christian places of pilgrimage are visited as a simple act of devotion or thanksgiving to a saint, or as penance.

For some the spiritual value of the pilgrimage increases with the difficulty of the journey, as was demonstrated in 1994 by one Hindu *sadhu* (ascetic) who rolled 200 miles (320 km) across India—the last 20 miles (32 km) or so uphill—on a pilgrimage to the shrine of the goddess Devi. Most pilgrim traditions include an element of worldly denial, which is expressed in two landmarks of Christian spiritual literature, *Il Purgatorio* by Dante (1265–1321) and *The Pilgrim's Progress* by John Bunyan (1628–88). In the former work the poet is guided on an otherworldly journey through Purgatory by his beloved Beatrice, who brings him to the Christian view of life itself as pilgrimage. The German churchman Johann Gerhard (1582–1637) wrote in his book of prayers: "Thus I, the object of the world's disdain, with pilgrim face surround the weary earth; I only relish what the world counts vain . . . Her freedom is my jail." This world-renouncing spirituality has at times encouraged a negative view of the world, which has come to be seen as a place of exile for humans, whose ultimate destination and true home is Heaven.

LEFT *The Persian hero Rustam undertook an epic journey when he went to the aid of the King of Kings. In the course of this he overcame seven challenges, the third of these posed by a dragon that he and his horse Rakhsh slayed. This miniature dates from 1486.*

The emphasis in pilgrimage may sometimes be on the destination rather than the act of journeying. In Islam great emphasis is put on the *hajj*, the pilgrimage to the holy city of Mecca in Saudi Arabia (see pages 188–189). The fifth of the religious duties known as the Five Pillars decrees that every Muslim should make the *hajj* at least once, unless they are physically incapable, or unless to do so would cause financial hardship to the family.

The idea of a pilgrimage without destination, when the journey traveled is the goal, was expressed somewhat desolately by the American poet Walt Whitman (1819–98), who saw "the universe itself as a road, as many roads, as roads for traveling souls."

A 7,360 ft. (2,243 m) mountain in the hill country of southwestern Sri Lanka, called Samanhela by the Sinhalese and known worldwide as Adam's Peak, has for centuries been the object of devotion because of its dramatic, conical shape and its summit, consisting of a rocky outcrop forming an oblong platform some 74 ft. by 24 ft. (22 m by 7 m). On this summit platform there is a hollow some 5 ft. 4 in. by 2 ft. 6 in. (1.6 m by 76 cm) in length, that has been interpreted by Buddhists, Muslims, Hindus, Daoists, and Christian visitors alike as a giant footprint.

In Buddhist writings dating from before 300BCE it was described as the footprint of the Buddha; Chinese writers have described it as the mark of a

LEFT *Hopi people in the American Southwest believe that their ancestors emerged from an underground world through a hole located in the Grand Canyon. Hopi means "peace," and, fittingly, they believe that all the earthly actions of people should lead to balance, harmony, and integration with all other living things within creation. They undertake a seasonal range of ceremonies, many of them secretive, in some of which the participants become the* kachina *messengers who first taught the Hopi their religion.*

god or of their first ancestor; in a Muslim legend it is the footprint that Adam left where he landed after his fall from Paradise. In the sixteenth century the Portuguese saw it as the mark of St. Thomas.

In order to reach the summit of Adam's Peak pilgrims are obliged to traverse steep ravines on steps carved into the rock before climbing a ladder fastened into the cliff-face. Heavy chains found on the southwestern face are said to have been placed there by Alexander the Great (365–323 BCE). After prayers, each attending pilgrim rings an ancient bell and takes water from a spring to end the ritual.

ABOVE *Adam's Peak is located in Sabaramaguwa province, Sri Lanka. Both Christians and Muslims identify the summit imprint with the place where Adam stood on one leg for 1,000 years as penance.*

Labyrinths and spirals

The earliest known labyrinth dates from the nineteenth century BCE in Egypt, where it represented the path through the underworld. Labyrinths are also known in Buddhist thought, where they are intricate paths to enlightenment. But the archetypal labyrinth for European culture is that built, according to Greek

Symbolism of the Maze

The idea of the labyrinth has long fascinated European minds. In early Christian thought the maze was a symbol of the path of ignorance, leading away from God. However, by the thirteenth century it had come to have a positive symbolism, as the path of the pilgrim strewn with difficulties. By the seventeenth century similar designs were also reproduced in secular contexts, in the hedge-mazes of great villas, reflecting a popular concern with finding one's way to a goal.

The labyrinth-spiral is depicted in the pavement floors of many medieval cathedrals. In Chartres Cathedral, France, the thirteenth-century maze on the floor of the nave is located in such a way that if the wall containing the west rose-window were to be hinged at the ground and bent down, the window would cover the maze exactly.

The maze has only one path to the center. It represents a spiritual journey, the winding path of the soul through human life, while the rose-window depicts the Last Judgment, the fate of the soul after death. The maze, positioned at the beginning of the nave, also forms an initiatory barrier to the sacred realm at the altar.

myth, by Dedalus for King Minos of Crete (see box, page 27). Here the labyrinth is a disorienting tangle of paths in which the unwary are lost, but which nevertheless contains a true path to the center. In the myth the Minotaur—part man, part bull, the result of an unnatural liaison between King Minos's wife Pasiphae and a bull sent by Poseidon—lurks in the depths of the Labyrinth, devouring the youths and maidens offered to it in sacrifice. The hero Theseus eventually finds his way to the center and kills the monster. He is able to find his way out by means of a golden thread that the king's daughter, Ariadne, has suggested he unravel from the entrance.

Here a labyrinth symbolizes the idea of penetration, through an initiatory test of personal qualities, to the center. Hence it came to be associated with spiritual progression and discovery of the self. Complicated and winding in form, a labyrinth represents confusion to the uninitiated but order to those who understand it.

The sense of movement in finding one's way through a labyrinth is similar in many ways to the movement inherent in the spiral, as the writer Jill Purce has pointed out. The one true path, often seen as that of the pilgrim, culminates in an encounter with the divine. The idea of the labyrinth-spiral, coiling back on itself, has led to images of a two-way movement, with seekers after the truth going in one direction and angels or divine messages coming in the other. Mystics have pondered the idea that the end of the spiral is also a beginning, or that the spiral leads out of this mundane world altogether. Thus many cultures attribute spiritual significance to whirling vortex-like dances, which generate extreme exaltation or an otherworldly trance state. The idea of the expansion of consciousness evoked by spiral ascent is met throughout the world, perhaps most dramatically in the ascending spiral minaret of the mosque near Samarra in Iraq (see page 9).

RIGHT *The labyrinth and nave at Chartres Cathedral, France. The labyrinth is 42 ft. (13 m) across and once had a central plate bearing images of Theseus, the Minotaur, and Ariadne. It stands on the site of an ancient hilltop forest where local druids once practiced religious rituals, and the crypt contains a well once believed to have held a representation of the Earth Mother. The structure's precise specifications and the waters beneath hint at the builders' mysterious beliefs.*

IMAGES ON ROCK

Ancient rock-art sites—both open-air and, less commonly, enclosed—form part of the sacred landscape of many Australian Aboriginal groups and are important in their mythology, both for the spirits said to inhabit such sites and for the supernatural events that are believed to have taken place there in the past. For example, in the mountains of the western Kimberley region of northwestern Australia the local Aborigines explain the existence at some sites of several layers of superimposed art as the work of tricksters who deliberately defaced sacred caves by drawing over the paintings left by the ancestors of the Dreaming (see pages 30–31) in order to assert their own ownership of the site. Rockpaintings may also mark territorial boundaries and the sites of significant real events (such as a particularly fruitful hunt), or they may be the work of individuals whose power has waned: this might help to explain the human handprint "signatures" at caves in Queensland.

Many of the rock-art traditions have been lost. We have the evidence itself, but no means of interpreting it. However, some practices have remained alive: for

example, in the 1930s an archaeologist investigating a shelter in Western Australia found freshly painted images of a dugong or sea cow, a freshwater tortoise, and the liver of a stingray. Throughout Australia paintings are occasionally retouched or renewed, sometimes as part of rituals intended to increase the numbers of kangaroos, alligators, yams, and other sources of food (see box, page 52).

Kakadu National Park, in the Alligator River region of northern Australia, has thousands of rockpaintings spanning several millennia. Some of the most striking were made in the twentieth

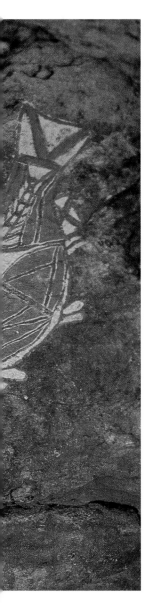

LEFT *Dramatic rock art is found throughout Australia, mostly on exterior rock-faces. This ancient "X-ray-style" painting of spirit figures and heroes from the Dreaming adorns Nourlangie Rock along the Alligator River in eastern Arnhem Land.*

The Rich Rock Imagery of Africa

Neolithic rock and cave art in Africa gives us vital evidence for the domestication of animals, and for the adaptation of wildlife to climatic change. Surprisingly, the African rock-art sites were discovered by Westerners before the European sites came to light.

Initially only wild animals were shown. The North African buffalo (*Bubulus antiquus*), which appears in rock engravings of the period from *c.*7000 to *c.*4500BCE, may be a Lord of Animals responsible for the movements of wild herds of various species of interest to human hunters; it makes a suggestive parallel with the bison found in the caves at Lascaux. Other wild beasts depicted include the elephant, rhinoceros, hippopotamus, giraffe, ostrich, and antelope.

From about 8,000 years before the present, domestication appears with increasing frequency. Pastoral scenes, with herds of cattle, sheep, asses, and goats, form a dramatic contrast with the wild beasts of the more familiar European Paleolithic paintings. Later, horses appear (first with chariots, then with riders), and finally camels. Various Saharan sites show attempts to domesticate beasts such as the giraffe.

In the Tassili region of the Sahara (see page 49), more than 15,000 examples of rock art are known, including a group of paintings, from *c.*6000BCE, characterized by stylized human figures with rounded featureless heads.

The wealth of cave art in southern Africa includes, in the Makumbe Cave, Zimbabwe, a superb painting produced accretively during a period from almost 2,000 to just a few hundred years ago, in a range of styles, depicting two large elephants, humans, a rhinoceros, and antelopes. The technique of superimposing images at different times, also found in Europe, supports the idea that the motivation was ritualistic rather than esthetic.

century by Najombolmi, a man who owned lands of the Bardmardi clan on Deaf Adder Creek. He worked for European hunters at buffalo hunting camps but also spent time traveling in the bush, painting. In the year before his death he became concerned by the decline of traditional beliefs and the abandonment of the land, and traveled to a site at Anbang-bang that had paintings of two men and their wives. Najombolmi repainted the couples and expanded the scene into two family groups.

Rock art is not, however, restricted to Australia. It can be seen throughout the world, and particularly in Africa, where some of the most remarkable art is found in the southcentral and southern part of the continent, produced over many centuries by the Bushmen (San) who were the region's principal human inhabitants before the migration of Bantu peoples after c.1600CE confined the San largely to the Kalahari and Namib deserts.

The greatest concentration of San art is found in the Drakensberg mountains of the eastern Cape, an area from which the San were pushed around the end of the nineteenth century by both the Bantu and European settlers, between whom they found themselves sandwiched. (San artists of this late period depicted scenes of themselves cattle-rustling from the herds of both groups of newcomers.)

The Drakensberg art includes engraved animals on stone and also painted images that reflect San mythology and belief, such as their reverence for the heavily built eland, the largest species of antelope. Some paintings depict ceremonies that appear to represent an individual's transformation into an eland-being through a shamanistic dance known as a *simbo*, which causes a state of trance in the

LEFT *Large colorful animal figures of giraffes and other wild species depicted on a wall of Nswatugi Cave in the Motopo Hills of modern-day Zimbabwe, produced by the artist using local minerals such as oxides and clay and probably bound to the rock's surface with blood or fat.*

participant. The painted rituals resemble, in form at least, practices still current among the San.

The Bantu peoples who had displaced the San in most of southern Africa by c.1800 left their own legacy of rockpaintings (much of it formerly attributed to the San by European scholars on the grounds that they were the only people of the region then still producing rock art). The Bantu art, centered on Zimbabwe, reflects a culture that practiced the sacrifice of infirm kings in order to ensure the continued prosperity of the land.

The power in the darkness

Prehistoric cave art, and particularly examples to be found at sites in western Europe and Africa, provides us with some of humankind's most powerful imagery of animal forms, suggesting a deeply felt relationship with the animal world that today is difficult for us to imagine.

The cave paintings of western Europe (in particular southwestern France and northwestern Spain) from the Upper Paleolithic period, some of them as much as 30,000 years old, are justly renowned.

Sometimes prehistoric artists suggested the twists and turns of moving animals with complicated naturalistic perspectives that would not be seen again for thousands of years.

Decorated with beasts and abstract markings, those works mostly date to the last phase of the Ice Age, ending about 10,000 years ago. A variety of techniques was used, from multicolored painting in red, yellow, and ochers (earth pigments), to blacks and violets from manganese oxides, to incised work in the cave walls.

Modern electric light, stairs, and pavements now intrude on many Paleolithic cave sites, but for prehistoric peoples the caves were filled with absolute darkness, and often consisted of tortuous networks of passages. From today's perspective it is hard to imagine that this underground landscape did not influence the artists' choice of what to portray.

In some of the shelters and caves the entrance areas are wide and dry, and served as living spaces. At Altamira in Spain and Le Poisson, La Madeleine, and many other caves in France, there are rockpaintings and engravings that were probably in close proximity to domestic life, as has been suggested by the discovery of the remains of hearths and animal bones and the debris of flint-knapping. Others, however, have been found at the end of deep passages that may wind far into the Earth, as at Rouffignac in France, where a special train is now provided to enable modern visitors to see the site. Squeezing through subterranean mazes, the artists must have crouched in flickering light (there is evidence of stone bowls filled with animal fat, their wicks made of grass, lichens, and juniper) to create their works.

Few human beings and no objects were depicted. Most of the imagery illustrates animals, and the frequency of mammoths, bison, reindeer, and other beasts of the hunt is consistent with the view that such cave art was motivated by "sympathetic magic," with the object of ensuring hunting success. However, other interpreters associate the cave sites with fertility, and in the popular imagination the underground darkness of these womblike places may be thought to reinforce this idea.

Some anthropomorphic figures amid the animals have been seen as spirit guardians, comparable to the shamans of later cultures. However, there is no

BELOW *This Aboriginal rock art depicting dingo hero figures, found in caves in Australia's Napier Range, has been produced using white ocher. Ocher—particularly red—was the most highly prized pigment among the Aborigines, valued for ceremonial use and body painting, and to create artworks on rock.*

RIGHT *An example of ancient art gouged from the sandstone of the Tassili-m-Ajjer plateau in what is today Algeria. The artist has executed the horned cattle on the rock surface in such a way that the play of light upon them suggests movement.*

conclusive evidence that the caves were ever put to ritual use.

In Australian Aboriginal belief the force that the ancestors left latent in the rock, earth, or natural objects is the creative energy by which the world and its features were originally formed. This stored-up primal power is known as *djang* and it can be evoked by rituals at particular places that will reunite the people with the ancestors who inaugurated them. When etched into a rock-face, an Aboriginal image becomes part of the very creation that it represents and through the use of natural materials it partakes of the natural order that the artist sets out to depict.

In the Napier Range of the remote Kimberley region there are rock-paintings in caves that depict an animal held in special regard by the Aborigines for its service as both a pet and a hunting aid: the dingo. In the form of the Melatji Law Dogs, two of these wild canines existed as spirits that embodied tribal law.

The story of the mythical wanderings of these two dingo heroes from water source to water source amounts to a mythological map of the real water resources in the territory of the Bunuba people. The story tells how the dogs dug in the sand and thereby threw up the King Leopold Mountains, before heading southwest to Windjana Gorge, where they imprinted themselves on a rock. Even the prized painting material of red ocher was attributable to one of the hero dingoes, for it was said to be its lifeblood which drained away into the valley floor at Parachilna in the Flinders Range after a deathly struggle with a giant gecko called Adno-artina.

While the Aboriginal work reflected both real-life animals in the natural world around them and more stylized, otherwordly spirit creatures, most of the animals illustrated by Paleolithic artists elsewhere can be recognized as the ancestors of modern

The Lascaux Caves

Southwestern France

In September 1940 four boys from Montignac explored a dark hole they had found in the hillside. Using a crude lamp to light their way, they scrambled down a steep slope of debris and into a large open chamber. The open space engulfed the light, but when they passed through a narrow archway into another, lower chamber, the lamp lit the bright reds, yellows, and blacks of a mass of painted animals on the ceiling. The boys had discovered a complex of caves, eroded over millennia from the limestone bedrock at Lascaux in the Perigord region in southwestern France's Dordogne Valley, containing one of the most extraordinary displays of prehistoric rock art ever encountered.

The high artistic quality of the paintings and engravings—which had probably been undisturbed for 17,000 years—was immediately evident. Less obvious was why apparently several generations of artists had adorned the caves with many hundreds of representations of animals.

The Lascaux artists often worked close to the cave roof (a feat requiring an artificial platform, such as a scaffold) to produce paintings that were very difficult to view from the cave floor, especially by the pale light of the artists' tallow lamps (hundreds of these have been found in the caves). The inaccessibility of such art implies that the paintings were not merely decorative, and the most widely held explanation for them is that they were linked with hunting.

Most of the pictures are of large game mammals such as bison, aurochs (an extinct bovine), horses, and deer, and some animals are depicted with wounds. It has been proposed that the paintings are "trophy arrays" of notable hunting successes. Another theory is that the artists were involved in a form of "sympathetic magic," supposedly drawing a beast to its death in the hunt by fixing its image and gaining control over its soul. The cave, it has been suggested, may have been the site of rites conducted by a shamanistic "master of animals," as is known to have happened in Africa and North America.

The Lascaux site is just one of several hundred prehistoric decorated caves and rock shelters so far located in southern France and northern Spain.

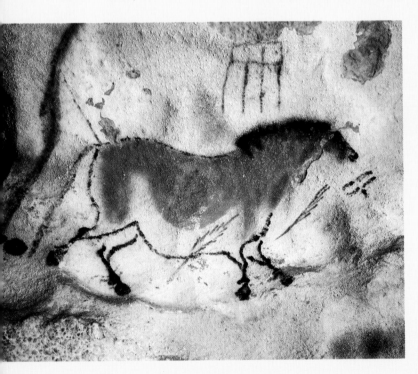

LEFT *One of the so-called "Chinese horses" from Lascaux's Axial Gallery, outlined and shaded in black charcoal. The name derives from a style reminiscent of later artists in China. The artistic technique frequently exploited the natural contours of the cave rock to create the design.*

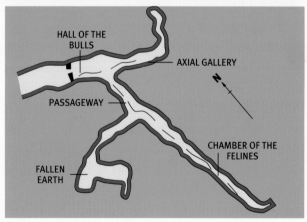

TOP *The Rotunda or Hall of the Bulls at the entrance has walls covered with outlines of aurochs, horses, and smaller animals. This aurochs on the north wall is a painting 18 ft. (5.5 m) long.*

ABOVE *Bulls, horses, reindeer, and smaller creatures are among the animals depicted that appear to roam across the wall of the cave, their images rendered in mineral pigments such as kaolin and hematite.*

ABOVE *The original Paleolithic entrance had long since collapsed and entombed the images when in 1940 the four boys found what was in fact a crack in the roof. The Hall of the Bulls is a very dramatic place and leads into the Axial Gallery, which is decorated with brightly painted animals, their color enhanced by the white calcite on the walls. The chamber then narrows until it opens into a gallery filled with images that include several engraved felines.*

"Increase Rocks"

Australian Aborigine peoples believe that some rocks and rockpaintings possess the power to increase the supply of game animals, plants, and other essential food sources in their area. In the Kimberleys Aborigines sometimes use their hands to rub standing stones associated with ancient beings from the Dreaming, in the belief that the dust that is thereby created will bring forth new life.

When Aboriginal people in the Oenpelli region of western Arnhem Land want to increase the supply of watersnakes, they beat a rock-painting of a watersnake with a bough to flush out its spirits, then tell the spirits to go to water-holes and become large snakes. At a site near South Alligator River, Aborigines build fires under the painting of a yam in the belief that the smoke will pick up the spirits of the plant and spread them over the land.

animals, such as the elk and deer, or identified as species that are now extinct, such as the mammoth. However, in a small recess of the cave of Les Trois Frères in southwestern France resides a creature that seems to have the feet and legs of a human but the torso, arms, and tail of an animal; the head is indistinct. The Abbé Breuil, a French archaeologist who worked in the early and middle years of the twentieth century, imagined and recorded this figure as a medicine man or "sorcerer," clothed in an animal skin and wearing a ceremonial headdress of animal horns. Other scholars of the time associated the image with hunting magic, seeing it as a magician or spirit who controlled animals. The interpretation of this figure, with its human and animal attributes, remains controversial.

Some experts perceive in the cave-art sites a symbolic landscape of imagery in which various galleries and passageways associated with different subjects are arranged in such a way as to convey fundamental ideas about life and nature. Sites such as Lascaux (see pages 50–51), with its richly decorated Hall of the Bulls and Chamber of the Felines, perhaps make this theory attractive, but unfortunately the mythologist Joseph Campbell's words are likely to remain true for the foreseeable future: "to the mystical function that each of these galleries served—for millennia—we have no clue."

It is generally assumed that the cave painters were male, but there is also a theory that the early interpreters of cave art underplayed the number of female, vulvic images, and in the process concealed some work that had been done by women. Various line markings have been read as records of menstruation, although the earlier hypothesis that they are calendrical is still plausible.

Rock-art rituals

When artists paint the surface of a rocky outcrop, they are imposing cultural expression on the ancient body of the Earth. It is widely believed that this conjunction of the human and natural worlds creates a source of great power and spiritual energy.

Rock-art sites sometimes function virtually as temples in drawing people together in worship. During the later seventeenth century, when Native Americans still conducted their ancient rituals in the open, the French priests Dollier de Casson and De Brehant de Galinée came upon a strange, human-shaped rock near Lake Erie that had been embellished with red ocher and facial features. In the area were many camps of people who had stopped to pay their respects to the stone and to leave offerings of skins and provisions in the hope of ensuring their safe passage across the often-treacherous waters of Lake Erie and Lake Huron.

An indigenous belief in the power of such sites continues today. For example, in northern Canada the Ojibwa people still believe that certain lakeside rockpainting and petroglyph sites are the haunt of spirits and tricksters; the Ojibwa either leave offerings of tobacco there or will travel quickly past on the opposite side of the lake. These sacred places are also sources of inspiration for shamans who seek to acquire knowledge from the spirit world through by dreams or visions. Perhaps similarly inspired, ancient hunters painted figures of animals and humans in shades of red, and sometimes yellow, ochre on the massive granite cliffs that line the innumerable waterways of the Canadian Shield region around the Great Lakes of Canada.

In southern Africa the San of the Kalahari and elsewhere often painted rocks with scenes of medicine men in rituals, sometimes dancing into a state of ecstasy in order to gain supernatural power. According to the San, many of the complicated abstract patterns that can also be found on the rocks were painted by the shamans. Recent research has demonstrated that the designs are similar to the neurological patterns produced when a human is in a state of trance.

Some people, such as the Tukano of South America, use similar patterns as the basis for their decorative art, and particular configurations are owned by different groups.

BELOW *The use of the handprint—a worldwide phenomenon, although this example is from a cave in Australia's Grampians—offers the perfect symbol, if not compulsive proof, of the connective nature between the rock, spirit world, and artist—as if the rock itself were being used to serve as a membrane between two realms of existence, the human world and that of the spirits.*

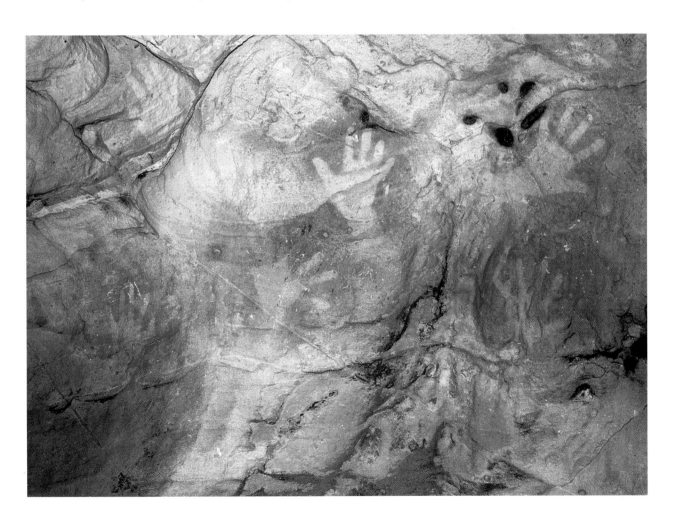

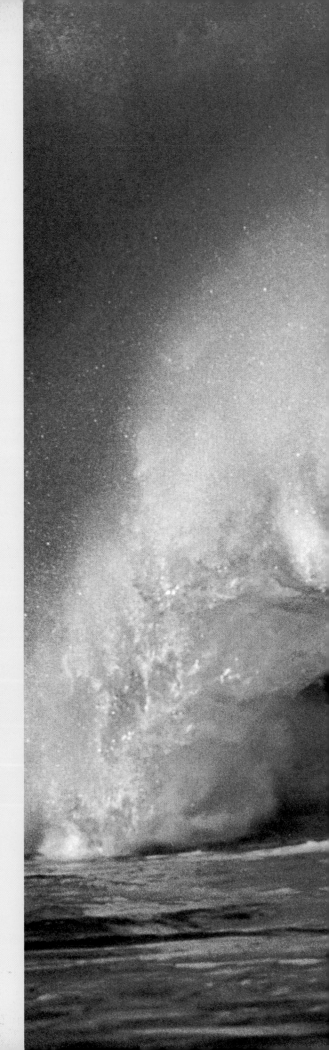

Earth Energy

From the highest mountains in the Himalayas to the holy springs of Ireland, features of the landscape have long been recognized by initiates as places where the Earth's spiritual pulse can be felt most strongly. This notion of the planet's energy is an extension of such empirically known natural phenomena as gravity and magnetism. Claims of success for dowsing and similar techniques conjures—even for many Western skeptics—a realm of quasi-electrical impulses within or beneath the Earth's crust. In many traditions such intimations of Earth energy have been overtly spiritualized. A seeker might retire to a mountain peak, a waterfall, or a cave in order to enter the perceived forcefield of the otherworld, believing that the energy encountered there will provide aid in the quest, and inner strength for the journey into the world of the spirit.

RIGHT *A wave breaks in Waimea Bay, Oahu, Hawaii. Thermal currents (heating at the equator and cooling at the poles), winds, tides, and the "Coriolis effect" (a result of the Earth's rotation) keep the oceans in perpetual motion, reinforcing the sense of the Earth as an animated ball of energy, informed by spirit.*

THE BODY OF THE EARTH

The belief in the living essence of our planet gains concrete and powerful expression when specific landscape features are interpreted as forming part of the body of a great supernatural being.

For the Thompson people of British Columbia, Earth-woman was long ago transformed into the present world: her hair became the trees and grass, her flesh became the earth, her bones became the rocks, and her blood became the waters. The Mesopotamian epic of creation, *Enuma Elish*, tells how the god Marduk killed his grandmother Tiamat, the goddess of watery chaos. He sliced her in two "like a fish for drying," then forced one half up into an arch to form the roof of the sky; he heaped the lower half with mountains, then pierced it to form watercourses. In Norse mythology the primeval giant Ymir rose out of the union of ice and fire but was slaughtered by Odin and his brothers, who created the earth from his body, rocks from his bones, stones and gravel from his teeth, lakes and seas from his blood, trees and vegetation from his hair, the sky from his skull, and clouds from his brains. In the Vedic hymn the *Rig Veda* the primordial man Purusha had his vast body pinned down by gods and sages prior to his sacrifice. They cut him into many pieces, from which the entire universe was created, including the sky from his head and the Earth from his feet.

Not surprisingly, cultures that view the Earth as a parent believe that it can provide direct physical nourishment. According to the Aztec Legend of the Sun, the original Mexica people were born in a cave and were suckled by Mecitli, the spirit of the Earth. Similarly in ancient Egyptian myth Hathor, the Earth and Mother goddess, was pictured as a cow, the provider of life-giving milk.

Caves and holes in the ground are in many regions viewed as vaginas, wombs, or other openings into Mother Earth (or, alternatively, sometimes exits from the underworld). The shrine of Kamakhya Devi in eastern India is a natural rockcleft that Hindus traditionally believe to be the vagina of the goddess who is said to menstruate once a year during a festival held in her honor. This direct correspondence between the natural landscape and the deities whose physical presence is believed to reside there is also

LEFT *An early 20th-century photograph shows a group of girls dancing around a phallic menhir in Brittany, northern France, in the hope of ensuring future fertility. In northern Europe there are thousands of upright stones that for millennia have been held to possess these powers. Popular wisdom advised young married women to sit on a menhir or recommended that barren couples dance naked among the stones.*

found in rock art where, for example, a painter or carver has seen a natural crevice as a vulva and incorporated it into a picture.

According to the creation myth of the Hopi people of North America, human beings entered the present world at an opening called the *sipapu*. This drama of emergence is acted out during the *wuwuchim* ceremony, a celebration of rebirth. The rite is held in secret once every four years in the sacred structure known as the *kiva* (see page 30). The *kiva* is conceived of as Mother Earth herself. A small hole in the center of the floor represents the *sipapu* and a ladder through a hole in the roof is seen as the umbilical cord leading out to the next world. During the ritual initiates make the transition to adulthood.

Stone monoliths are regarded as phallic in many cultures. In rural Brittany childless women made pilgrimages to ancient stone menhirs, seeing them as concentrations of male sexual potency: by offering up prayers to the stones they believed they would become more fertile. Similarly in India the god Shiva is represented by a phallic pillar known as a *lingam*—one of many associations between divinity and virility.

In Petra (Jordan), capital of the Nabatean kingdom that flourished *c*.150BCE–*c*.150CE, two obelisks stand on the summit of a mountain. The Arabian people who lived between what are now Syria and Saudi Arabia carved the sandstone away to leave the pillars, which stand some 20 ft. (6 m) high and 100 ft. (30 m) apart. The landmarks appear to have a religious purpose and may represent male and female divinities. Almost certainly they were symbols of fertility, and the site is known to modern Bedouins as Zibb Attuf, "The Place of the Merciful Phallus," suggesting a continuing tradition of sexual associations.

The world's navel

The most sacred stone of ancient Greece once stood in the oracle chamber of Apollo's shrine at Delphi, on

The Journey to the Center of the Earth

The stories of the French writer Jules Verne (1828–1905), who is often regarded as the father of modern science fiction, tended to be based on scientific theories, inventions, and accounts by travelers, and show his fascination with themes of geographical space and territory. A recurrent motif is the *omphalos* or central point. Verne's perhaps most successful work, *A Journey to the Center of the Earth* (first published in 1864), is a geological epic in which, typically for Verne, prosaic science and poetic fantasy are skillfully combined to produce a compelling account that inverts the more commonplace fascination of adventures in outer space. One influence on the novel was the theory posited by John Cleves Synmes, of the US Infantry, that the Earth was hollow and made up of five concentric spheres, with openings several thousands of miles wide at the poles. Interwoven with this idea was the theory expounded by the Frenchman Charles Sainte-Claire Deville, a distinguished geographer who was also a friend of Verne, that all the volcanoes of Europe were interconnected by a network of subterranean passages.

the southern slope of Mount Parnassus. According to the Greek poet Hesiod, writing in the eighth century BCE, the egg-shaped stone had been placed there by Zeus and stood next to the tripod on which the priestess sat to deliver her prophesies, possibly inspired by narcotic vapors emanating from the depths of the Earth. The Greeks regarded this stone as the center of the world and called it the *omphalos*, or navel; in doing so they symbolically connected the stone with the body of the goddess Gaia, who was seen as the Earth itself.

Another *omphalos* was located on the island of Crete, a sacred place where the umbilical cord of Zeus was believed to have fallen after his birth. The sites of these two navel stones, at Delphi and on Crete, symbolically brought together the supreme god Zeus and the Earth goddess Gaia, and were seen as the dual source of all the world's creative energy, the wellspring of life itself.

In some cultures the navel is believed to be manifested in natural features of the Earth. Sometimes weathered mountains, their peaks reaching up to the heavens, are said to mark the cosmic center. Mount Gerizim in Palestine was described in the Hebrew Scriptures (Old Testament) as the navel of the Earth, and the name of Mount Tabor derives from the Hebrew word for navel, *tabur*. The rock on which Jerusalem was built was also seen as a kind of navel: according to Hebrew tradition, it was the spiritual center of the holy lands, the pivot of creation; it is also sacred to Muslims as the place where Muhammad ascended into Heaven.

The cosmic center, which may also be marked by a tree, pillar, or other symbolic focus, gives a reassurance, in the landscape, of a world in which harmony and order have positive meaning.

There are potentially as many symbolic world centers as there are social groups. The Pueblo Indian Tewa people, for example, see every village as a microcosm of the world—at the center of the village is the most sacred spot, which translates as "earth mother earth navel middle place." This is set within a series of objects oriented to the cardinal points: four plazas, four shrines, and four sacred mountains.

Many megalithic monuments throughout Europe make explicit reference to human anatomy in their construction and decoration. At the passage-grave of Gavrinis, built on a small island in the Gulf of Morbihan in Brittany, twenty-three upright stone slabs that line the passages are completely incised with complex abstract designs. Each design is a set of increasingly larger arcs that extend outwards from a vulvic shape in the center. Certain researchers have interpreted this pattern as a belly with an *omphalos* protruding at the top, executed in an attempt to connect the dead with the navel of the Earth. The domed mound of Silbury Hill in Wiltshire, England (see pages 138–139), might also be said to resemble the belly of a goddess: the *omphalos* is the circular summit of the hill.

The cosmic pillar

A vertical axis linking this world with those above and below appears in systems of belief throughout the world in three dominant images. The World Mountain and the Cosmic Tree are probably the best known; the third is the Fire, with its column of smoke ascending to the sky. In architecture the pillar often represents the archetypal cosmic axis, the center line about which other objects rotate and to which they refer. Pillars may also express ideas that do not relate to the center: ancient Greek columns, for example, may have symbolized sacred groves of trees where the gods dwelled. Cosmological significance is evident in numerous pillar forms, from the totem pole, the ritual ladder, and the lotus stalk to the *lingam* (phallus) of the Hindu god Shiva; the cosmic pillar is also represented in spires and pinnacles, continued as an imagined line inside a building or extending from the highest point in the roof.

Such pillar imagery generally relates the Earth (and sometimes an underworld) to the sky, but to be completely understood it must be interpreted in the cultural context from which it emerges. The totem

BELOW *The decorated and incised passage at Gavrinis tomb, east of Carnac in Brittany. The interior is aligned to the midsummer solstice, but the motive for this is unknown. The spiral pattern, however, is believed to represent the journey of the soul as it travels through death to rebirth, in much the same way as the powers of the Sun appear to be resurrected daily.*

Delphi

Mount Parnassus, Greece

Delphi lies below cliffs on the southwestern slope of Mount Parnassus and was once the holiest place in ancient Greece. Believed to be the navel (*omphalos*) of the world, it was there that two eagles met when released by Zeus from opposite ends of the Earth. According to Homer, the god Apollo made the place his sanctuary after ridding it of the great serpent Python—probably a form of the Earth goddess. The Delphic oracle combined the powers of the male Sun and the female Earth. It is not known when the famous oracle was established, but from the sixth century BCE Delphi with its shrine of Apollo became one of Greece's most renowned sacred sites.

A temple was built to honor the god and over centuries a vast complex developed. According to legend, Apollo's temple was made first of beeswax and feathers, later of bronze, and finally of stone. The oracle, however, remained Delphi's focal point.

The priestess (Pythia) issued her cryptic soothsaying messages from a chamber deep inside the temple that housed the *omphalos*, a carved stone said to be the center of the world (see pages 57–58). It was believed that the prophecies were inspired by powerful "spiritual" vapors, or intoxicating fumes, which rose from a large cleft in the earth beneath the stone. (The use of narcotics by the priestess is probably the more likely explanation.)

After *c.*300BCE the oracle began to lose authority and in *c.*390CE the Roman emperor Theodosius had the temple closed as being anti-Christian.

LEFT *During the 5th and 4th centuries* BCE *the site at Delphi grew into the greatest of all Greek oracles—even mighty foreign kings came to ask their fortunes. Through fees and offerings Delphi built up the richest collection of treasures in the Greek world, but the treasures were plundered by the Roman emperor Nero in 67*CE*, and after a long decline the oracle was shut down by Theodosius. At the center of the site is the Temple of Apollo, now reduced by earthquakes to a few pillars (left); the priestess sat in its inner sanctum. Above the temple were a 2nd-century stadium (for games and musical competitions) and a 4th-century theater, its seating still well preserved and capable of hosting an audience of 5,000.*

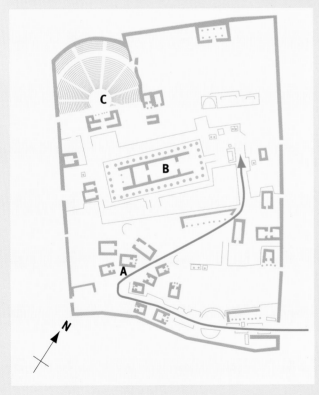

ABOVE LEFT *The sanctuary of Athena Pronaia was built in the 4th century* BCE *after an earlier temple was destroyed by an earthquake. The structure stands slightly away from the main area of the oracle. It was originally supported by magnificent Doric columns, but only three remain.*

ABOVE RIGHT *The omphalos stone—a rounded cone marking the navel of the world. The meaning of the strange carvings is not known; it may be geomantic.*

LEFT *Plan of the temenos (sacred area). Visitors washed in the Castalian Spring, then climbed the paved Sacred Way (shown in red) and zigzagged uphill via a series of carefully planned views, each with its own emotional impact, past the offerings, statues, and treasuries (A) of various individual cities, such as the Treasury of the Athenians, to the imposing Temple of Apollo (B). Behind this was the theater (C). Inside the temple stood statues of Zeus and Apollo; the sides of the building were filled with riches: tripods of gold given by Tyrant of Syracuse and donations of sculptures.*

poles of the Native Americans, for example, combine the image of the cosmic pillar with vivid and bold depictions of the sacred animal insignia of the clans to which they belong. Mounting to the sky, the totem poles declare the accumulated ancestral glory of the people who live in the houses below.

Trees are perhaps the most obvious objects in the natural world that reach to the heavens and they have offered endless inspiration for builders in nearly every culture, providing not only material for construction but a wealth of images: of verticality or solidity, of spreading branches, of rising sap or life-giving fruit. The first-century BCE Roman architect Vitruvius asserted that the first columns actually were trees.

The tree is a fundamental image in shamanic religions, in which a visionary specialist—the shaman—enters a trancelike state and is said to fly to other worlds where spirits dwell. In Central Asia the ritual ascent is often described as "climbing the Cosmic Tree," its multiple branches representing different levels of the universe. The Kwakiutl people of North America's Pacific Northwest coast wrap a cedar "cannibal pole" in red-cedar bark to endow it with *nawalak* (supernatural power). Projecting through the roof of the communal dwelling, the 40 ft. (12 m) post represents the copper Pillar of the World, said to uphold the heavens. It is this pillar that a shaman "climbs" to reach distant realms of the universe, and it is also the insignia of the god Baxbakualanyxsiwae ("the man-eater at the mouth of the river").

Images of a cosmic axis are particularly strong in Asia, where they can be traced back to the ancient Indian cosmology of Mount Meru, which stands at the center of the world (see pages 180–186). The Indian gods grasped this mountain-axis and used it to stir the primordial ocean, in this way initiating the creation of the universe. An important related image is the *gnomon*, the post that casts the shadow on a sundial. In ancient India the *gnomon* was erected as a pillar and had two functions: it cast the shadows by which the true cardinal directions were established,

and it was an architectural representation of the king of the gods, Indra, who "pillared apart" Heaven and Earth. Both Mount Meru and the *gnomon* are represented in the *shikhara*, the central tower of a temple. Each time a temple is built it is a symbolic reiteration of the act of separation that allows life to proceed. As long as the primordial chaos is separated into distinct vertical parts, such as heavenly, earthly, and the lower demonic realms, the world may continue.

The symbolism of the *yurt* (domed tent-dwelling) from Inner Asia refers to a cosmology based on the cardinal points and a three-layered universe. Here the

Structures Striving for Heaven

The main features of Gothic-style medieval European church architecture are all vertical in emphasis. Pointed arches, flying buttresses, rib-vault ceilings and spires are directed upward as if reaching to Heaven. These features first came together in 1144 in the revolutionary abbey-church of St-Denis near Paris. The first great Gothic spire was on the south tower at Chartres Cathedral (1194–1220). Yet, owing to the difficulty and expense of the work, many more spires were designed than were completed (Chartres was to have six, rather than its actual two).

Unlike the restful harmony embodied in the Greek temple, the Gothic tower uses sharp tracery, interruptions of line, and spiky pinnacles to express religious aspiration. The architectural historian Nikolaus Pevsner has written that Gothic architecture achieves a precarious balance between the vertical and the horizontal. The spire—the culmination of all the elements—represents a logical necessity to complete the effect of upward movement that starts at ground level. The balance and contrasts between the upward drive and the horizontal pull may be seen as reflecting the tension of the Christian soul striving for holiness.

pillar is invisible, yet absolutely vital. The Mongolian *yurt* consists of felts tied over a round wooden structure of lattice walls and a roof made of poles radiating from a central hollow ring. The outer ends of the poles are tied to the walls, while the inner ends are slotted into the central ring. Supported by two posts, the ring is left uncovered and serves a practical purpose as a smokehole.

The line from the hearth through the smokehole to the sky forms the vertical axis, and it is from the position of the hearth that the four cardinal directions are reckoned. The hearth-fire is, at one and the same time, both domestic and sacred. It is protected from impurities and aggressive actions, and symbolizes the ongoing life of the family inhabiting the *yurt*. For someone to declare, "May your hearth-fire be extinguished," is the worst of evil spells, equivalent to wishing the extinction of all descendants. Like smoke on a still day, prayers ascend to the sky, which is said to be the source of all blessings. The sky is also thought to receive sacrifices in the form of vapors from meat cooked on the hearth.

The *yurt* is an example of an archetype—the domed hut at the ideal center of the world, containing an axis to the heavens—that is found all over Asia, although the meanings given may differ. In ancient India a variant was the cupola on the central summit of the temple, as seen on the seventh- to eighth-century CE shore temples of Mamallapuram in southern India. The cupola represents both the hut of the wandering forest ascetic and the cap on the vertical shaft of the cosmic pillar.

In the Far East the nearest equivalent to the *yurt* is the pagoda, a development of the Buddhist *stupa* (see pages 160–164). The Chinese pagoda is attached to a temple, and has an image of the Buddha on the ground floor, beneath which is a crypt containing buried treasures. The pagoda may be hollow or it may have several floors, carrying either a series of images or perhaps having one giant statue that rises up through a number of stories. The elegant series of ever-smaller roofs and balconies receding into the sky probably developed from the thirteen discs or "umbrellas" that Indian *stupas* acquired around the eleventh century. But the pagoda may have had a native antecedent in the domestic house: this was a single square room, over which was a study, and above that an attic granary.

Pagodas are often sited strategically to block the entry of evil spirits from the northeast—the direction from which devils are thought to appear. Cosmic significance may be indicated by an uneven number of floors—usually seven, nine, or thirteen—relating to the number of skies in the universe. In more recent centuries pagodas have had several uses, from watching out for enemies to announcing the pomp and power of town authorities.

The Japanese pagoda usually has five roofs widely overhanging a square base, and is topped by a thin many-layered finial (*hosho*), the sacred pinnacle of the temple. The pagoda is often surrounded by pine trees, whose silhouette it resembles and the spiky leaves of which are believed to act as a conduit for a heavenly deity (see page 156).

LEFT *The Stone Garden at Taizo-in Temple in Kyoto represents inner peace. Such austere creations were a Zen development to foster contemplation. The rocks represent mountains and the gravel the patterns of the energized seas.*

Mapping the Environment

The Wopkaimin people of the Mountain Ok tribe in central New Guinea display game-animal bones and other tribal mementoes on the walls of their houses in such a way that they map the position of the local animals in both their natural and a social environment. Ancestral relics and the mandibles of sacrificial pigs come from the village area, and are placed in the center of the display; the relics, the most important objects, are placed at eye level, and the pig bones just below. Wild-pig bones come from the bottom zone of the rainforest, so are placed at the bottom of the display. Marsupials live in the upper zone, so their bones are at the top. The bones of cassowaries, birds found in both zones, are distributed in both the upper and lower parts of the display.

As the array builds up it becomes a symbolic map of the landscape in which the Wopkaimin live and hunt, reflecting the numbers and habitat of the animals hunted. By studying the array the Wopkaimin can gain a graphic impression of their environment, information that will help them to plan their future hunting strategies.

Monuments of the mythic mind

An individual's opinion about the world around them is determined by experience, cultural background, and spiritual outlook. The views of the world expressed in the early Judaic and Christian traditions were largely the product of the Hebrew Scriptures. For example, one sixth-century drawing represented the Earth as a rectangular box, the tabernacle of Moses: in the box was a mountain, the Earth, surrounded by ocean, and the lid of the box was the sky. Some medieval maps show Jerusalem as both the spiritual and physical center of the world. Until the seventeenth century the Earth was regarded in the West as the focal point of God's creation.

A culture's sense of identity might be reflected by cosmological focal points. The physical Inca empire also consisted of a mental image of a series of lines radiating from Cuzco, their course marked by sacred monuments. Delphi, likewise, represented the sacred heart of the Greek cosmos: it was the navel of the Earth (see pages 57–58), which itself was envisaged as the body of a goddess, Gaia.

Just as the Earth can be viewed in many ways, so different environments may be endowed with varying degrees of spiritual significance to create what has been termed a mythologized landscape. In many cultures features of the land may be significant elements in a repository of sacred knowledge and ancestral wisdom that is often crucial to survival. For example, the Pawnee of the Great Plains of North America once hunted within a territory that was denoted by five sacred sites, where the game animals were believed to assemble. As long as the hunters kept within the area demarcated by these sites and made offerings at them, they maintained their close spiritual relationship with the creatures upon whose meat and hide they depended. The oceanic environment of the Polynesians is traditionally viewed in a similar way: for them, maritime lore is not merely awareness of observable phenomena gained by experience, but sacred wisdom from the gods bestowed on the navigators for whom it was essential for survival.

The peoples of Australasia and Polynesia all recognize specific natural features of the landscape—fishing grounds, rocks, trees, rivers, caves, and ridges—as places that their ancestors visited and named. In this way, cultural knowledge and history is communicated to any descendant who passes by.

Many traditions convey sacred and practical ideas simultaneously. A Nunamiut boy learns about his

Caves in Mesoamerican Belief

The cave played a highly important part in Mesoamerican belief and ritual. The Sun and Moon were said to have been formed in a cave, and the first Nahuatl-speaking people were believed to have emerged from the ground at a mountain known as Chicomoztoc or "the place of the seven caves." Some researchers have identified Chicomoztoc with Arizona, and have suggested that the Nahuatl-speakers were distantly related to the prehistoric Anasazi people of Arizona who inhabited the natural caves found in cliff-faces (see pages 68–69).

As in many cultures, caves were used as natural shrines to gods and earth spirits. The Aztec god Centeotl was allegedly born in a cavern, and cotton and edible plants were said to have grown from different parts of his body. Tlaloc, the god of rain and earth, was honored with the yearly sacrifice of four children who were sealed within a cave, and inside the Yopico pyramid at Tenochtitlán the flayed skins of sacrificial victims were placed in an artificial cave as offerings to a vegetation god.

Such was the perceived power of the cave that it influenced the choice of site on which to construct the Pyramid of the Sun, the most important monument in Teotihuacan, the pre-Aztec "city of the gods." Built in the first century BCE, the pyramid was set directly over an earlier sacred place, an underground cave and shrine. The inhabitants hoped that, through the choice of such a location, the ancient power of the Earth would be harnessed to the new monument as it reached up toward the sky.

Further south in the Americas, caves play a prominent role in Incan belief. According to the Incas' origin myth, the ancestors of their people—three brothers and three sisters—emerged from a group of three caves at Pacariqtambo ("the place of origin"), near Cuzco (Peru).

local Alaskan terrain in detail before taking his place in the hunt. Topographical information is conveyed in myths of the spirits, tricksters, and heroes who are said to have populated the hunting grounds. Through the mythic drama he builds up a symbolic picture of his area to guide him when he takes to the trails.

Paths to the underworld

Openings into the body of the Earth, by their nature dark and mysterious, elicit widely differing emotions. Some see them as damp, airless, and claustrophobic, infested with bats and other night creatures. No one, it is believed, would choose to live in such an

BELOW *Cappadocia in Anatolia is situated in the once-volcanic plateau north of the Taurus Mountains and has been home to settled communities for 10,000 years. The landscape has been carved by winds to leave curious cones of rock, in addition to caves and underground "towns" hewn by people needing to hide from the invaders who crisscrossed the steppes.*

Canyon de Chelly

Southwestern United States

UNITED STATES

Canyon de Chelly

PACIFIC OCEAN

MEXICO

Canyon de Chelly cuts deeply into the red sandstone beds of Defiance Plateau in northeastern Arizona. It was formed by a large desert wash that flows out of the Tunicha Mountains, winding sinuously until it disappears in juniper and sagebrush flats almost 30 miles (50 km) away. The canyon walls have been sculpted by centuries of weathering into myriad shapes, from sheer cliff-faces to spectacular mounds and hollows. This region of the Southwest is known as Four Corners; here four modern states meet amid ancient desert and rugged mountains.

In places where large areas of rock had broken away to create horizontal crevasses, an ancient agrarian people named the Anasazi (the "Ancient Ones," often called the Basketmakers, and the precursors of the Pueblo Indians) were able to take mud mortar, stones, and sticks and build multistoried dwellings that clung to the canyon walls. Some of these settlements could be reached only with the help of ladders or precarious footholds driven into the rock. Why they built in such a way is not known, but their cliff-side houses remain in place today in Canyon de Chelly, Pueblo Bonito in Chaco Canyon, the tableland at Mesa Verde, Tsegi Canyon, and elsewhere.

The Anasazi people also painted and engraved images—animals, humanlike figures, spirals, and other geometric designs—in caves or rock shelters throughout the canyon. They had first appeared in the region about 2,000 years ago, and after *c.*500CE they began to move from scattered villages into the well-populated cliff-dwellings. By *c.*1200CE their influence had spread through the southwest, but within a century they had abandoned the canyon-dwellings and moved on. After centuries of disuse Canyon de Chelly was temporarily reoccupied in the eighteenth century by Navajo people entering the area from New Mexico.

LEFT *White House settlement (so called because of the gypsum clay coating the upper section) is just one of some 400 in the Canyon de Chelly area created by the Anasazi c.1050CE. The settlement consists of two sections: one on the canyon floor built against the cliff-face and the other high above in a rock shelter within the cliff itself. The two sites were once connected by a four-story building. The larger, lower structure had between forty-five and sixty rooms and one kiva. Rockpaintings adorn the walls of the shelters. The Navajo later placed burial chambers within the ruins.*

ABOVE *Spider Rock, standing nearly 800 ft. (245 m) high, is the canyon's most dramatic geological feature. It is revered by the Navajo and Hopi as the lair of the Earth goddess Spider Woman, who serves as a link between the human world and that of the gods.*

LEFT *Canyon de Chelly has been a refuge for thousands of years. Woven baskets found in caves suggest the Anasazi were present between c.2500 and c.2000BCE. By 450CE they had begun to build houses under the protection of the cliffs—the beginning of a trend that climaxed in the monumental cliff dwellings.*

LEFT *At the head of the canyon the waters of Chinle Wash run between sandstone cliffs some 30 ft. (10 m) high. As the canyon winds its way through the plateau, the cliffs rise ever higher. Halfway, where Monument Canyon joins, the plateau rim is almost 1,000 ft. (300 m) above the canyon floor. Here the water of the wash is absorbed by the deep sand, except during storms when flash floods may rush the length of the canyon.*

environment, unless they had been compelled to, as in the case of Paleolithic peoples, who are thought to have sought shelter from the elements and a means to barricade themselves against fierce animals. Others, though, respond more positively to the openings' ancient and numinous connotations.

It is often assumed that Paleolithic cave artists held nature in awe and penetrated the darkness in search of spiritual enlightenment. However, fear of caves and crevices could well be a purely modern phenomenon. To early peoples they may have offered the promise of shelter and comfort in their womblike passages and clefts. People accustomed to living in a world without artificial light may have felt at ease in total darkness.

Nevertheless, it is probable that caves prompted contrasting emotions, and also that these found expression in beliefs about creation and death. As has been shown, myths of emergence are often set in caves or openings in the Earth—settings suggestive of birth. A cave shrine on Mount Ida in Crete is one of the sites claimed as the birthplace of Zeus; and according to the Anyanja tribal group from southern Africa, all humans and animals emerged from a hole in the ground at a place called Kapirimtiya, east of Lake Nyasa, leaving their footprints in a rock.

However, caves also lead to the gloomy regions of the underworld, land of the dead. Gilgamesh, the legendary Mesopotamian hero-king of the second millennium BCE, was compelled to travel more than twelve leagues through a dark and terrifying passage into the depths of Mount Mashu before he finally reached the subterranean home of the Sun.

Fertility symbolism associated with caves and dwarf rain gods appears in Mexico. In China caves were often sacred burial places for emperors, who were reborn from them.

Mountains of heaven and hell

Mountains are the points on Earth that come closest to the heavens, and in many cosmologies they are the center of the world, forming links between Earth and sky. A summit is often a sacred place, where mortals may draw close to the spirit world. Bear Butte, a high ridge in the plains of South Dakota, is regarded as sacred by local Native Americans and is used for vision quests (see pages 214–215) and other rituals.

According to the Hebrew Scriptures, Moses spoke to God and received the Ten Commandments atop

LEFT *In Japan many places in the landscape are sacred, for they are believed to be imbued with* kami *or "beings of higher place." The high, snow-capped cone of the dormant volcano Mount Fuji is one of Japan's most sacred mountains, and in a time-honored annual ritual of reverence it is climbed by thousands of pilgrims.*

Mount Sinai, a peak whose identity remains uncertain. It was on Mount Carmel that Elijah triumphed over the priests of Baal, on Mount Horeb that he heard the word of God, and from the Mount of Olives that Jesus ascended into Heaven.

Mountains are also seen as abodes of gods and goddesses, especially in areas where the peaks are veiled in clouds. According to the Pima people of California, a powerful deity, Siuhu ("Elder Brother"), lives within a deep labyrinth in the mountains adjacent to Pima country; he acts as a protector and is responsible for rain, crops, and tobacco.

In the Japanese Shinto religion mountains such as Mount Fuji are not simply the dwellings of deities but, according to some, their physical embodiments. The Navajo likewise view certain mountains as the bodies of their most important nature spirits: a male

ABOVE In this seventeenth-century Hindu painting from Rajasthan, the Lord of Mount Govardhana, the god Krishna, holds aloft the mountain to shield the women and herdsmen of Mathura from a storm sent by the Vedic god Indra who is angry that the villagers have abandoned him for Krishna, the deity of a new religion.

who rules all plants and wildlife, and a female in charge of water and water creatures. The male figure is believed to stretch along two mountain chains, the Chuska and Carrizo: his legs lie along the Carrizo, his neck at a mountain pass, and his head at Chuska Peak. The female lies across the valley with her feet and body resting on various mesas and her head supported by Navajo Mountain. Some peoples see the rocks of a mountain as bones, the streams as blood, the vegetation as hair, and the clouds as breath.

Hindus and Jains regard a golden mountain called Meru as the center of the cosmos. The roots of Mount Meru are believed to be in the underworld, and the mountain is said to be wider at the top than the bottom, like an open lotus blossom. The abode of the gods, it is represented in Hindu temples as the roof-tower that surmounts the shrine.

Markers of the center of the world in many cultures (see pages 60–61), mountains are also seen as the symbolic ends of the Earth, sheltering the territory of the people who live in their shadow. The protection afforded, though, may be contingent on pilgrimage and sacrifice, such as that performed by the Aztec citizens of mountain-ringed Tenochtitlán.

In north European folklore mountains are often said to be the dwelling-places of kindly (but mischievous) dwarves expert in metalwork and in the forging of magic rings and swords.

The power of the Earth explodes into fierce and vivid reality when volcanoes erupt. It is difficult not to imagine the mythical fury of underworld beasts and the rage of gods as fire and ash surge into the sky in towering clouds, then rain destruction on the land below. The Greeks believed that the 100-headed monster Typhon was subdued by the gods and chained to the land beneath Mount Etna and that, as the monster surged against its chains, it moved the earth and blasted the air with fire and smoke.

BELOW *Few events on Earth can equal the power of a volcanic eruption. These ash-laden clouds are billowing from Mount Etna in Sicily, believed by the ancient Greeks to lie above the lair of the monster Typhon. Lava, momentarily so destructive, nevertheless brings with it regeneration through rich, highly nutritional new mineral deposits.*

Volcanoes were sometimes viewed in a more positive light. In a myth of the Tsimshian people of British Columbia the trickster spirit Raven brought light to humankind from a volcano that was active into the eighteenth century. However, even if volcanoes brought fire and light and, for later generations, renewed fertility in the soil, their destructive impact guaranteed fear and respect. In Hawaii sacrifices were thrown into the crater of Kilauea in order to ease the wrath of Pele, the goddess of volcanoes. The preferred gift was a suckling pig. People still throw offerings of food into the crater, and some witnesses claim to have seen Pele in the guise of an old woman before an eruption.

When a volcano is dormant or extinct, as is Mount Fuji, it often continues to have the status of a supreme being. The flanks of the Nicaraguan volcano Ometepe are dotted with prehistoric stone images, graves, and burial urns, all pointing to a belief in its supernatural power.

Millions of years of erosion have stripped away the cones of some volcanoes to leave strange gaunt lava cores soaring high above the land. These ancient long-dead hulks continue to arouse a sense of mystery. Devil's Tower in Wyoming—a giant gray column of solidified magma venerated as a sacred shrine by native Lakota (Sioux), Kiowa and other Great Plains peoples—was the site chosen by Steven Spielberg for the first alien spaceship to land in the movie *Close Encounters of the Third Kind*.

Treasures of the Earth

The life of the rocks that formed the Earth ends when they are worn away over time by weathering and broken down into various sands and clays. Red ocher, one of the weathered compounds of iron, is a natural earth pigment that has been used for rock art ever since the first Paleolithic artists decorated the walls of their caves, as well as being a sacred substance used in rituals and for ceremonial body painting (see pages 44–53).

A Face Twisted by the Mountain

The Iroquois people of eastern North America have a secret healing organization known as the False Face Society. During rituals members wear carved wooden masks that represent the various Iroquois spirits who are believed to exist as disembodied faces in the forest. The origin of one spirit, Twisted Face, is said to have involved a dramatic encounter with a mountain. According to legend, Twisted Face was a giant who lived near the Rocky Mountains. One day he met up with the creator and argued that he, the giant, had made the Earth. In order to settle the argument the two decided to see which of them could move a mountain by magic. The giant called out to the peak, and it moved slightly. Then the creator called out, and the mountain rushed toward him. As it approached, the giant turned around and it smashed him in the face, breaking his nose.

Because metals, like human beings, were an earthly substance with spiritual potential (through smelting), they were listed in a cosmic hierarchy and associated with the seven known planets: lead was linked with Saturn, tin with Jupiter, iron with Mars, copper with Venus, mercury with Mercury, silver with the Moon, and gold with the Sun.

Minerals and metals sometimes play a role in myths and folklore. For example, according to an Iroquois creation myth, a mysterious stranger thrust a flint-tipped arrow into the ground and made the

OVERLEAF *The peaks of Lapchi Kang at dawn (Chobo Bhamare on the right), viewed from Dukpu Danda, in Helambu, Nepal. It was here and in other similar mountainous places that Shiva was said to meditate. Such sacred sites are* tirthas *or fords between this world of ordinary experience and the divine realm.*

Stones with Secret Power

Jewels are commonly regarded as symbols of the hidden treasures of knowledge or truth, and their shaping and cutting signify the soul shedding itself of the physical body's corruption.

Individual jewels have acquired a variety of symbolic meanings. In Russian folk belief the blood-red ruby was a cure for hemorrhages, and in Muslim lore a ruby supported the angel who held up the Earth. Emeralds were believed to cure many ailments and were said to have the power to calm stormy seas.

Hindus claim that the first sapphire was formed from one of Brahma's tears. According to the Hebrew legend of Aaron's Rod, which blossomed and bore fruit as a sign of Yahweh's power, the rod was made of sapphire and engraved with ten letters representing the ten plagues that were sent to strike Egypt.

In Persia the diamond was once seen as a source of evil, whereas in other traditions its brilliance and hardness give it a warmer spiritual significance.

daughter of the first woman pregnant; the child to whom she gave birth was an evil trickster called Flint. In British folk belief it was traditionally thought that flint chippings were the tips of arrows shot by fairies.

Unusual mineral patterns in rock formations are often said to indicate sites where supernatural events took place. In the early twentieth century some North American Ojibwa people were paddling down a river when they saw veins of white quartz snaking through a multicolored granite rock, and they interpreted the pattern as marking the body of a spirit-being. Other people in the region believed that shiny flat crystals of mica set with quartz and feldspar crystals in outcrops of pegmatite were the scales of the underwater *manitou* ("divine spirit") Mishipishew.

Certain Aboriginal groups in Australia believe that a sky god hurled crystals to the ground and that their sacred origin has given these rocks the power to assist shamans in finding lost souls. According to Buddhist belief, crystals are a symbol of spiritual knowledge. Throughout Western culture these solids penetrable by light are still the stock-in-trade of fortune-tellers, owing to an ancient interpretation of them as fragments of a star or of the throne of a god.

In antiquity analogies were sometimes made between the formation of metals and the creation of human life. Alchemists both in China and in western Europe thought that minerals grew in the body of the Earth like fetuses and that, given time, common metals would change into gold, the ultimate symbol of perfection.

Gold is remarkable because of its extraordinary luster, durability, resistance to rust, and the fact that it is malleable enough to be pounded to the thinnest leaf. It has always decorated the elites of the world, both during their lifetimes and after their deaths, and is almost universally regarded as a symbol of wisdom and immortality. The ancient Egyptians regarded gold as a divine substance and believed that the flesh of the gods was made of gold, their bones of silver (a metal rare in Egypt and one that therefore had to be imported). The use of gold in the death masks of pharaohs reflected their belief that they became gods after their death.

Iron was associated by Herodotus with "the hurt of man" and by the ancient Egyptians with the bones of the destructive god Seth. In West Africa, by contrast, ironmaking was the craft that made possible the hard-edged tools with which people tamed the landscape. Among the Dogon and the Yoruba iron was considered a gift from Heaven, and the secret of blacksmithing was imparted by divine ancestors.

The soft body of the Earth holds the nutrients for almost all natural life. "Earthdiver" origin stories, especially common among Native American groups, draw attention to the soil's vitality. According to such myths, scraps of mud carried up from the bottom of the primordial sea by otters, ducks, or other water creatures are magically transformed into the first dry land. The sacred role of the soil in the origins of life is also emphasized in accounts of the creation of human beings. Ancient Athenians believed that their original ancestor, Kekrops, was a half-man, half-serpent formed from the soil. In South America the Aché of Paraguay still place a newly born baby on the soil to create a symbolic bond between the child and the sacred Earth.

Certain deities celebrate the sustaining role of the soil in agriculture. According to Homer and Hesiod, Demeter was a goddess of the soil who made love to the hero Iasion in a field "in the fat land of Crete" and thus produced the crops essential to survival.

The soil within a particular field may be felt to possess a unique fertile essence. The Chuvashes, a Finno-Ugric people, practice a fertility rite in which

BELOW *Blocks of freshly cut peat mimic the shape of Errigal, the highest peak in the Derryveagh range in northwest Donegal, Ireland. The creation of fire from the Earth has strong elemental symbolism—though in modern times the exploitation of peat is tempered by its status as a non-renewable resource.*

they "steal earth." This ritual is important because the spiritual potency, and hence the fertility, of soil is believed to vary from one cultivated field to another. An unsuccessful farmer might "steal" a clod of earth from a successful field to improve the land in his own field. The Chuvashes also believe that the "field mother," the sacred essence of the soil, can be transmitted from field to field on the hooves of a horse.

In Burma soil is held in such high regard that it is taken to be one of the seven earthly metals, along with gold, silver, iron, copper, lead, and tin.

The coming together of soil and rain, which is fundamental to fertility, is itself sacred to many agrarian peoples. Hopi mud-dancers cover themselves in mud and charcoal for curing and rainmaking rituals, and may chase and smear onlookers with mud in order to draw them into this celebration of life.

The deep spiritual importance of mud art may be appreciated in Mud Glyph Cave in Tennessee. Here

ABOVE *The basalt formations of the island of Staffa in western Scotland's Inner Hebrides. Over many millennia the power of wave action along these coasts has gouged out sea caves from the bedrock. The most famous example in Staffa is Fingal's Cave, named for the Celtic hero Finn mac Cumhaill who, say the stories, did not die but sleeps with his warriors in a cave where one day they will awaken to save Ireland in its hour of need.*

the visitor must wade and crawl through long narrow passages to reach an extraordinary complex of images that have been scraped and gouged out of the mud with fingers. These are believed to date from the fifth century CE and include costumed figures and animals, among them some powerfully suggestive serpents and winged creatures. They were probably made by ancestors of the Cherokee or Creek peoples, who believe that humans were created from the mud of the Lower World by a powerful being.

The spirituality of rock

From the perspective of a human lifetime, rock has seemed to possess an immovable, eternal nature. This may explain its association, in many cultures, with the supernatural and the divine. Rock stores heat, cold, water, and (as gemstones) light, and much of its symbolism comes from these properties, and from its unyielding solidity. Its sacredness is reflected not only in prehistoric megaliths but also in its use for objects such as amulets and for sacrificial knives.

Supernatural beings are often said to reside in rocks. The Sami of northern Russia believe that certain unusual stones known as *seite* are inhabited by spirits that control the surrounding animals. An account from 1671 describes a ritual in which the spirit within the *seite* was propitiated by a reindeer sacrifice in order to ensure good hunting. In the forests of northern Russia the hunting and gathering Tungus people believe that a dangerous spirit of the woods, the Forest Master, can take the form of a rock, so they avoid any rock that resembles a human or animal, for fear of disturbing him. Elsewhere in the world small rocks or stones are sometimes piled up and viewed as representations of a deity; in the south of India, for instance, rocks heaped in village shrines are regarded as the *ammas*, local goddesses who guard villages.

Stones themselves are widely believed to have sacred or magical properties, and prayers or offerings are often made at prominent or strangely formed outcrops associated with spirit energy. In Brittany and elsewhere ancient standing stones and other monoliths are traditionally believed to contain the power to make barren women fertile (see page 56). Those who succeed in kissing a particular stone at Blarney Castle, Ireland, are said to receive the gift of eloquence; this idea is based on the oracular symbolism of stone, in Celtic tradition and elsewhere. Small painted stones decorated in prehistoric times and discovered at the foot of rockpainting sites in western Canada may have been charms: the use of stones as talismans is found almost everywhere.

In ancient Greece people would traditionally leave piles of small stones on top of herms, the roadside obelisks (often phallic) that represented the god Hermes, the patron deity of communication and travelers. In doing so they hoped to win the god's favor or protection on their journey.

Stones may become powerful symbols of identity for a people. At Delphi in Greece a carved stone marked the *omphalos*, the center of the world (see pages 58–61). Scottish kings were enthroned at Scone in Fife on a sacred "stone of destiny" reputed to be the very one on which the patriarch Jacob laid his head when he dreamed of the destiny of the Israelites. Legend has it that it reached Scone after being carried

The Stone of Destiny

Scotland's Coronation Stone, or Stone of Destiny, is a block of sandstone weighing 336 lb. (152 kg) and inscribed with a Latin cross. This inanimate object is steeped in mystery and intimately connected to Scottish national identity.

In antiquity the stone was reputedly kept in the Temple of Jerusalem, thus lending the monarchy a biblically inspired legitimacy. Blessed by St. Patrick, it was brought to Scotland from Ireland and was used to inaugurate dozens of rulers, culminating with the Dalriadic kings of Scotland at Scone in the ninth century CE. Following Scotland's defeat by England's King Edward I, in 1296 the stone was removed to Westminster Abbey in an act that symbolically transferred sovereignty. Since then, every monarch in England, and subsequently of the United Kingdom, has been crowned while sitting above Scotland's ancestral enthroning stone in the abbey's Coronation Chair. Only in 1996 was the stone returned to Scotland, where it is now on display in Edinburgh Castle, in the capital city and home of a new self-governing parliament.

from the Near East to Ireland, original homeland of the Scots, where it was used in enthronement rituals. When the Scots were defeated by King Edward I of England (who ruled 1272–1307), he moved the stone to London, incorporating it into a new coronation throne to symbolize his subjugation of Scotland.

Prominent outcrops of rock feature significantly in the mythologized landscape of many cultures. For hunting and gathering peoples they may be the places where supernatural ancestors went about their daily tasks. Sometimes rockmarkings are identified as footprints or other human traces, and taken as proof of

an ancestral being's passing. In the plains of South Dakota the Lakota left offerings of tobacco and beads on an exposed rock said to bear human footprints, and the Australian ancestral beings Djanggawul and his two sisters were believed to have had sexual organs so long that they dragged along

the ground when they walked about during the Dreaming, leaving permanent marks on the landscape and conjuring many features into existence.

It is often believed that spirits inhabit strange rock formations. In northeastern North America the ocher image of a horned figure painted by the Algonquins on Painted Rock Channel at the Lake of Woods is thought to represent a rock-dwelling spirit similar to the Ojibwa *maymaygwayshiwuk*, tiny beings who were believed by some to be the painters of the red ocher images found across Ojibwa country in the Great Lakes region. These *maymaygwayshiwuk* are said to live in the crevices of the cliffs that line the lakeshores, whence they might creep out to steal fishing gear or play other tricks on travelers. The Mi'Kmaq (Micmac) people of Nova Scotia tell of a similar being called the *hamaja'lu*. In one tale a group of travelers happen upon the *hamaja'lu* tapping away at rocks and making pictures. On closer examination, the travelers find that the pictures are of themselves. Similarly the Aboriginal peoples of northern Australia claim that a race of supernatural tricksters, the *mimi*, live in cracks in the cliff-face of the Arnhem Land escarpment.

In some places the rocks themselves are regarded as animals, humans, or supernatural beings that have been transformed into stone. In the Kyushu district of Japan a stone formation set high on the cliffs of the hills of Matsuura is seen as a lady of the royal court, turned to stone as she watched her husband sail off on an expedition to Korea in 457CE. She still stands there, leaning forward with her dress trailing behind her, gazing after the disappearing ship.

In the Kimberleys of northwestern Australia the Aborigines view an entire rock formation as the *wandjina*, the ancestors of the Araluli people, who

LEFT *These large red granite boulders in the arid Australian Outback were eroded from the bedrock over millions of years—a reminder of the distant beginnings of earthly creation. Known as the Devil's Marbles, the Aborigines regard them as the eggs of a Rainbow Snake.*

are believed to have been turned to stone as they stood fishing for rock cod. The Judeo-Christian tradition recounts how the wife of Lot was turned into a pillar of salt during the family's flight from the destruction of Sodom: slender salt-rock outcrops are a notable feature of the area in which the Biblical story is set (see pages 99–102).

High rock outcrops are commonly seen as places close to the heavens, and as such they may be revered as the home of divinities. Examples include Spider Rock in Canyon de Chelly, Arizona (see pages 68–69), and the numerous outcrops in Europe dedicated to the god Apollo or the archangel Michael (see pages 140–141).

The forest sanctuary

Rooted firmly in the Earth and reaching toward the heavens with their branches, trees are natural links in the cosmos. With lifespans that often outlast those of human beings, they act as potent symbols redolent of time, maturity, and endurance.

According to a postmedieval legend, Joseph of Arimathea arrived at Glastonbury, England, in 63CE, planted his staff in the ground on Wearyall Hill and watched it blossom into a hawthorn tree. Certainly there was a tree here, known as the Holy Thorn, that bloomed at Christmas, and although it was cut down by a Puritan in 1643 its descendants survived; in 1951 a new Holy Thorn was planted on the hill.

The annual cycle of deciduous trees, through budding, flowering, leaf-fall, and the bearing of fruit, provides visible proof, on the largest scale, of the creative force within nature. Trees have therefore come to be seen as symbols of fertility. The Yarralin people of the Northern Territory of Australia have a

Dreaming site for their *karu*, or uninitiated males, at a billabong near Lingara. The trees that grow around the site supposedly sprang from the semen of a group of *karu* who had stopped there; each of the trees is said to be an individual *karu*, and they are led by a large dead tree known as the "boss" *karu*. Men gather clay from the billabong and grind it with scrapings

RIGHT *In this sacred grove dedicated to the goddess Oshun in Nigeria a spirit figure has been carved into the bark of the tree. Oshun, a river goddess, befriends and blesses women with babies and is associated with love and beauty.*

of bark to create a potion that they believe will attract women. Women also have Dreaming trees, some of them at sites where they can receive the spiritual seed that is necessary for birth.

Many of the gods and goddesses of ancient Greece were believed to reside in sacred groves, to which people would retire for prayer or contemplation. The early Germanic peoples regarded oak groves as sacred, and would enter them to ask questions and listen for the answers in the rustling of the leaves. Today many neo-pagans call their outdoor meeting places "groves."

In the form of the Tree of Life, the tree is a powerful image of cosmic integration: it sends its roots down into the underworld, grows its trunk upward to the sky, and spreads its branches in a leafy bower over all humanity. In many creation myths that feature multiple worlds or levels of existence, the tree stands solid as the single unifying feature, a conduit for the flow of divine energy. The image is found across a broad span of civilizations, and there are many variations on the theme.

In some traditions the tree flourishes in paradise, or atop a sacred mountain. At its roots a fountain of spiritual refreshment may gush. A serpent coiled around the base of the trunk may symbolize a spiralling earth energy (or else destruction). Birds nesting in the topmost canopy may represent souls, or heavenly messages; fruits may signify the celestial bodies. Forming a network of communication, the tree was sometimes believed to offer a route to the first people who clambered up its trunk and through its branches to the present world. Cabbalistic and other occult traditions reverse the cosmic tree, depicting the roots nourished from the sky.

In Scandinavian mythology the giant ash tree Yggdrasil unites the cosmos: it draws sacred water from springs and wells at its base and supports a host of supernatural beings in its branches. On the highest branch sits an eagle scanning the world for Odin, chief of the gods, who was to hang himself on the tree as a sacrifice in order to gain knowledge of the

Goddesses of the Tree

Egyptian tomb paintings often depict the sacred tree above or beside a spring that bubbles with the waters of life. A woman is sometimes shown embodied in the tree, her task being to provide food and drink for the inhabitants of the underworld.

The Yakut of Siberia also have a tree goddess. They relate how the first man, on setting out to explore the world, saw a giant tree that joined Heaven, Earth, and the underworld and talked to the gods through its leaves. Feeling lonely, the young man asked the spirit of the tree to help him; a grave-eyed woman rose up from underneath the roots and offered him milk from her breasts. After the first man had drunk, he was filled with so much power and energy that no earthly thing could harm him.

runic symbols used in divination. There is an analogy here with Christ's sacrifice, and indeed medieval iconography often shows the Crucifixion on a tree rather than a cross.

In many cultures the tree is regarded not only as a symbol of cosmic unity, but also as the source of life. The Herero people of southern Africa believe that the first humans, as well as cattle, came from a tree called Omum-borombonga, in the grasslands south of the Kunene River. The tree is still alive, and when people pass it they leave offerings of small green twigs. And to this day pregnant women in several parts of Africa wear sacred tree bark in the belief that it will help them conceive.

In Guyana and areas of Venezuela the survival of humankind is said to have depended on a single tree. According to legend, the first people found that all the world's food was out of reach on one great tree; they chopped at it, and when it fell, water flowed from the trunk. The cuttings they took were said to

Darwin's "Tree of Life"

In his theory of natural selection Charles Darwin (1809–82) laid down the basis of modern theories of the evolution of species. There is a famous analogy in *On the Origin of Species* in which Darwin compares living creatures to a great tree that he calls the Tree of Life. The green and budding twigs represent the existing species while the old wood represents fossils. As the tree grows, the living twigs branch out on all sides. Successful branches shade and kill the surrounding weaker offshoots, just as successful species and groups of species have overcome their competitors. Most of these young limbs die and drop off, although some remain as thin and straggly branches, representing the threatened species. A few twigs become great branches, and a small number become major limbs, which support a dense foliage of new twigs and leaves at the top of the tree.

According to Darwin, "As buds give rise by growth to fresh buds, and these, if vigorous, branch out and overtop on all sides many a feebler branch, so by generation I believe it has been with the great Tree of Life, which fills with its dead and broken branches the crust of the Earth and covers the surface with its ever-branching and beautiful ramifications."

have become the first garden, a creation that has long been used to signify a state of paradisal bliss ("paradise" derives from the Old Persian word *paridaida*, meaning "encircled garden or park"); the symbol of the garden is frequently fruit—with some types sharing the cosmic properties of the egg.

The vine is an ancient symbol of fecundity in various traditions, but in the Mediterranean lands it is also associated with sacrifice: it is the emblem of the Greek god Dionysus, who became linked with sacrifice under the influence of the cult of Orphism.

The pomegranate, with its many seeds in a juicy pulp, is a fertility symbol with overtones of love, marriage, and the bearing of many children; it also suggests the oneness of the cosmos. One of the most positive of fruit symbols is the peach, which in the East is linked with immortality, longevity, youth, and protective magic. The acorn was sacred to the Scandinavian thunder god Thor, as part of a cult of the sacred oak tree.

Spirits of nature

Some philosophies (such as the Western Newtonian tradition) argue that the physical world is inanimate matter. However, many peoples elsewhere in the world sense that the substance of all earthly things is imbued with spiritual power, and that any item—even a stone or household pot—has both a material form and a living essence.

The peoples of Melanesia and Polynesia have a cultural concept of *mana* as a force immanent within anything from prized weapons to the personal power of a shaman and his ritual equipment and potions. Aristocratic families possessed great *mana*; the most important chiefs in Tahiti were never allowed to touch the ground when they traveled, because their *mana* was said to be so powerful that each patch of earth they made contact with would become a sacred place.

A reverence for nature lies at the heart of Japan's Shinto religion. Divine spirits or *kami* are everywhere, populating all natural things, especially those with unusual size or form, such as mountains or distinctive trees. They have a profound creative and harmonizing power that can never be understood fully, because it transcends our faculties of cognition.

BELOW *Votive offerings found in ancient forests attest to the fact that some of the world's oldest places of worship were wooded. The Celtic druids practiced their rites in groves of oak trees, and their word for sanctuary was identical to that used for grove or woodland glade. The Volga tribes in Russia also held ceremonies in sacred groves, each dominated by a central tree under which sacrifices were made.*

Native Americans also have a powerful sense of the sacredness of all creation. The Lakota concept of *wakan* refers to a spiritual essence which may reside in a whole range of objects from stones and trees to trade goods: at one time they called their firearms *maza-wakan* or "sacred iron." Among the Mi'Kmaq (Micmac) of Nova Scotia, if someone finds an unusual stone, or some other strange object, it may be prized as having *keskamsit*, or magic good luck, endowed by the creator spirit Kisurgub.

It was once assumed by Westerners that only aborigi-nal peoples saw the sacred in everything: their perception of a soul (in Latin, *anima*) within material objects was described as "animism" and was seen as a primitive form of religion, perhaps even the first expression of the religious impulse that in more developed societies had evolved via polytheism into monotheism. Sir Edward Burnett Tylor, the first scholar to carry out a broad survey of animistic beliefs, stated in his *Primitive Culture* (1871) that religion represented humanity's formalization of its relationship with the spirits that, it was perceived, "possessed, pervaded, crowded" everything in nature.

In ancient Greece animistic ideas were developed into a concept of nature as a living organism. Greek philosophers believed that the cycles of nature indi-cated that the world was alive, and that, because these cycles were regular and ordered, the world must also be intelligent. They thus viewed the natu-ral world as an animated being; according to the Greek philosopher Plato (*c*.427–347BCE), the creator endowed the world and all it contained, including every animal and plant, with a soul, the seat of which was the center of the Earth. In his philosophical work *Timaeus* Plato provided an account of the origin of the world and of nature that remained influential until the Renaissance. In this treatise Plato developed his concept of the *anima mundi* or "world-soul." He described the world as "the fairest and most perfect of intelligible beings, framed like one visible animal comprehending within itself all other animals of a kindred nature."

Members of the twelfth-century academic School of Chartres, in France, further animated and personified Plato's world-soul in their quest to relate the physical world to the sacred. The interest they took in the world-soul arose from their curiosity about creation. The school taught that by observing natural laws and striving to live in harmony with nature, humanity might grow closer to God.

This relationship between humans and the flora and fauna of the natural world is expressed in the religions, ceremonies, and arts of peoples across the pre-industrialized cultures of the world. In the Western world one surviving reminder is the Green Man, a nature spirit associated with the woodlands of Europe. His popularity was such that his image was carved in medieval churches. Known in England as Jack in the Green and in Russia and the Balkans as Green George, he is usually depicted wearing horns

ABOVE *A painted wooden mask from the Bapende people of Congo in heavily rainforested Central Africa. Such stylized evocations of animal heads are believed to concentrate great spirit power in the head of the wearer, protecting him from evil.*

and wreathed in foliage. His ability to control the rains was recognized in Russia on St. George's Day, when a man disguised as Green George was covered with branches and pushed into a stream in order to ensure summer rain.

The Green Man (sometimes shown as a woman or animal) exudes a potent symbolism. The sometimes agonized face is either enveloped by or spews forth leaves, branches, vegative growth, and even fruit such as grapes and acorns from its orifices. Whatever the real meaning behind this figure, its usually pained expression appears to hint at the involuntary nature of the growths, as if indicating that it cannot hold back the fresh life that results from its own decay. The Green Man offers a fitting symbol of life's cycle of death and rebirth.

BELOW *A foliate face, a variant of the Green Man, carved in the 14th century as a roof boss in the eastern cloister walk in Norwich Cathedral. Such imagery is not uncommon in medieval churches, perhaps reminding worshipers of the woodlands paganism that made way for Christianity and monastic settlements. In a similar vein, the Green Man's death makes way for new life.*

THE WATERS OF EXISTENCE

As water is essential to all life, its frequent association with spiritual and creative power has an obvious logic. Consecrated water is often used in rituals as a medium to bring about or symbolize a spiritual awakening, and baptism of one form or another is widely practiced as a rite of passage. To pass through water as a symbolic act of death and rebirth is commonly part of initiation rites marking the beginning of adulthood. The initiation rite of the Yolngu people of northern Australia reenacts the swallowing and regurgitation of two boys by Yurlunggur, a great serpent venerated as the source of rain.

In Christian baptism a new person is believed to arise from the waters, reborn within the body of the Church and the spirit of Christ. In early Christian societies baptism usually involved a person undergoing total immersion in streams and rivers, but by the fourth century the Church had introduced the practice of baptizing by trickling "holy water" over the recipient's forehead from a font blessed with the sign of the Cross.

The baptismal rite consciously parallels Christ's own death and resurrection, which, according to Christian theology, was prefigured in the Old Testament story of Jonah and the whale. Jonah was in flight from God until his traumatic ordeal in the belly of

LEFT *The falls at Niagara are the epitome of the elemental power of water. According to the local Iroquois people, the falls were created after a conflict between sky and earth powers—the Thunderer spirit and the Great Snake Monster. After the Thunderer killed the snake, its massive body fell into the river and became wedged in the rocks, forcing the Niagara to rise above it and fall in a cascade that offers a permanent reminder of good's triumph over evil.*

Ishtar, Dumuzi, and the Waters of Life

Water plays a significant role in the ancient Mesopotamian story of the Akkadian goddess Ishtar's (Inana among the Sumerians) descent to the underworld. The tale was first recorded in Bronze Age texts and later inscribed on clay tablets in the palace library built in the late eighth century BCE at Nineveh, the capital of the Assyrian empire.

The Mesopotamians believed that a boundless saltwater ocean surrounded the universe, and that Heaven and Earth had been formed by means of a cataclysm that churned up the primordial ocean. Some peoples talked of Marduk having achieving this by splitting open the ocean goddess, while others explained how the ocean goddess Nammu engendered a cojoined male sky and a female Earth, which were then parted and filled with life by her son Enlil. The cosmos itself was regarded as having various layers, including an upper realm or Heaven, the Earth, a freshwater underground ocean, and often an underworld where the dead were believed to dwell, unable to return to Earth.

When Ishtar, or Inana, the goddess of love, fertility, and war, forces her way into the underworld to retrieve her lover Dumuzi, she is stripped of her powers and treated as one of the dead, a situation that causes great problems on Earth, which is deprived of her gift of procreation. Only when Ea, or Enki, god of water and wisdom, intervenes to rescue her by arranging for her to receive life-giving water can she be revived and return to life on Earth.

The judges of the underworld, however, extract a price for Ishtar's freedom. Her lover, the god Dumuzi, must take her place in the realm of death for half of the year.

---

the "great fish," a symbol of the transfiguring energy of the cosmic waters of creation.

Ritual bathing has a physical as well as a spiritual function: we cleanse our bodies as we wash away our sins. Worshipers often touch themselves with water or wash before entering a sacred place, a practice shared, among many others, by ancient Greeks and modern Muslims and Hindus.

The ritual bathing of sacred objects is performed with similar intent. The ancient Greeks bathed statues of their goddesses every year to reaffirm their powers. Today the king of Saudi Arabia performs an annual ritual washing of the Kaaba stone, the sacred black rock that stands as the focal point of the Muslim holy city of Mecca (see pages 188–189), of which he is the guardian.

Water surrounding a place—contained in a dyke, moat, or ditch—offers physical protection, but is also traditionally believed to create a sacred enclosure, ensuring that the inner space remains pure.

The cosmic ocean

As discussed, a belief in the primeval importance and creative potential of life-sustaining water can be found at the heart of many of the world's creation stories. This is particularly well developed in the Near East, the concept of a cosmic ocean being found in both Persian and Indian traditions.

According to the holy book of ancient Persia, the *Avesta*, all was once a large flat expanse stretching away to a surrounding sea, windless and unwrinkled by waves. Order was hurled into confusion when evil irrupted into this world, its dynamism creating everything with which we are familiar today. This included the formation of water, which was gathered up by

OVERLEAF *Llyn Padarn in Snowdonia, Wales. Areas such as this are common settings for Celtic tales, for the mountains represent places of sanctuary and the deep mysterious lakes are thought to lead to another realm that the Celts often referred to as the Otherworld.*

the wind and swept into a great cosmic ocean called Vourukasha, from where it fell down to Earth as rain to run through streams to a host of seas. Under the surface of the Earth two great rivers returned rainwater to Vourukasha and completed another new cycle of life. Amid the waters of this cosmic ocean grew the Saena Tree, its branches bearing the kernels of every different type of plant. Living in the tree was the great Saena bird, which flapped its wings and caused seeds to fall to Earth, where they took root. Also rising from the ocean's depths was the mysterous Hom Tree in which the essence of the eternal life of the human soul was kept. The falling rain not only watered the Earth into teeming life, it also helped to give it definition by crisscrossing its surface with rivers and streams that ran into surging seas and separated the landmass into continents. And alongside the banks of the River Veh Daiti arose the first animal, a white bull, and the first man, Gayomartan.

The Indian *Vedas* spoke of creation as the act of making order out of chaos. Fundamental to such Hindu concepts is the notion that the external world is the product of the creative play of *maya*—the force of illusion whereby what humankind understands to be reality is in fact the dream of the creator god and magician, Brahma. Therefore the world as we know it is not solid and real but illusory; the universe is in constant flux with many levels of reality. Water identifies perfectly with *maya* because it is constantly changing as it flows from place to place. Water is both a symbol and an agent of illusion.

In Indian creation stories preexisting matter is rearranged rather than created. Universal consciousness, known as *brahman*, willed into being both the waters and a seed to float on them. The seed became an egg that contained Brahma, also known as Narayana because he was born of the waters or *naras*. Brahma later used his meditative powers to split open the egg and proceeded to create the rest of the universe.

As Hinduism developed over the centuries, cults embellished the creative roles of the subsequent gods Vishnu and Shiva, and in the popular creation stories of the Vaishnavites Brahma was cast as the creative force of Vishnu. It was said that Vishnu used his *maya* to create a vastness of primordial waters, where he then rested upon the hundred-headed serpent Ananta-Shesha who represented eternity.

In India, the preeminence of water is a recurrent theme—even fire was condensed into a vast sea in one early story, while in Hindu descriptions of the cosmos the Earth remains set in a salty sea.

Waters from within

In many traditions the source of the sweet waters that issue from the Earth as springs, wells, and waterfalls is the supernatural underworld. Wells and springs are often said to flow from the spiritual womb of the Earth and to possess the power to heal, confer wisdom, or grant wishes. At Bath in western England (see pages 96–97), archaeologists have found hundreds of "curse tablets"—imprecations scratched on lead pieces and thrown into the sacred spring of the

BELOW *In one celebrated Indian myth the entire universe existed within the meditation of Brahma the creator; the heavens, the world, and its peoples were the thoughts of the god. According to this version, Vishnu came into existence out of nothing, created the endless primordial waters and reclined on the hundred-headed serpent Ananta-Shesha, who represented eternity. As Vishnu rested, a lotus arose from his navel and opened to reveal Brahma, who produced and maintained the universe by the power of his thoughts. Vishnu continues to rest in the snake's coils until the next cycle of life.*

ABOVE Venus and the Fountain of Eternal Youth, *a detail from the 15th-century manuscript* Modena De Sphaera. *Spanish explorer Ponce de Leon sought in vain for the magical spring during his 16th-century journey through the territories of Florida and the Caribbean.*

Romano-British deity Sulis-Minerva, goddess of wisdom. In the symbolic imagination of the Zuni people of the Southwestern United States, springs are joined to the distant oceans as the runners of willow trees are to a single plant. According to the Zuni's origin myths, the Daylight People, the first humans, came up into this world from the underworld below through the waters of a spring.

As a source of life, springs and wells often act as symbols of love and marriage, sexuality and procreation. In the European tradition nymphs and fairies are widely believed to frequent their waters, beguiling lovers and strangers and giving rise to the notion of wishing wells.

The Tsimshian people of the northwestern coast of North America, relating how light came to the world, describe how the light-bringer Raven transformed himself into a leaf at a spring where the daughter of the chief of Heaven came to drink. The chief's daughter then swallowed the leaf and became pregnant, eventually giving birth to the great hero-trickster figure of Raven in his human form.

Throughout the world many sacred wells are said to have the power to make barren women fertile; closed wells, on the other hand, symbolize virginity. Wells can also be seen as dangerous places, because springs and wells are alleged to provide openings to the underworld. According to Irish mythology, for example, the hero Diarmuid grappled with a wizard at a magic well and fell into its depths, emerging in a supernatural land peopled with new adversaries.

There is an important group of holy wells in Ireland, exemplified by the Otherworld well of Seghais, which is interpreted as the source of the two great rivers the Boyne and the Shannon. Myths tell of a beautiful woman, acting as guardian of the well, whose favor was sought by visiting warrior chieftains: drinking from the well and intercourse with this woman were symbolically identified with attaining wisdom. Around the site were nine hazel trees, whose magic nuts supposedly dropped in the well to cause "bubbles of inspiration." A supernatural salmon in the well ate the hazelnuts, thereby becoming the Salmon of Wisdom (*eo fis*); anyone who can catch and eat it is endowed with bardic powers.

Holy wells are also found in Wales, some with healing properties, others serving as cursing wells. One of the latter is St. Aelian's Well at Llanelian yn Rhos, whose cult flourished in the early nineteenth century: the victim's initials would be scratched on a tablet of slate, or written on parchment sealed with lead, and placed inside the well. The idea recalls the curse tablets used by the Romans at Bath.

The quest for a fountain or spring that would ensure eternal youth is a theme that occurs in many traditions worldwide. Some peoples from western North America relate how the creator was about to bring humankind into being and summoned two buzzards to build a ladder to Heaven. He instructed the birds to make two springs at the top, one for drinking, the other for bathing. Whenever an old person reached the top and used the springs, their youth would be restored. The buzzards began their task but the trickster Coyote pointed out that if people had the promise of youth they would be eternally climbing up and down the ladder, without making friends or families. The buzzards realized that Coyote was right and destroyed their work.

LEFT *The Ffynnon Sara healing well at Derwen in Clywd, North Wales. Celts frequently left votive offerings at wells they considered to be sacred. Only Celtic goddesses, never gods, were associated with fresh water.*

The Bath Springs

Southwestern England

For at least 10,000 years hot mineral springs have gushed from the ground at the site of Bath, the point where a low clay ridge rises above the Avon River, Somerset, on one of its meanders through the Cotswold hills. The city there is said to have been founded by King Bladud who, after being cast out from his family for having leprosy, became a swineherd. During this time he noticed how his pigs were cured of their skin ailments after wallowing in the hot muddy spring. When he, too, tried this, his condition was also healed. In this way the pagan ancient Britons discovered the curative properties of the springs, which were sacred to Sulis, a goddess of water and healing whose name derives from the Celtic word for the Sun; it has been suggested that this refers to the heat of the springs.

The Romans identified Sulis with their own Minerva, resulting in a new healing deity who dispensed justice and retribution. Around 70CE the main spring, which they called Aquae Sulis (Waters of Sulis), was turned into a temple complex with baths for pilgrims and those seeking cures. Worshipers prayed to the Romano-British goddess for healing, protection, and the punishment of malefactors. Other deities were also worshiped, including a triad of Celtic Mother Earth goddesses, the Suleviae.

LEFT *The King's Bath was built by the Normans over the lead sanctuary created by the Romans around the spring, for the sacred status of Bath was still recognized 500 years after the Romans' departure. While the springs were used in the medieval period, it was only in the 17th and 18th centuries that Bath developed as a fashionable spa resort, when the King's Bath became the social focus.*

BELOW *The plan of the Roman baths of Sulis-Minerva shows the original spring to the north of the complex (at the bottom of this picture). In the center is the main bath. The goddess's temple, an austere building with a pediment supported on four Corinthian columns, stood to the northwest of the old spring.*

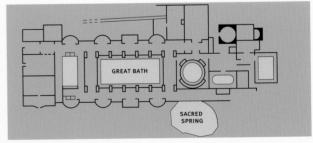

ABOVE *The Great Bath adjacent to the Pump Room. Built in 1790 during Bath's heyday as a spa resort, the Pump Room drew attention to the presence of extensive Roman remains in the city. An antiquarian, James Levine, began to explore the area in the 1860s, and the open-air Roman bath seen today was fully exposed only during the 1880s. Finds from the spring and culvert include many coins and inscribed leaden tablets, providing evidence that visitors asked the goddess for help in recovering possessions or punishing enemies.*

LEFT *The Roman bath, lined with lead mined from the Mendip hills, was rediscovered in 1755, but was not fully excavated and rebuilt until the 1880s.*

The rich symbolism of rivers

A river is an ancient and widespread metaphor for the course of human life, from birth, conception, or previous existence (the source) to death, the afterlife, or reincarnation (the river's outlet to the sea). In Buddhist thought the river of life must be traced back to its source in order to attain enlightenment. More generally, the parodoxical image of a river flowing upstream represents the return to a pristine, paradisal state of being.

For the ancient civilizations that were dependent on irrigation, rivers were major symbols of fruitfulness and contentment—as in the image of the four rivers of paradise flowing from the Tree of Life to the cardinal points.

Streams and rivers may form the boundary between life and death, the most famous example being Styx and Acheron, the rivers of Hades. In Japanese Buddhist and Shinto teaching the Sanzunokawa River is said to separate the dead from the living. Rivers also divide the visible world from magical regions such as the otherworld of old Slav tradition, which has often been envisaged as lying on the far shore of a fiery river.

Often regarded as sacred, rivers may even be seen as deities in their own right. The Tigris and Euphrates were worshiped by the ancient Hittites, and the Yoruba of West Africa believe that the Ogun River is the transformed goddess Yemoja. Whereas the Earth is often seen as a goddess, river water is sometimes viewed as the body of a god. In a deluge story told by the Ifugao people of the Philippines, the elders treated a dried-up river as being dead and in its grave; as they dug to find its soul, they opened a great gushing spring that soon covered the Earth.

The great Hindu pilgrimages in India are focused on three sacred rivers, the Yamuna, the Sindhu (or Indus), and, most particularly, the Ganges, which is venerated as a goddess, Ganga (see pages 100–101). Some of the rituals involve uniting the sacred essence of Ganga with the symbol of Shiva, bringing together the female river goddess and the male god of fertility.

Supernatural beings are also believed to reside in rivers. For example, among the Finno-Ugric tribal peoples of northwestern Europe water spirits are at once annoying tricksters, evil demons, and providers of fish and other food resources. The Votjaks of

LEFT *In ancient Egyptian religion water featured prominently. Life originated in a dry void within the universal waters and death was introduced when Osiris drowned. This boat, depicted in the tomb of Sennefer at Thebes, may be a vessel on which to journey into eternity.*

Russia call the festival of Twelfth Night "the following of the water spirit." On the morning after the festivities people may throw offerings of meat, bread, or porridge into the river—or even sacrifice a duck—in order to appease the spirit and to ensure a ready supply of food.

Like all waters, rivers are both dangerous and nurturing, as seen in those great rivers that seasonally flood but deposit a rich layer of silt when they subside. The Nile in Egypt, the Tigris and Euphrates in Mesopotamia, and the Indus in India provided, literally, the fertile soil for the first civilizations.

Sacred lakes and holy purity

The sea is the ancestral origin of life—formless, inexhaustible, latent with potential. This expanse of water is also a maternal image of great power, a metaphor for unfathomable wisdom, and, in psychology, a symbol of the unconscious.

Oceans can transform themselves from calm to frenzy within a matter of minutes. All maritime cultures tend to view them as a source of plenty, but also as an environment beset with dangers—not only storms, but also threats lurking in an otherworld below the water's surface.

In Norse myth the oceans were the blood of the giant primordial being Ymir, and ancient legends speak of giant sea goddesses, Hafgygr and Margygr, who wrecked ships. Early European maps of the world often show sea monsters in the oceans, inspired by the wildly imaginative accounts of seafarers.

The hold of the sea upon all who live beside it is captured in the somber stories fisherfolk tell of the spirits that haunt their daily lives. According to the Estonians, a version of the Baltic water spirit Nåkk would sometimes appear as a horse galloping along the seashore, enticing children to ride him to their doom in the waves. On other occasions the same spirit would bewitch the eyes of his victims so that they were unable to tell the land from the sea and were thus lured to their deaths.

A Watery Embrace for the Dead

Burial rites have long been performed on sacred rivers in many parts of the world. In Europe folktales and legends also refer to human sacrifices being made beside rivers and at sacred springs.

The LoDagaa people of northern Ghana throw into rivers the bodies of those who have died spiritually unclean deaths, in order to cleanse the community.

In India the act of scattering ashes on the holy waters of the River Ganges permits the soul of the deceased to bathe in the body of the goddess Ganga. The point at which the Ganges meets its first tributary, the Yamuna (Jumna), is a particularly sacred place. The ashes of Mahatma Gandhi, the great spiritual and political leader, were scattered at this spot.

In China the souls of the drowned were thought to haunt rivers, looking for living bodies they could occupy.

Most lakes, with their freshwater resources, teem with life, but the Dead Sea offers a stark exception. Situated in the middle of a desert, the Dead Sea is, as the name suggests, an eerie and lifeless place, which, through the Hebrew Scriptures, has taken on the symbolism of a spiritual wilderness. It is in fact a landlocked saltlake that lies about 1,300 ft. (400 m) below sea level, with summer temperatures rising to well over 40° C (104° F). The only life forms able to survive in its extremely salty waters are a few bacteria and specially adapted plants. Evaporation and the variable flow of the rivers that feed the lake cause its water level to rise and fall by up to 2 ft. (0.6 m). As a result, salt gets deposited on the terrain, creating an undulating landscape of salt mounds and pillars.

The Biblical cities of Sodom and Gomorrah are believed to have been situated on the lake's southern shore, and its bleak salt-encrusted landscape was

The Ganges River

Northeastern India

The Ganges is the spiritual artery of India. It is regarded as the personification of the goddess Ganga, daughter of the mountain god Himalaya and a wife of Shiva, who is said to have descended to Earth after King Bhagiratha pleased the gods by years of worship in the Himalayas. To prevent crashing waters from causing a disaster on Earth, Lord Shiva, meditating on Mount Kailasa (Kailash), supposedly caught the river in his hair. With the onset of the monsoon season in mid-June each year, the story of the river's descent from Heaven is celebrated in the festival of Ganga-dussera.

The 1,500 mile (2,507 km) river originates at Gomukh, more than 13,000 ft. (4,200 m) up in the Himalayas below the peak of Shivalinga, a holy place where pilgrims may hear the voices of spirits created by the winds that rush across the ice-face. The icy stream flows swiftly down the mountain, cutting through gorges before joining with other sources until it finally becomes the great river. It wanders across a broad flat plain where it provides the agricultural lifeblood of irrigation water, until it finally empties into the Bay of Bengal by way of the largest delta in the world.

The heavenly origin of the Ganges makes its water holy as the essence of the goddess, or female energy, known as *shakti*. Drinking water from the Ganges and bathing in it are therefore sacred rituals. People from all over India converge on Rishikesh, the first settlement after the river's course through the Himalayas, and on Hardwar, a town farther south where the water is believed to be holiest. Hiuen Tsiang, a Buddhist pilgrim who trecked overland from China to India in the seventh century CE, witnessed "hundreds and thousands" of people cleansing themselves on the ghats at Hardwar, and many people still travel there to fill their pots with water that they drink at weddings and funerals.

Varanasi (Benares) is sacred as Shiva's city, and its greatest temple is Vishvanatha, dedicated to him as Lord of the Universe. Buddha himself gave his first sermon near the city around 500BCE when it was known as Kashi or City of Light.

Although dams now control parts of the Ganges, harnessing energy and preventing floods, the river still carries prayers, offerings and ashes to the sea.

LEFT *Thousands journey to the city of Varanasi to commit the ashes of the dead to the Ganges, for both the city and the river are a* mokshadvara *or "door to liberation." To have one's funeral here is to ensure a direct path to Heaven. The body must be burned before sunset on the day of death, and the cremation pyre is thought to permit the spirit to proceed to rebirth.*

ABOVE *Dasaswamedh Ghat at Varanasi, where stone landings and steps, as well as temples and palaces, stretch for 4 miles (6 km) along the Ganges in order to cater for the pilgrims who attend this most sacred of places. While people cleanse themselves of the karma of previous lives, smoke drifts along from the cremations taking place on ghats designated for the purpose.*

LEFT *For the faithful who flock to its shores, the Ganges offers the hope of a better future. At sunset temple bells ring out and people launch boats of leaves filled with flower petals and lighted candles onto the waters, in the hope that these will carry their prayers to the heavens.*

drawn on for the account of their destruction. Unwilling to punish the only virtuous people in Sodom—Lot and his family—God allowed them to escape on condition that they never looked back. When Lot's wife stole a parting glance, she was turned into a pillar of salt.

Indirectly the Dead Sea has been the inspiration for a more modern ideology. The ancient Hebrew and Arabic manuscripts known as the Dead Sea Scrolls were discovered in caves close to the lake. Some believe them to have been the work of the Essenes, a sect that flourished about 2,000 years ago. The interest in the Essenes today stems in part from the claim that their lives were in step with the natural world and recognized the sacred unity of all life on Earth.

A lake in myth is often an occult medium, linked with female enchantment and with death, the abyss, and the night passage of the Sun (from observation of its apparent disappearances into water). Many of these elements interweave in the Arthurian legends.

The Lady of the Lake ruled a land that was entered through a body of water. She reigned over both men and women (though later tales describe only an all-female realm) but rarely ventured into mortal lands, communicating with Lancelot and Arthur's court via messengers.

She generally supports the Round Table because Lancelot is her foster-son, whom she stole from his mother after his father died and then raised in fairyland. When he came of age, she equipped him with his knightly accoutrements and he took his place in the world, slaying each knight who challenged him.

Throughout the tale, water confirms its dual associations with both life and death. At the end, when Arthur dies at the lakeside, the tale's Celtic origins are implicit in the appearance on a barge of three queens, reminiscent of the Celtic triad of goddesses (see page 96), who place Arthur in the vessel and sail away from the shore.

LEFT *A common notion of the Celtic Otherworld was that the dead found it by journeying across water. As stormclouds gather over Lough Conn in County Mayo, western Ireland, both primeval and mystical qualities intermingle evocatively.*

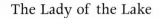

The Lady of the Lake

The Lady of the Lake, a prophetess with magical powers, is first mentioned in Arthurian legend in the *Conte de la charette* by Chrétien de Troyes (1179). She appears as the guardian of the knight Lancelot and the forger of his sword; she gives him a magic ring, set with a stone that enables him to break spells, as well as a white lance which can penetrate steel.

The Lady of the Lake is the opponent of the enchantress Morgan Le Fay. Originally she bore no name, but in later stories she was identified variously as Viviane, Niniane, and, in Sir Thomas Malory's *Le Morte d'Arthur*, Nemué. She is pursued by Merlin, whom she imprisons in a tree, tomb, or cave.

In some other versions she sees the future but declines to prophesy as this would result in more people dying. The romances disagree about her precise dwelling-place, variously depicted as the sea, a place beyond the sea, a lake isle, or a place beneath the mirage of a lake—all images associated with the Celtic Otherworld.

The Lady of the Lake's court is made up entirely of women (except for Lancelot), and this echoes the Celtic notion of the Otherworld as a Land of Women. Her sponsorship of the deadly warrior Lancelot and the harsh treatment of Merlin strengthen her associations with death. Her key attribute was that of transforming people into their opposites, making heroes out of cowards and cowards out of brave warriors.

The well-known role of the Lady of the Lake as giver of Arthur's sword is, however, found only in Malory. In his version she thrust up her arm to offer Arthur the magic sword. Later she reclaimed it as Arthur lay dying by the lakeside and ordered Bedivere to throw it in, whereupon her hand emerged, grasped the hilt and then flourished the sword three times before vanishing with it below the surface.

Connecting with the Universe

The natural landscape, as well as being our richest and readiest source of metaphor, has also borne on its surfaces, both above ground and underground, some of the most impressive and enigmatic artifacts that humankind has ever created.

Dotted around ancient stretches of terrain are monuments whose function continues to intrigue archaeologists and anthropologists: avenues of rocks leading to massive henges; vast artificial mounds and hills; straight tracks in the desert plotted with precision but leading seemingly nowhere; curious alignments and edifices apparently based on a sacred geometry; and untold numbers of other monuments whose precise purpose may remain a mystery forever.

These works, whether constructions or pictures, give the lie to the commonplace notion that art progressed inevitably from primitivism to subtlety, through stages of increasing sophistication. These are images that speak to us directly but mysteriously, like many ancient artifacts, across vast tracts of time.

RIGHT *In many cultures rock art is interpreted as having a supernatural origin. The Dogon people live in hillside villages on a plateau in modern Mali, Africa, led there long ago by a mythic snake. These cliff-face paintings animate their landscape with spiritual meaning.*

IMAGES FOR DIVINE EYES

Images created on the surface of the Earth may be so large that they cannot be seen in their entirety from ground level. Some of the world's most remarkable examples of such designs are to be found on the Nazca pampa, a desert plateau in the foothills of the Peruvian Andes mountain range. The brown-black oxidized desert surface was scraped away to uncover the lighter-colored subsoil—much in the same way as images were cut into the chalk downs of southern England (see page 108)—to form long narrow lines or tracks.

The "artists" who worked on this site also created giant images of geometric forms, such as spirals and triangles, with outlines, too, of monkeys, frigate

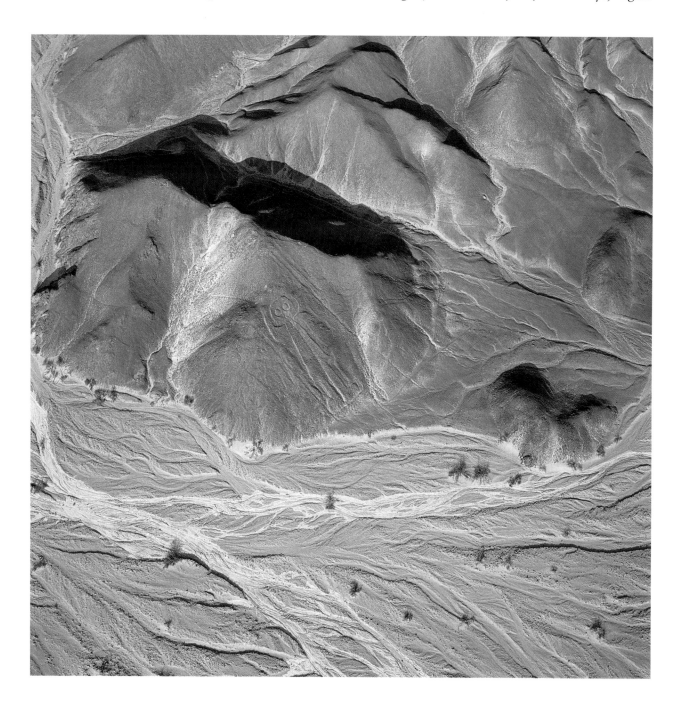

birds, spiders, and other creatures. These great earth drawings, discernible only from the air, were probably made by the Nazca people, whose culture flourished *c.1–c.*650CE. The size of the images has attracted much attention and prompted various theories as to their purpose, ranging from the proposition that they are associated with Nazca astronomical or calendrical systems (unlikely, in view of the fact that few astronomical alignments have been found) to the more fantastic suggestion that they were intended as navigation beacons for alien landing craft. The truth may be related to both these ideas: perhaps the designs were intended to be seen only by the deities believed to dwell in the heavens.

There is some evidence that in the distant past the Nazca lines were ritually swept. Our interpretation of this is illuminated by the observations of anthropologist Gary Urton, who recorded an Andean ceremony in which the plaza outside a church was swept in strips, each one belonging to a different kinship group in the village; after the sweeping had been completed, a statue of the saint to whom the church was dedicated was brought out and paraded.

The Inca people, who established an empire stretching from Ecuador to Chile known as the Land of the Four Quarters, built long straight roads, parts of which incorporated the older Nazca lines. These straight lines or *ceques* (sighting lines) intersected at the Sun Temple in the capital city of Cuzco (which in the Quechua language means "navel"). The layout of the city was in the shape of a giant feline (the jaguar played an important role in Andean myth). A series of *huacas* (sacred or significant sites) along the *ceques* was used to make sacred alignments.

LEFT *A strange figure stands out on a hillside of Peru's San Jose-pampa, one of many unexplained drawings on the Earth's surface found throughout the region and known as the Nazca lines. One theory is that the drawings form pathways of lines used for ritual walks, as various routes are known to have been built for religious purposes throughout the Americas.*

The deserts of the southern United States also furnished a massive natural canvas for ancient artists. Near Blyth in California several giant human figures and an animal were scraped out of the gravel terrace west of the Colorado River. The origin of these images remains unknown, but one figure in Arizona resembles Hâ-âk, a monster in the creation mythology of the Pima people.

Some of the many burial mounds found in the modern American states of Wisconsin, Michigan, and Iowa take the form of great effigies of human beings, birds, reptiles, and other animals. One group of 900 mounds recorded at Harper's Ferry, Iowa, in the nineteenth century, included effigies of more than 100 animals and around seventy birds, as well as many other forms that were unidentifiable owing to erosion. Further destruction occurred when the land in which these mounds stood came under human cultivation, and all but the most remarkable effigies were eradicated.

Pictures on the Earth

Rituals involving the Earth itself are to be found in many of the world's cultures. When the Lakota people from the Great Plains of North America conduct a "sweatlodge" ritual (see pages 214–216), earth is removed from the center of the lodge to make a pit where the hot stones are placed. The excavated earth is used to make a sacred path with a small mound at one end called *unci*, or "grandmother," a symbol of the Earth. When the ritual is finished, the sacred ground is abandoned to the elements. Similarly the intricate and painstakingly prepared sandpaintings used in Navajo curing rituals (see page 12) are simply swept away after use.

In Australia ground sculptures are formed as part of mortuary or healing rituals. Among the Yolngu people of northeast Arnhem Land, members of the Liyagawumirri clan design a map that shows the springs and wells believed to have been created by the Djanggawul sisters, ancestral heroines from the

Hill Figures of England

At several places in the downlands of southern England ancient sculptors created striking images by cutting away the thin layer of grassy turf to reveal the white chalk beneath. One of the finest of these chalk figures is on Whitehorse Hill at Uffington in Oxfordshire (shown opposite), where the turf was cut away to create a great horse 374 ft. (114 m) long. It is not known who made the figure, which was once attributed to King Alfred the Great of Wessex (849–99CE), who was born at nearby Wantage. The animal resembles the stylized horse images on British coins of the period immediately preceding the Roman invasion, but it may be older than that. It lies in an area that contains numerous significant prehistoric monuments; for example, an ancient track, the Ridgeway, passes near by and the horse is close to Wayland's Smithy, an immense standing stone. The horse has survived (and quite possibly changed in form) through the periodic removal of grass and weeds.

The origin of another famous chalk effigy, the 260 ft. (80 m) tall giant near Cerne Abbas in Dorset, is uncertain. The figure has a large erect penis and wields a club. In local tradition he is linked with fertility, and May Day dances were once held on the hilltop above his head.

Dreaming (see pages 30 and 81). The sculpture is used as a grave and as a place to dispose of spiritually polluted food (that is, any food belonging to those closely related to the deceased). More monumental is the *larrakan* of the Gidjingali people, a final burial rite in which the dry bones of the deceased (dead for some years) are packed into a decorated hollow log. This coffin is then interred within the stomach area of a giant 33 ft. (10 m) long sacred totemic being (*wongarr*) called Ngarapia, created in a ceremony on the morning of the burial day.

Images may also be made by incising marks into the topsoil or vegetation to reveal a different coloration below. The White Horse of Uffington and other hill figures of England (see box, left, and picture, right) were made by removing the turf from chalklands to expose the underlying white chalk, and it is known that a similar method was also practiced in North America, although no images survive.

Turf mazes are a typically English form of incised earth imagery, although there are fascinating parallels in other cultures. Probably the oldest of the eight extant examples is the Walls of Troy maze near Brandsby, in Yorkshire, which is still tended to keep its outline sharp. The turf mazes are unicursal (that is, there is only one route through them, a single winding path leading to the center). More complex in form is an example at Alkborough, Lincolnshire, on a hill above the Humber Valley. Probably cut in the thirteenth century by monks from Spalding Abbey, the maze is known as Julian's Bower, a reference to the tradition according to which Aeneas's son Julius supposedly introduced mazes to western Europe. (Aeneas was the exiled Trojan who, in the Roman poet Virgil's *Aenid*, was said to have founded the royal line that later built Rome.) Based on twelve concentric circles, the design resembles the twelfth-century maze on the floor of Chartres Cathedral, France (see pages 42–43).

Interpretations of the function of turf mazes concentrate on their uses for various dancing and walking rituals, connected with spring fertility rites. It is possible that the sudden changes of direction required by the convoluted route are associated with dizzying changes in consciousness, akin to the effect of hallucinogens, or, at a more mundane level, the exhilaration of dance.

Rock effigies and medicine wheels

On many high remote hills in the northern plains and prairies of North America, rocks and boulders originally deposited by glaciers were arranged by prehistoric artists into geometric patterns or the outlines of human beings and animals. Even where they have not subsequently been disturbed or destroyed by farmers, the precise age and origin of the stone images are difficult to determine, but oral traditions often record the legendary or mythical events behind their construction. For example, on a high knoll near Punished Woman's Lake in South Dakota, early European settlers discovered the larger-than-life-size stone effigies of a man and a woman, together with an unidentified figure, a number of cairns, and some shallow pits. When the local Lakota people were asked about the history of the effigies, they explained that the two figures were a woman who had run away from the husband she was forced to marry, and the man who was her first love. The monument was said to mark the spot at which the lovers were slain by the jealous husband.

BELOW *The White Horse chalk figure at Uffington in Oxfordshire, England. A popular local explanation for the carving is that it was created to commemorate St. George's victory over the dragon at nearby Dragon Hill. Modern scientific dating, however, suggests that the original trenches date back some 3,000 years, to the Bronze Age. The typical Celtic iconography might indicate a link with Epona, the goddess of horses.*

The Serpent Mound

Northeastern United States

The Serpent Mound is one of the most striking and mysterious of all Native American monuments. It was built out of yellow clay on a base of clay and stones some 2,000 years ago by people of either the Adena or the Hopewell cultures, forerunners of the Mississippian culture that created thousands of ceremonial and burial mounds in the East's river valleys.

Built in the form of a snake with what appears to be an egg in its mouth, the coiling earthwork is more than 1,254 ft. (382 m) in length and stands on a narrow promontory in the fork of Brush Creek and a smaller tributary in Adams County. Steep wooded slopes on one side and a sheer cliff 160 ft. (50 m) high on the other side make the promontory itself an impressive sight—one that dominates the landscape.

The antiquarian Stephen D. Peet was among the first to propose that the mound was the effigy of a deity. In 1890 Peet wrote that "the shape of the cliff would easily suggest the idea of a massive serpent, and this with the inaccessibility of the spot would produce a peculiar feeling of awe, as if it were a great Manitou ["divine spirit"] which resided there."

In Native American mythology the divinity known as Horned Serpent, Antlered Serpent, or Water Monster is the guardian of sources of life arising out of the Earth, especially water, as well as a manifestation of primal energy and power. The promontory overlooks an entire water-catchment area, and the "egg" originally contained a small circle of burnt stones. A fire lit there would have been visible for miles and may have been intended as a sign that the serpent spirit of the waters was active and watchful.

By 1886 the mound, already damaged by treasure-hunters, sightseers, and soil erosion, seemed destined to be turned into a cornfield. But P.W. Putnam of the Peabody Museum at Harvard University restored it, and from 1900 visitors were able to appreciate the effigy fully by looking down from a viewing tower.

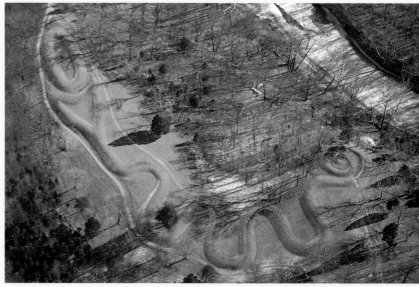

ABOVE *The Serpent Mound was first interpreted by E.G. Squier and E.H. Davis in 1848 as part of the Smithsonian Institution's survey of ancient monuments in the Mississippi Valley. The serpent was a universal sacred symbol used by the Egyptians, Assyrians, Celts, Hindus, and others, causing the two men to speculate about Old World influences in the mound-building.*

LEFT *The precise meaning is elusive, but the coil of the tail in the Serpent Mound might signify the Earth's sacred forces and the "egg" about to be swallowed might represent an imminent solar eclipse.*

FAR LEFT *Snakes and serpents are powerful supernatural beings in many Native American mythologies. This prehistoric Mississippian gorget from the eastern woodlands depicts a curled rattlesnake associated with the underworld. The Cherokee who later lived in the area believed in a rattlesnake monster called the Uktena.*

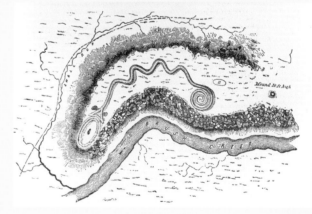

ABOVE *Squier and Davis published their survey of the mound in* Ancient Monuments of the Mississippi Valley *(1848), a groundbreaking study from which this engraving is taken. The mound is one of hundreds, many in the form of birds and animals, built in the region by people of the Adena or Hopewell cultures.*

Two similar legends of warrior deaths are associated with boulder designs hundreds of miles apart in Cluny, Alberta, in Canada, and Snake Butte, South Dakota, in the United States. Near Cluny a human figure lies part of the way along a line of boulders linking two cairns. It is said to mark a battle that took place in 1872 between the Blackfoot and Blood peoples. In the 1960s a Blackfoot elder identified the figure as that of Young Medicine Man, a Blood who was killed by Walking With A Scalp, a Blackfoot. The cairns allegedly mark where the duel began and ended, and the boulders indicate the course of the warriors during the combat. The effigy is on the spot where Young Medicine Man fell.

The top of Snake Butte has a similar grouping of cairns, effigy, and boulder path. The site is known locally as the place where a Lakota warrior wounded an Arikara enemy who fled and eventually fell dead. The cairns are said to denote the place of the fight and of the warrior's death, while the boulders represent drops of his blood. Near this construction, which is about half a mile (800 m) long, the image of a turtle is said to represent the sacred animal of the victor. However, the discovery elsewhere of numerous outlines of snakes and turtles, prominent creatures in traditional Native American religion, suggests that the boulder forms may in fact have been sacred in both origin and purpose.

On high land in the northern plains the stones sometimes form giant circles, often with massive cairns at their centers and rows of stones leading out to the edges like the spokes of wheels. No one knows

why these effigies, known as "medicine wheels," were built, but some appear to have been used in rituals associated with astronomical events. Surviving oral tradition provides little evidence of astronomical reckoning, but the alignment evidence from medicine wheels suggests the movement of stars and planets was significant to the earliest Native Americans.

Near the summit of Medicine Mountain, one of the highest peaks in the Big Horn Mountains of Wyoming, the "wheel" has twenty-eight "spokes" and is almost 100 ft. (30 m) in diameter. There are six small cairns around the circumference of the circle. The form of this medicine wheel closely resembles the design of a Cheyenne Sun-dance lodge, a round building with a central post and twenty-eight rafters. The lodge was reserved for sacred rituals connected

with the Sun, and it is possible that the medicine wheel was constructed with a similar purpose. It certainly appears to have some link with the solar cycle: one prominent cairn and the center of the wheel are aligned with the position of the Sun at dawn at the summer solstice.

A modern form of medicine wheel has arisen in recent years from a complex mix of Native American spirituality and Oriental mysticism. Among groups

BELOW *An ancient medicine wheel overlooking Long Canyon at Sedona, Arizona. The rich colors of the rock provide this place with an energetic atmosphere, and the Yavapai people revere the site, entering the canyons only for ceremonials. Tribal stories explain that the "grandmother of the supernatural" lives here in a cave.*

ABOVE *Wolf Creek Crater in Western Australia, just over half a mile (800 m) long, is one of several large craters created across the planet thousands of years ago by meteors striking the Earth. Most of this rocky space debris disintegrates in the Earth's atmosphere, but the larger pieces fall to the ground. Fortunately, most are too small to cause any significant damage. Local mythology normally explains the existence of such indentations as due to a destructive act of the gods, such as the hurling of a thunderbolt.*

such as Sun Bear's Bear Tribe Medicine Society, the wheel has become a focus for meditation, like the mandala used by Hindus and Buddhists. The participants in this modern medicine-wheel ritual gather thirty-six stones, each signifying a part of the universe, and create a huge circle representing the cosmos. The leader of the group, Sun Bear, places the skull of a sacred animal in the center as a symbol of the creator spirit, from whom all life radiates.

Stones from deep space and time

Stones that fall from the sky represent a unique visitation from the heavens and are often thought to be charged with spiritual energy. The impact of meteorites on the imagination is demonstrated by the extent to which they feature in religious beliefs. According to some accounts, the Persian god of light, Mithra, whose cult became popular throughout the Roman Empire, emerged from a burning cosmic rock that was probably a meteorite. The cult of the Earth Mother goddess Cybele, which centered on Pergamum in Asia Minor (modern Turkey), had as its focal point of worship a silver statue encasing a small black stone, almost certainly a meteorite. The statue was considered so powerful that in 204BCE, on the direction of the Delphic oracle, it was taken to Rome in the belief that it would aid the Romans in their war against Carthage.

Millions of Muslims have a sacred duty to make a pilgrimage to Mecca to pay homage at the Grand Mosque to the Kaaba, the most sacred shrine of Islam. Built into a corner of the Kaaba is the Hajaru 'l-Aswad or Black Stone, which is thought to be a meteorite but was supposedly brought down to Earth by the archangel Gabriel. Pilgrims walk around the Kaaba seven times before entering the shrine and kissing or touching the stone.

Rocks of terrestrial origin are often associated with the sky. In Africa the Numana people of the Niger River region worship small pebbles that they believe to be pieces of the sky god that have fallen to Earth. The pebbles are placed on top of cones of earth and sacrifices are offered to them.

Stones bearing the fossils of plants or animals provide evidence of evolution, but even before the scientific age they were objects of fascination. Prehistoric peoples were undoubtedly struck by their unusual appearance, for it is not uncommon to find them at prehistoric sites, sometimes deliberately incorporated into stone artifacts. The mystery exerted by fossils remains strong in those societies where scientific explanations are not widely known. For example, belemnites, fossils of the pen-shaped bodies of a squidlike creature that are found on beaches in the Baltic Sea, are regarded by some Finno-Ugric tribal peoples as the fingers of a water spirit.

Fossils may also be treated as sacred objects. In a well-digging ceremony in Indonesia a ritual marriage is performed for an ammonite, a fossil of a shellfish held sacred to the gods, and a basil plant, representing a garden—a union believed to keep the waters sweet and flowing.

In medieval Europe there was a belief in the "philosopher's stone," an elusive substance sought by alchemists in order to turn ordinary metals into gold. However, the true aim of alchemy was far more profound: the discovery of the divine medium (not necessarily a stone) that could effect the transformation of spirit and matter into a state of ultimate perfection—the physical transmutation of the metals was simply an indicator providing the alchemist with a way of knowing that he had discovered the transforming medium. Glassmaking offers an interesting parallel: its practitioners, in the Middle Ages, used

"secret knowledge" to turn sand and stones into the colored glass that constituted such an important element in Europe's cathedrals, for its influence had a truly transformational effect on the human spirit.

The psychologist Carl Jung regarded alchemy as a paradigm for the development of human nature. The philosopher's stone was for him a psychological process: the transformative experience of self-realization, or individuation. Similarly, the rites conducted within different cultures enable people to have key experiences and make connections with the universe around them.

BELOW *The track of a burning meteor—popularly known as a falling or shooting star—can be seen disintegrating in the Earth's atmosphere amid a colorful display of the Northern Lights. To Arctic peoples, such lights in the night sky represented the souls of the dead.*

MODELS OF THE COSMOS

The design and construction of sacred buildings is the largest-scale form of art. It is surely also the most ambitious, as humans seek to recreate the realm of the gods on Earth in a three-dimensional space that worshipers can enter physically as well as spiritually. Throughout the world, in diverse traditions and theologies, sacred architecture continually strives to reproduce the patterns, structures, and alignments of the universe.

In some cultures the sacred is isolated from the secular by the simplest of huts inside a fenced enclosure. In other traditions magnificent towers, spires, or *stupas* (domed Buddhist reliquaries) thrust upward to the heavens, giving material form to the spiritual journeys of mystics, shamans, and saints. Many sacred buildings bring space and time together by providing an arena for the reenactment of myths and rituals that link the beginning of time to the devotees' own present.

From the earliest times humans have believed that the cosmos contains far more than the world immediately around them. The sky is often considered the realm of perfection, and the goal of much sacred architecture is to reproduce this perfection on Earth.

Cities and temples are often held to represent a form of Heaven on Earth. Jerusalem in Israel and Varanasi in India are considered holy cities because they are thought to reproduce a heavenly prototype. The Hindu temple at Sri Rangam in southern India was supposedly brought from Heaven to Earth, just as the Kaaba at Mecca (see pages 188–189) is seen by Muslims as an exact model of a heavenly temple.

South American Skies

In the Inca world-view, as in other South American beliefs, astronomical phenomena are saturated with spiritual significance. This is reflected in part by the celestial character of major deities such as Inti (the Sun god) and Mama Kilya (the Moon goddess). However, the Milky Way was also important, and the stars themselves were interpreted as minor deities.

Preeminent was the Pleiades, known as Collca (the "granary"), for this cluster of stars was the celestial protector of agriculture and fertility. From Cuzco's central plaza the sunset on April 26 was observed between two pillars set on a peak to the west; these pillars were a *huaca* and the *ceque* they stood on (see pages 106-107) aligned (over the horizon) with the sacred spring Catachillay, another name for the Pleiades.

The Incas also attached importance to certain "dark cloud" constellations made up of dense clouds of stellar dust.

Earth and skies

The first recorded astronomers lived during the time of the earliest civilizations in Mesopotamia. It is difficult to know to what degree these Old World stargazers were motivated by religious or intellectual curiosity. In the New World, however, the texts and images of the Maya and Aztec civilizations certainly reveal that knowledge of the heavens, and of complex and precise calendrical systems, conferred a sacral status that was used to extend priestly power and social control.

The distinction between astrology and astronomy derives from the European scientific revolution of the seventeenth century. Astrology focused on the direct influence of the stars and planets on earthly events, whereas astronomy had an empirical basis. Before then, however, astral divination was an instrinsic part of the study of the heavens.

The Babylonians and other early civilizations of Mesopotamia placed great importance on the interpretation of omens, as we know from many inscribed clay tablets that have been discovered. The configuration resulting from molten lead when it was poured

BELOW *An image from the Jain religion of India and Pakistan that depicts the cosmos or* loka *as a complex, multilayered disc of concentric continents and oceans. At the center of this cosmos is Jambudvipa, the inner* continent of the mortal world, itself divided into seven regions at the core of which is sacred Mount Meru. Outside Jambudvipa are two other continents and two salt oceans teeming with assorted life.

on to water, or the pattern of veins on the liver of a sacrificed beast, was taken as an indicator of the future, and a guide to conduct. In the same way the behavior of the stars and planets was full of significance for the conduct of human lives and of society.

The Babylonians are credited with having identified the Zodiac, a belt of twelve constellations through which the Sun appeared to travel on its annual orbit of the Earth, and from this the Western and Hindu zodiacs were subsequently derived. But present-day Western astrology has its roots specifically in the Greek system of nearly 2,000 years ago (the word zodiac comes from the Greek *zodiakos kyklos*, meaning "animal circle"). Scholars in both Babylon and Greece calculated the 18.6-year eclipse cycle with reasonable precision, but it was a Greek, in the fifth century BCE, who first put forward a model of the solstice and equinox points, thereby laying down the framework for an exact solar calendar.

The ability to locate the planets on the celestial sphere (that is, relative to the solstice and equinox points) was a great step forward, freeing scholars from the earlier reliance upon the four points of

BELOW *The ceiling of the Hall of Prayer for Good Harvest in the Temple of Heaven in Beijing reproduces the geometric structure of Heaven, according to Confucian belief. At the first ray of Sun at the winter solstice, the emperor, the Son of Heaven, would offer prayers for a bountiful harvest in the coming year.*

the compass, the zenith (a point directly above) and the nadir (a point directly below) as a framework for observation.

Because of the wobble of the Earth's axis over millennia, the signs of the zodiac no longer correspond with the constellations from which they take their name, and this discrepancy has led to many popular misconceptions.

Astrology is still the most popular form of divination in the West, in its "natal" (birth sign) manifestation (its "horary" manifestation interprets a situation of current alignments, at the time of seeking advice). However, the craft has lost status since the scientific revolution demolished the theory of geocentricity, according to which the Sun moved around the Earth, the central point of the cosmos. Theology was able to absorb the startling new cosmology, which to many (Newton included) revealed that God had created the heavens and the Earth according to principles more profoundly complex than people had hitherto suspected. Astrology, however, which depended heavily on geocentricity, was less easily defended. In England one founder member of the Royal Society, established in 1662, denounced astrology as a "disgrace to reason," and later that century the government censored astrological publications (albeit on political as much as scientific grounds).

Celestial geometry and architecture

The alignment of a sacred building is rarely a random procedure. It may be aligned to a tree, along a river, or toward the site of a holy event that took place in the past. Perhaps most often of all, the building is aligned in relation to the trajectories of the Sun, Moon, stars, and planets. Such an alignment may be crucial for the building to serve as a meeting point between the earthly realm of humans and the celestial realm of the gods.

Many sacred buildings, from Greek temples to megalithic passage-graves, face the rising Sun as the source of new life and power (traditional domestic

Star Symbolism of the Earth Lodge

Most Native American peoples believe that they emerged from the Earth, but among the Pawnee of the Great Plains the first humans are said to have been born from the marriage between the male Morning Star and the female Evening Star. Great power had been bestowed on the stars by the supreme and changeless creator, Tirawa.

Each Pawnee village is held to have been founded by a star. A hereditary village chief is that star's representative in the community. The circular earth lodge provides the ceremonial center of a settlement that aligned with the cardinal directions and was constructed according to mythical beliefs about the stars.

The sunken floor of the earth lodge is approached down a slope and entered from the east, where a post represents the Morning Star, god of light, fire, and war and older brother of the Sun. A post at the western end represents the Evening Star, goddess of night. Each day, Morning Star shines his beam into the lodge through the entrance, repeating his first mating with Evening Star.

A post to the north of the lodge is the North Star, the chief star; a southern post is the Milky Way. An altar at the west is the garden of Evening Star, where corn and buffalo are constantly regenerated. In front of the altar is the throne of Tirawa and at the center of the lodge is a firepit—the open mouth of Tirawa, who enters the lodge in a shaft of light through the smokehole. Rituals are accompanied by sacred singing, which reaches its climax as this light moves across the interior and falls directly on to the fire.

Much of Pawnee tribal mythology relates to sky and star powers. In times gone by charts were maintained that identified constellations and were believed to incorporate the powers of the stars and bring them to the people when used in complex ceremonials.

houses or hogans do, too, among the Navajo of the American Southwest). In most Christian churches a similar point is made. One enters from the west and progresses toward the altar at the east, moving from darkness to light and from death to life.

Early English churches often deviate slightly from true east, a variance that can be traced to the position of the rising Sun on the day of the saint to whom the church is dedicated. Sometimes accurate alignment is deliberately avoided, to convey a special meaning. In some English cruciform churches the chancel is skewed to represent the head of Christ falling sidewise on the Cross.

Celestial alignments seem to have become more elaborate with the growth of cities and empires.

Navajo Stargazers

When Navajo people fall ill, they sometimes call on a stargazer to perform a curing ritual. The stargazer seeks to discover the cause of the sickness from the Holy People, supernatural beings who live in the skies. First he talks to the patient and his or her family and friends, and may chant or pray in the patient's hogan (dwelling). He may make a sandpainting, carefully outlining a sacred star and features of the land in white, blue, yellow, and black powders. At some point in the ritual, the stargazer leaves the hogan and walks into the darkness carrying a quartz crystal. Alone, he chants and prays to a sacred being such as the Gila lizard, or to a star spirit, and then raises the crystal to the sky and gazes deeply into it, seeking out a bright star. When he sees strings of light streaming from the crystal, the stargazer has a vision of the cause of the illness, perhaps in the form of an animal or human or as lights of particular colors. The stargazer is able to use this inspiration from the Holy People to prescribe the rituals and medicine needed.

Ancient Chinese cities were laid out as a model of the universe, following a north–south axis reflecting the celestial meridian. At the center, corresponding to the position of the pole star, was the royal palace. The city thus recreated the celestial order on Earth, with the emperor as central figure (see page 118). From Sumeria to Mexico, ancient cities repeatedly show a parallel between celestial alignments and centralized political power.

The relationship between astronomy and architecture was often sophisticated and precise, as can be seen in the structural alignment of Mesoamerican temples and observatories to the movements of Venus or the Pleiades (see pages 142–143). Similarly, it has been suggested that the narrow shafts built within the great Egyptian pyramids may be aligned with the belt of Orion (see page 232).

Sacred buildings may also directly represent the year. In the traditional Vedic Hindu altar 360 bricks stood for the number of days of the year and 360 stones for the nights. Some buildings are designed as a calendar, as was probably the case with Stonehenge and the Big Horn Medicine Wheel in Wyoming, formed out of boulders placed on the ground. In Cuzco, the capital city of the Incas in what is now Peru, the Sun Temple was situated at the ritual center of the city. Forty-one *ceques* (sighting lines) radiated from the temple, passing through significant sites (*huacas*) that were both astronomical and linked with events in the Incas' history. The surrounding region contained 328 points along or adjacent to these sacred alignments, corresponding to the number of days in the Incas' year.

Mandalas: circles of existence

Of all the models of the cosmos the most compact is the mandala used by Buddhists, Jains, and Hindus. A diagram that represents the structure of the universe, it is used in rituals and as a meditational device; it can serve as an external plan as well as something to be internalized mentally, to make the body of the

mediator into a microcosm of the universe. As a plan the mandala combines the circle (the original meaning of the word mandala), representing the celestial realm, with the square, representing the shape of the material world on Earth. The sides are oriented to the four cardinal directions, while a dot at the center represents Mount Meru, the cosmic mountain and axis of the universe (see pages 180–186).

ABOVE *The Zodiac of Denderah is the best-preserved depiction of the Egyptian zodiac. It formed the ornate ceiling of a small chapel or* naos *in the Temple of Hathor at Denderah, built out of sandstone during the Ptolemaic period, 333–33BCE. The shape clearly implies that the sky envelops an Earth that is round. The sky was thought to be composed of water, just as the Nile River was, and the world was therefore believed to exist within a universal ocean.*

The mandala underlies the structure of the temple throughout the Hindu, Jain, and Buddhist worlds. It is used as the plan of the temple, so that the building reproduces the hidden structure of the universe and also comes to function as a three-dimensional meditational device. At the center of the temple is the inner sanctuary, above which rises a tower symbolizing Mount Meru.

Implicit in the idea of the mandala is the belief that something may have numerous different aspects simultaneously. The Buddhist temple of Borobudur in Java (see pages 128–129) is laid out on a perfect mandala plan and is at the same time *stupa* (reliquary), altar, cosmic axis, center of the world, body of the Buddha, and teaching of the Buddha.

By reproducing through sacred architecture what was thought to be the divine structure of the universe, many ancient civilizations believed that this offered humankind the best possible model to follow for life on Earth. This view applied to the city as well as to the temple and it made the spiritual and political dimensions of power virtually identical. In Mesoamerica the city was often laid out as an exact model of a heavenly city. The Aztec capital of Tenochtitlán was constructed according to a divine ideogram (see page 219), while at Teotihuacan (see pages 166–167), the entire city, with thousands of temples, was itself equivalent to one great temple.

Similarly, Romulus founded the city of Rome by ploughing a circular furrow around the Palatine Hill. This circle was called the world (*mundus*) and was divided into four quarters like the cosmos. In historical times this legendary action was repeated at the foundation of every new Roman city, when a priest, or augur, would draw a circle on the ground and quarter it with lines running to the four points of the compass. The line from east to west represented the course of the Sun, while the north–south line was the axis of the sky. Through prayers the augur would project this alignment outward over the whole area of the future city.

The human body, proportion, and place

Buildings have often been seen as reproductions not only of the cosmos but also of the human body. This correspondence may even be thought to constitute part of the building's sacredness. Megalithic tombs were sometimes constructed in the form of the human body, their inner space resembling the womb

The Immovable Center

Judaism, like Islam (see pages 186–189), retains one single center for a large community of believers that is scattered throughout the world. It was the destruction of the Temple of Solomon (see pages 190–191) and the subsequent dispersal (Diaspora) of the Jewish people that, ironically, laid the historical foundations for this deliberate centralization, and no other religion has retained its focus on a center through such historical vicissitudes.

The Temple of Solomon itself was built on the site where Abraham went to sacrifice his son Isaac, and where, according to one Jewish text, God had fashioned the entire world, from the center outward.

A rabbinical text, the *Midrash Tanhuma*, states that just as the navel is at the center of the person, so the land of Israel is at the center of the world, the city of Jerusalem at the centre of Israel, the Temple of Solomon at the center of Jerusalem, the Holy of Holies at the center of the Temple of Solomon, and the Ark of the Covenant at the center of the Holy of Holies. In front of the Ark of the Covenant is the foundation stone of the world.

from which it was perhaps believed that the deceased would be reborn.

The Greek temple complex at Delphi (see pages 60–61), like Mecca's Kaaba (see pages 188–189), was called the navel of the world, while the Hindu god Shiva's phallus (*lingam*) is at the center of every temple dedicated to him. Among the Dogon people of Mali in West Africa the vernacular plan of a house represents a man lying on his side during the sexual act. The kitchen is his head, the central room his belly, and the grinding-stones are his sexual organs.

The correlation between building and body is especially strong in some of the religions based on a key mythical or historical personage. The Christian church represents the body of Christ, who is himself divinity incarnate. The cruciform plan of many churches represents Christ's body on the Cross. The Catholic priest celebrates Mass at the head, where the blood and flesh of Christ are consumed: Christ represents not only divinity but also humanity. In Byzantine churches the body symbolism is more generalized, the nave representing the human body, the chancel the soul, and the altar the spirit.

A similar symbolism prevails in the Hindu temple. The classical Hindu temple is built according to the *vastupurusha* mandala, which transforms a site's specific natural features into something cosmic and universal by incorporating the human body, gods, and planets and projecting their form upward into the temple building. This mandala is a diagram of sixty-four or eighty-one squares, in which the head, trunk, and legs of the original cosmic man (Purusha) are drawn; deities are placed in the various squares. A dedicatory rite represents the planting of the "seed" of the future temple in the earth—the sacred area that will remain at the heart of the fully "grown" temple as the womb-like *garbhagriha* (inner sanctum).

A related Hindu interpretation of the temple sees the entrance as the mouth, the dome as the head, the finial in the top of the dome as the fontanelle in the human skull (the soft part of the skull that closes after birth), and the inner sanctum as the container of the human soul. The journey into this sanctum is therefore also a journey into one's inner self. Some of the most important Hindu temples further emphasize divine and bodily origins by claiming to stand where parts of the goddess Devi's body are said to have fallen after her suicide and dismemberment.

Frequently, a sacred building literally contains the human body. Both Buddhism and Christianity have a strong cult of relics, and shrines have often been built on the site of an event in the life of a significant figure. Buddhist *stupas* enclose a relic, usually a portion of the body of the Buddha or a saint. Similar relics lie at the heart of many Christian shrines and churches, where bodily relics—even the deceased's embalmed body—of saints and martyrs are enclosed in an altar, surrounded by the tombs of worshipers.

The approximate geometry of sacred architecture encapsulated in the *vastupurusha* mandala also occurs in other traditions. In the first century BCE the Roman architectural theorist Vitruvius expounded an architectural geometry based on the proportions of the human body. In the fifteenth and sixteenth centuries his ideas were revived in Italy. Renaissance scholars read Vitruvius to understand Roman architecture, and developed his ideas into theories of harmony concerning arithmetic, geometry, and music.

The Renaissance fascination with proportion was, however, foreshadowed by other forms of

OVERLEAF *Samye monastery in Tibet is the oldest in the country. It was built in the eighth century* CE *under the auspices of two Indian holy men and their patron, the king of Tibet, who sought to create an entirely new place of religious power and significance. Samye's architecture represents a fresh vision of the universe. The settlement constitutes a gigantic mandala with outer circular walls and buildings inside that reflect the Buddhist cosmos. At the center is a large multistoried temple that represents Mount Meru, known as Sumeru. Flanking it are four* chortens *or sanctuaries executed in different colors and styles, and representing the four continents. Protecting the various entrances are figures of lions and statues of guardian beings.*

architecture. One interesting example is the Romanesque church at the abbey of Cluny in France (1080). The plan was based on a modular unit of five Roman feet and the modules were further grouped according to theories of mathematical perfection, including Plato's succession by squares (one, three, nine, twenty-seven . . .) and Pythagoras's series of numbers that were believed to underlie the structure of the universe as well as music and beauty in the arts (the so-called golden section, a ratio between two dimensions such that the smaller is to the larger as the larger is to the sum of the two).

These diverse Eastern and Western schools of thought are united in sharing a belief in a liberating spiritual power, whether it occurs through systematic harmony, or is a cosmological concept pointing to a concentration or focus of power in one central place where space and time come together.

In vertical space the centre is the point of opening from one level to another and is often represented in architecture as a pillar, *stupa*, mountain, or ladder to Heaven. Altars similarly constitute a center, as the point at which a sacrifice can move between the plane of the Earth and that of the gods. A center can also lead downward: while reaching up to Heaven, the Rock in Jerusalem also holds down the chaotic waters in the abyss beneath the Earth.

In horizontal space the center is the point from which the organized and habitable world takes its bearings. In ancient China, just as in the Aztec capital of Tenochtitlán and the Inca capital of Cuzco, it was not only the temple but the entire city that was called the center of the world.

Relationships between sacred buildings and the concept of the center varied. The synagogue and the mosque each look to one geographical center as the site of a past event (see box, page 122); on the other hand, Delphi was deemed the "navel" of the Greek world, yet temples were not oriented toward Delphi.

Many traditions make it clear that the center is not so much an absolute concept as a relational one, the point toward which a community's life, thought, and activity are oriented. In these cultures there can be multiple centers, with each city, temple, and house having its own pillars, altars, and shrines. Nomadic Mongols even carry their center around with them and reestablish it every time they set up their round tent with its central hearth under the smokehole leading directly to the sky (see pages 62–63).

The center is not only a spatial concept, but also a point of origin in time. The Walbiri Aborigines of Australia erect an elaborately decorated post in a hole in the ground at a ceremony to increase the fertility of ants. As dancers move toward this pole across a series of concentric circles drawn on the ground they approach the point of contact with the Dreaming of the ancestors, which lies at the deepest part of the hole. In other cultures rites of construction and consecration may project a sacred building into the center of the universe by reenacting the creation. Such rituals probably took place in ancient Sumeria in a divine drama at the consecration of the temple and its annual rededication.

This treatment of time and space among largely nomadic cultures shows that although buildings are a powerful spiritual focus, a degree of centrality can be created anywhere at any time. The power of the center can be diffused and reproduced in pictures of shrines, gods and saints in homes and elsewhere— even one's own body can be a shrine and a center. Ultimately the center is not a building but a state of mind or a state of grace. As the labyrinth suggests (see page 42), the journey to this understanding of the center is difficult and dangerous. One of the roles of sacred architecture is to guide the devotee toward this destination.

RIGHT *A thangka or scroll painting depicting a Wheel of Life (*Bhavachakramudra*) being turned by Yama, Lord of Death, who can be interpreted as symbolizing the human tendency to cling to material existence. The six stages reflect the human lifecycle of death and rebirth. At the center are the symbols of the cardinal faults of greed, hatred, and delusion.*

Borobudur

Central Java

The Buddhist temple at Borobudur in central Java, begun in the eighth century CE, is probably the world's most elaborate architectural expression of the temple as mountain. Built on the summit of a small hill, it achieves its impact at close quarters, not from any intense skyward thrust, but from its immense mass, its ornamentation, and the subtly orchestrated progression of the visitor's ascent.

Like similar examples at Angkor in Cambodia and Pagan in Myanmar (Burma), the temple follows the groundplan of a mandala (cosmic diagram), facing the four cardinal directions. A square base is surmounted by five square terraces, followed by three circular levels. The square terraces are surrounded by galleries of bas-reliefs in a vigorous style, while the circular layers are set with a total of seventy-two perforated *stupas*, the whole crowned at the top by a large, enclosed *stupa*. A stone staircase runs up the center of each side.

The entire temple is an expression in stone of Buddhist metaphysics and doctrine, and provides a visible and experiential aid to the believer's quest for release. The terraces permit the pilgrims to circumambulate and stage processions, sanctifying and protecting the temple. The pilgrim does not penetrate inside the mountain, as with most Hindu and Egyptian temples, but instead ascends it on the outside, moving from illustrations of the world as we know it, to the level of inner vision on the upper terraces. The journey to the summit of the cosmic axis is also a journey to the ultimate insight of Buddhism.

ABOVE *This aerial picture of Borobudur shows the ascending levels progressing toward the uppermost— symbolizing the Buddhist* nirvana *(enlightenment). The terraces of the temple contain a multitude of carvings, with the sculptures on the square lower galleries designed to be circumambulated in a clockwise fashion, because this is considered an auspicious direction. A continuous narrative of stories from the various lives of the Buddha is presented in the stone reliefs. The second to fourth levels depict the spiritual wanderings of the disciple Sudhana. At the end of the square terraces, moving on to the round ones, Sudhana enters the realm of the future Buddha, Maitreya, on Mount Meru.*

LEFT AND FAR LEFT *On the circular levels each* stupa *contains the statue of a meditating Buddha, visible, albeit with some difficulty, through the latticework. The topmost* stupa, *at the axis of the universe, contained a statue (now lost) that was probably of the primordial Buddha (Adi Buddha), the ultimate source of the universe. This statue, which symbolized ultimate formlessness, would have been invisible to the pilgrim.*

BELOW *A plan of the temple, revealing the mandala form that underlies the entire structure. As if meditating upon a mandala and attaining the ultimate spiritual goal, the visitor to the temple progresses by ascending the steps through different levels—from outer edge to cosmic center—until the highest point is reached.*

STANDING STONES AND SACRED ALIGNMENTS

Standing stones, dug out of the landscape, dragged to sites at varying distances from their places of origin and set upright for now-obscure purposes, have an almost anthropomorphic quality. Almost inevitably, folk legends have crowded around them—as they always do around a monument once its purpose has been forgotten. A typical story is the Cornish tale of young women being transformed into the stone circle called the Merry Maidens as punishment for having danced on the Sabbath.

The term megalith ("huge stone") is applied to any prehistoric massive undressed block of stone, of the kind widely, but not exclusively, erected in northwest European landscapes during the period 3200–1500BCE. A menhir (from the Breton words *men*, "stone," and *hir*, "long") was a type of mega-lith—a simple upright stone of the kind most often found in western Europe, particularly Brittany, either alone or as part of a whole complex, such as a circle, half-circle, or alignment.

Many of these menhirs were large enough to command the landscape. In Brittany the Grand Menhir Brisé at Locmariaquer, which today lies in pieces on the ground, was once almost 70 ft. (22 m) high.

The quarrying of standing stones was an operation requiring great ingenuity in an age of primitive tools. It is possible that wedges of timber were forced into cracks in the rock and soaked with water, causing them to expand and widen the split. Another likely technique was the lighting of fires along faultlines,

BELOW *The thousands of stones at Carnac are nearly all arranged in parallel rows. The Kermario Lines seen here consist of ten rows of stones stretching some 4,000 ft. (1,200 m). Their purpose is unknown but scientists have established that a magnetic field emanates from the vicinity.*

followed by a sudden cold soaking. Transportation was undoubtedly laborious, involving hundreds of men working in unison.

The most impressive megalithic alignments of all are at Carnac in Brittany, the site of more than 3,000 prehistoric stone monuments. Quarried from local granite, the stones were commandeered for ritual purposes by the Romans, who carved images of their gods on some of them.

Other, similar alignments are found in smaller densities in southwest England (there are sixty or so on Dartmoor, for example), and even as far afield as Southeast Asia. Some of the rows at Carnac end in circular or rectangular stone configurations, while others end with a single stone set at right angles to the main axis. It has been suggested that these end-stones were in some way intended to block the passage of the spirits of the dead. A parallel to this is the use of low walls inside the gateways to temples in Indonesia to obstruct the spirits, which it is believed can move only in straight lines.

The purpose of prehistoric standing stones is obscure, and it is difficult to chart a confident course between conflicting speculations, many of them relating to astronomy, fertility, the Mother goddess, and sacred ritual. Although weathering has made its mark over the centuries, even at the time of erection it is probable that each stone had its unique character, and here and there one cannot help seeing in a particular set of surfaces and indentations a human or animal face. This idea has led a number of experts to suppose that some of the stones may have been intended as images of the gods.

In western Europe many ancient stone formations were destroyed by the Christian Church, particularly in France and Britain. As late as 1560 a stone circle on the religiously important Scottish island of Iona, reputed to have a sacrificial victim buried under each of its twelve stones, was demolished. Other monuments survived because they were in church grounds —for example, the stone circle in the cemetery of Midmar Kirk, Aberdeenshire.

Living Memorials

An ancient tradition of erecting megaliths as burial monuments and for other commemorative purposes has continued into modern times in the southern hemisphere.

In the eighteenth century the king of Ambohimanga in Madagascar ordered a stone to be erected in celebration of his marriage; it took two months to transport the megalith from its mountain location. In 1907 a Dutch colonial adminstrator photographed a megalith being erected on the island of Nias near Sumatra in Southeast Asia, intended as a home for a tribal chief's spirit. As recently as 1960 several stones were erected to celebrate Madagascar's independence from France.

In some parts of Madagascar even quite recent stones are seen as phalluses, and women hoping to have children try to throw pebbles on top of them, believing that if they succeed in their aim their prayers will be answered.

However, old legends live on. The belief that standing stones are a source of fertility and healing powers has inspired many people to visit the churchyard of La Pierre de St. Martin in Pitres, France, where they tie pieces of cloth on a Cross that stands in front of a solitary megalith. Elsewhere some menhirs have been carved with the Cross and thus "converted" to serve as Christian shrines.

The great circles

The largest and most spectacular megalithic monuments are the circles of standing stones in northwest Europe dating from the Neolithic period. They are so deeply bound up with their landscapes that they seem almost to have grown out of the earth. Still dominating windswept moors and pastures, they resemble vast open-air temples or ritual enclosures, and are perhaps best exemplified by the lintel-capped stones still to be seen at Stonehenge (see pages 134–135).

Although no evidence of their function has yet been unearthed, it has been speculated that the circles were originally used for pagan sacrifices, Druidic ceremonies, or Mother goddess worship. In the absence of written records, however, such interpretation of these prehistoric monuments remains controversial. The great stone circle of Stonehenge in southern England, one of the most mysterious of such sites, has been interpreted as temple, meeting place, burial site, observatory, and calendar, and may have been all of these. It certainly seems to have celestial associations: at the northwest of the site an opening appears to be aligned to the midwinter setting of the Moon, while at the northeast an avenue leading from the center gives an alignment to the midsummer sunrise so that at dawn at the summer solstice an observer standing in the center of Stonehenge will see the Sun rise over the heel stone situated outside the circle.

One megalithic complex, at Callanish on the Isle of Lewis in the Outer Hebrides, off Scotland, acts, in association with its surrounding landscape, as a vast lunar calendar. The Moon at its most southerly point in its nineteen-year cycle appears to skim the horizon when seen from the prehistoric site. Nobody knows now what purpose, if any, these astronomical relationships fulfilled. However, one British civil

RIGHT *Tracking the phases of the Moon preoccupied many ancient cultures. The standing stones of Callanish, dating from 2500BCE, may have served as a huge lunar calendar, for there are lines to the Moon, Sun and stars. Its suffix name Tursachen means "stones of mourning."*

engineer, after measuring hundreds of megalithic sites, has claimed that all the major stone circles in Britain are related in some way to the phases of the Moon, and in some cases may have helped ancient peoples to predict the movements of the tides.

What is beyond doubt is the great importance that these henges must have had for those who built them, since an enormous effort was required by the small and scattered population in order to quarry, transport, and erect the huge megaliths. The motivating impulse must have been intense, akin to something like missionary zeal.

Long after the original functions of these sites had been forgotten, they continued to be centers of activity—and often controversy. The Romans used Maumbury Rings in Dorset as an amphitheater; and in the 1640s, during the English Civil War, this site shielded Parliamentary troops. A village sprang up in the centre of Avebury (see pages 138–139), which now grapples with the sometimes conflicting demands of a village economy, tourism, and conservation. Stonehenge is a focus of dispute because fears for its preservation have led to a ban

The Jantar Mantar and the Lunar Calendar

The thirteenth-century CE Jantar Mantar at Delhi, India, is a celestial observatory connected with the phases of the Moon. The astronomer-astrologers of the time, known as *jyotishas*, were brahmin priests who wished to establish a religious calendar based upon lunar movements in order to determine the most auspicious time for sacrifices.

Faced with the problem that the apparently monthly lunar cycle is in fact irregular, the *jyotishas* set out to find a longer one, when the Moon's movements repeat themselves exactly. They found this to be nineteen solar years, which they reflected in the observatory's structure. There are now many Hindu calendars, all linked to the phases of the Moon.

Stonehenge

Southwestern England

The ruins of Stonehenge, a Neolithic monument on Salisbury Plain in Wiltshire, show the last of several forms that the monument has had over many centuries. Beginning *c.*3000BCE as a simple ditch and earth bank, by *c.*2100BCE Stonehenge had become the imposing megalithic structure whose remains are visible today.

The monument was believed from early times to have calendrical significance. It was observed long ago that the avenue to the northeast, with its "heel" stone, aligns with sunrise at the summer solstice, a fact that has been taken as evidence of Sun worship; it is possible that there was originally a winter solstice alignment also. In the 1960s American astronomer Gerald Hawkins suggested it was actually a complex instrument for predicting solar and lunar eclipses.

The construction of Stonehenge, no less than its astronomical sophistication, has been an object of wonder. In the second phase of building, about eighty bluestone pillars were brought to the site (possibly by sea and along the Avon River) from the Preseli Mountains in southwest Wales, a distance of about 240 miles (385 km). One folk legend claimed that these non-local stones were brought to Stonehenge by magic. It is possible that the mountain they came from had sacred significance.

There is little evidence to support the belief that the so-called Altar Stone, a dressed sarsen in the center of the henge, was originally used for sacrifice. It may simply be a toppled upright. The inner "horseshoe" within the original thirty-stone outer sarsen circle would have had five trilithons (a trilithon consists of a horizontal capstone atop two stone pillars), dressed smooth and secured by mortise-and-tenon joints. The central trilithon is the tallest, measuring 10 ft. (3 m) wide and more than 25 ft. (8 m) high.

LEFT *By the 19th century many of the stones had fallen or were missing. The outer sarsen would originally have consisted of thirty stones with a continuous lintel and an inner "horseshoe" of five trilithons. Only seven of the megaliths have never been disturbed. Today eleven have been straightened and six reerected, allowing this most impressive of ancient monuments to recapture many of the qualities of Earth kinship and mystery it has embodied for millennia.*

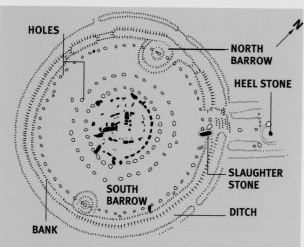

HOLES

NORTH BARROW

HEEL STONE

SLAUGHTER STONE

SOUTH BARROW

DITCH

BANK

ABOVE *The midsummer dawn is celebrated at Stonehenge by the Ancient Order of Druids, (founded in the 19th century), following William Stukeley's proposal in the 1720s that Stonehenge had been a Druid temple—previously it had been seen as Roman or Danish. However, the henge, like many other monuments once attributed to the ancient Britons, predates the Celtic presence in southern Britain.*

LEFT *A plan of the entire complex of Stonehenge. The oldest part of the monument, the outer bank and ditch henge of c.3000BCE, encloses the megalithic structures erected nearly a millennium later. Although a number of graves have been found within the monument, there is no evidence that human sacrifice took place at the site.*

on Druids and other neo-pagan groups celebrating the summer solstice at the site.

Europe's Neolithic megalithic monuments were constructed at various times between the fifth and second millennia BCE. The most numerous type of monument is actually the burial chamber. This may take the form of passage-graves with a long entrance, such as Newgrange in Ireland; court-graves, so named after their large semicircular entrance, found in Ireland and Sardinia; and dolmens, in which two or more upright stones support a horizontal slab.

The design of some tombs clearly links astronomy to rebirth. The passage-grave resembles a vagina leading into the womb, and some tombs have entrances shaped unmistakably like a vulva. This interpretation is borne out by the facing of the burial mound at Newgrange with white quartz, making the tomb resemble an egg. In many religions today the tomb is also a place of regeneration and rebirth, and it seems likely that this was also the case for many Neolithic peoples. At Newgrange at the winter solstice, the rays of the rising Sun penetrate nearly 100 ft. (30 m) along the passage to the back wall. This was very carefully calculated, as the uphill gradient of the passage was compensated for by a tiny opening in a "roof-box" that let in the sunlight. It is as if the deceased, just like the dying year, will be reborn at the touch of the returning Sun.

Although megalithic cultures are best recognized from the concentrations of examples found in prehistoric western Europe, they also embraced ancient Mesoamerica as well as Southeast Asia and Oceania. The word generally describes very simple styles of building that use the shape of natural stone, but the term is also sometimes applied elsewhere when massive stones were used with more elaborate techniques of carving and dressing. This is the case at a number of Olmec sites in Mexico and the early Inca site of Chavín in Peru. At the mysterious site of Tiahuanaco, located at an altitude of 13,000 ft. (4,000 m) in the Bolivian part of the Andes mountain range, long lines of massive upright stones formed a continuous wall around a large square and an entrance was carved through a single block of stone to form the Gateway of the Sun.

Megalithic monuments were also widespread in ancient Asian and Pacific cultures. In modern times they are particularly prominent in parts of tribal India, on the islands of Nias, Bali, and Sumba in Indonesia, and in Polynesia. As in ancient Europe, they perform a range of functions. Among the Sora of India the shaman's assistants raise a menhir at each person's funeral, representing that person's continuing existence in the underworld (see page 229). At the funeral of a chief in Nias or Sumba enormous massive stones of up to thirty tons are laid horizontally across dolmen supports.

In modern Bali, as in ancient Polynesia, a row of menhirs wrapped in cloth is placed in an enclosed temple courtyard as a lodging for visiting ancestor spirits. Both cultures built rectangular stone pyramids, of which the largest in Polynesia—on Tahiti—had a base of 266 ft. by 72 ft. (81 m by 22 m).

In Polynesia megaliths were also used as aids for navigation between tiny islands amid the huge Pacific Ocean. Sailors would study the sequence of stars as they came up against the stone. In Kiribati nine stones on the shore point accurately toward three neighboring islands, apparently showing the degree of drift associated with different currents.

Lost megalithic cultures

Bronze Age cultures that flourished in the western Mediterranean in the second millennium BCE have left mysterious megalithic remains in the Balearic Islands and on Sardinia. These ancient cultures were probably unrelated, but in both cases their builders were skilled craftsmen who erected imposing structures of finely dressed granite, limestone, or basalt blocks that fitted together without mortar.

On Majorca and Minorca there were once thousands of the limestone towers known as *talayots*, the vestiges of a culture that evidently continued into

Roman times. A great many of them were destroyed by the expanded use of land for agriculture, but where they survive they usually stand in groups, sometimes enclosed by a wall. They look like fortified compounds, but their original use is a mystery. Whereas some have small chambers within the thickness of their walls, many others are solid.

It has been suggested that these constructions may have been defenses against invasion, or funerary monuments, or simply the foundations of buildings that have decayed with age. On Minorca a *talayot* usually stands within a stone enclosure and is accompanied by a *taula*, an immense upright slab of dressed stone upon which another has been laid horizontally to form a T-shaped structure.

It is widely believed that the *taulas* had some ritual function or were central supports for ceremonial halls. Most of the information about the people who built these structures comes from the *navetas* or *naus* ("ships" in Catalan)—stone tombs resembling an upside-down boat that were built near the *talayots*. The *navetas* have yielded the remains of many dead, together with their burial goods, including early Bronze Age pottery and copper and bronze objects.

The *nuraghe*, a prehistoric conical tower built from great blocks of volcanic basalt or granite, is a common sight on Sardinia. It is generally accepted that the island's 7,000 or so *nuraghi*, concentrated in the southcentral and northwestern regions, were built between *c.*1500 and *c.*400BCE. They were evidently occupied, because they contain chambers with vaulted or flat ceilings and spiral staircases leading to upper stories. Possibly for defensive reasons, each *nuraghe* is visible from at least one other. The largest *nuraghi* are more than 45 ft. (14 m) in diameter and 65 ft. (20 m) high, with walls up to 15 ft. (4.5 m) thick. Among artifacts found within them are tools, weapons, and domestic utensils. Other objects, of clay, metal, and obsidian, may have had a religious purpose. At Serra Orrios, a *nuraghe* village near Dorgali, there are nearly eighty buildings, including temples and a theater.

Sardinia's Su Nuraxi

A large isolated hill covered with scattered stones once rose above a plain at Su Nuraxi near the village of Barumini in southcentral Sardinia. However, after a violent thunderstorm, floodwater washed away the soil and revealed that the hill was actually a vast *nuraghe*, flanked by four large towers and several smaller ones connected by a wall. The structure stood amid dozens of mainly circular small buildings resembling mushrooms.

Archaeological excavation suggests that Su Nuraxi was built in phases over several centuries, with the main tower constructed *c.*1500BCE, the four flanking towers *c.*1200BCE, the enclosing wall *c.*900BCE and the remaining structures after that. Research indicates that the settlement was destroyed by the Carthaginians in the sixth century BCE.

Ceremonial landscapes

Stone circles and tombs continue to evoke mystery and wonder, epitomizing to this day the deep and enduring spiritual relationship between humankind and the Earth. But this bond is not reflected solely in the structures built upon the ground; it has also found expression in the search for hidden relationships between significant sites, most notably in a widely found belief in sacred alignments and leys.

In 1925 Alfred Watkins (1855–1935), a businessman and photographic pioneer, published *The Old Straight Track*, in which he observed that many ancient sites—megalithic monuments, churches, holy wells, and cairns—appear to lie on straight alignments for dozens of miles through the English countryside. One alignment in Wiltshire, with Salisbury Cathedral near its center, appears to link several prehistoric features including Stonehenge. Watkins discovered that a syllable that often appears in the

Avebury and Silbury Hill

Southwestern England

Avebury is a massive Bronze Age henge in Wiltshire, built *c.*2600BCE. An outer circle made up of some 100 standing stones was surrounded by a ditch and embankment 1,400 ft. (430 m) across. To form this ditch, tons of chalk gravel were scraped out with antler-pick tools. Inside were two smaller circles side by side, each of around thirty stones, and a cluster of larger stones in the middle. A village was later established at the center of the henge and only a quarter of the stones remain in place today.

William Stukeley drew and described the monument in the eighteenth century, shortly before much of it was destroyed to provide farmland and building materials. He identified two avenues of stones. One, still visible, leads from Avebury to a stone circle on Overton Hill that has now disappeared. The other (no longer visible) curved sinuously to the southwest. Stukeley called these avenues "serpents" and described Avebury as a serpent temple, shaped as an alchemical symbol of divine power, although this interpretation now seems doubtful.

Avebury is surrounded by the greatest concentration of large prehistoric monuments in Britain. Near by are the West and East Kennet long barrows —passage-tombs dating from *c.*3600BCE—and the mysterious Neolithic Silbury Hill.

Silbury Hill is a massive manmade mound that rises some 130 ft. (40 m) above the valley floor of the Kennet River in the chalklands of the Marlborough Downs in Wiltshire. It has long aroused both respect and curiosity: an important Roman road detoured around it, and the antiquarian John Aubrey wrote in 1663, when he conducted King Charles II on a tour of nearby Avebury, that "his Majesty cast his eie on Silsbury-hill about a mile off; which they had the curiosity to see, and walkt up to the top of it." According to local legend, the hill was the tomb of an ancient king, Sil, buried with his horse.

RIGHT *The great enclosure of Avebury is today bisected by the lines of roads, and the village breaches the outer ditch. Nonetheless the site retains an aura of ancient power. The circular bank is 1,396 ft. (427 m) in diameter and rises to 20 ft. (6 m) in height. Note the conical mound of Silbury Hill close by.*

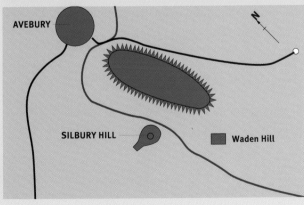

AVEBURY

SILBURY HILL Waden Hill

ABOVE *Southwest of Avebury is Silbury Hill, at 130 ft. (40 m) high the largest artificial tumulus in Europe. It was once held to be a burial mound, but excavations found a solid core of stone. Built c.2750–2660BCE, its purpose remains unknown, but suggestions include an omphalos marking the navel of the world, the womb of a pregnant Mother goddess, or a chieftain's memorial.*

LEFT *The proximity between the circle and the hill leads many people to believe they must somehow have been related. One suggestion is that the mound was a point from which to summon people to rituals at Avebury.*

names of places lying along these alignments is "ley" (pronounced "lea"), meaning a cleared glade, and so he called these lines "leys." His theory was that they were primarily practical, originating in ancient times as a network of landmarks to guide travelers. The leys passed through prominent hills and mountains where beacons were once lit to mark their course. Watkins's British followers, who formed The Old Straight Track Club, went further, interpreting leys as part of a web of physical and spiritual energy lines,

rather like those recognized by Chinese geomancers, running through the terrestrial landscape and ultimately aligning with the stars.

One such line, which passes through the stone circle at Boscawenun, near Penzance in Cornwall, links the site of a hermitage on St. Clement's Isle off the Cornish coast to the position of the Pleiades, as seen during September. As well as lying on the trans-European St. Michael ley, St. Michael's Mount in Cornwall is at one end of the longest ley in Britain, which coincides with the path of the rising Sun on May Day and runs through the megalithic complex at Avebury, Wiltshire.

The fact that Christian church buildings frequently share alignments with heavenly bodies is in part due to the early Church policy of Christianizing local traditions. In England in the 1950s the Reverend Hugh Benson surveyed almost 300 churches to show that rather than all aligning east, toward the rising Sun and the direction of the resurrection, a significant proportion of them were actually aligned to the point of sunrise on the day of the saint to whom the church was dedicated. Cornwall's ancient St. Piran's Church was aligned to a prehistoric earthwork some two miles away—the point where the Sun would have risen on August 15 in the seventh century.

Other investigators have made their own studies of European landmark alignments. Josef Heinsch, who worked in his native Germany and Czechoslovakia, discovered leys linking the sites of churches built on pre-Christian sites. In the early 1970s the French investigator Lucien Richer discovered an extraordinary alignment of holy sites that spanned Europe from the island of Skerrig Michael off southwest Ireland to Mount Carmel in Israel, via St. Michael's Mount in Cornwall, Mont St. Michel in France, and Delphi, Athens, and Delos in Greece. On the ley, and built mostly on outcrops, are many of the important sanctuaries to St. Michael, the standard bearer of the archangels, and Apollo, the Greek god of light.

LEFT *St. Michael's Church at Glastonbury Tor, Somerset, England. Many legends are associated with this site, including some of King Arthur and the Holy Grail. Others believe that the tor is part of a network of sacred alignments and that Glastonbury is a place where the visible and invisible worlds are in harmony.*

Chichén Itzá

Yucatán, Mexico

Chichén Itzá is the greatest of the ruined cities of Mexico's Yucatán peninsula. The city was built by the Itzá group of Maya *c.*600–*c.*830CE, and its name means "Opening of the Wells of the Itzá," a reference to two sinkholes that were considered divine. It was probably captured by the Toltecs in 987, but abandoned *c.*1200, at a time of increasing instability.

Early cities and temples are often oriented in some way to the north-south axis, the pivot of the celestial drama of the movement of stars and planets. In ancient Mesoamerica such orientation was extreme —sometimes entire cities were constructed as precise functioning astronomical instruments. Chichén Itzá, located in completely flat terrain, contains one of the best examples of astronomical architecture—the mysterious asymmetrical Caracol observatory.

The astroarchaeologist Anthony Aveni has identified distinct groups of buildings according to orientation, notably at 17 and 22 degrees east of north. These orientations are related to events such as the setting of the Pleiades, the rising and setting of the Sun at the equinoxes, and the movement of Venus, conceived as the feathered serpent Kukulcan who dies as the evening star and is reborn as the morning star. The shafts and openings of the Caracol enabled very specific astronomical sightings: all point in different directions. Mayan astronomers achieved astonishing results without the wheel, optical instruments, or clocks, relying on architecture that by means of slits in walls enabled sighting by eye.

LEFT *The pyramid of El Castillo was dedicated to the feathered serpent god Kukulcan. Just before sunset at the annual spring and autumn equinoxes the Sun picks out a wavy line of seven segments along the sloping balustrade of the stairway on the shaded north side of the pyramid. The pattern undulates directly down to the carved head (right) and makes the serpent appear to come alive and descend from the temple. The structure has nine terraces (for the nine underground worlds of the Mayan cosmos) culminating in the temple at the top, accessed via four staircases. The main staircase on the northern side has ninety-two steps, if the heads are included, and the other three have ninety-one each; the total of 365 steps equates to one for each day of the Mayan year.*

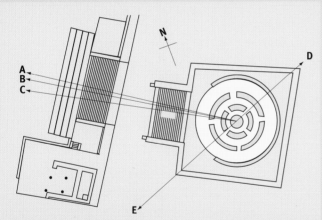

ABOVE *The Caracol observatory takes its name from its internal spiral staircase (caracol is Spanish for snail). A cylindrical tower on a two-tiered platform, it originally had six horizontal sight tubes or shafts, but only three survive. The ancient Mesoamericans were particularly interested in the movements of the Sun and in the disappearance and reappearance of Venus, the bright planet whose associated god, Kukulcan, stood for warfare and blood sacrifice. The Caracol was used by Mayan astronomers partly to demarcate significant points in the celestial path of Venus, and their accurate calculation of Venus's year was based on data collected over 384 Earth years.*

ABOVE, LEFT *A plan of the observatory showing the major lines of astronomical orientation. (A) sunset at midsummer; (B) the northernmost setting point of Venus; (C) sunset on the day of the Sun's zenith passage (that is, when the Sun passes directly overhead); (D) sunrise at midsummer; (E) sunrise at midwinter.*

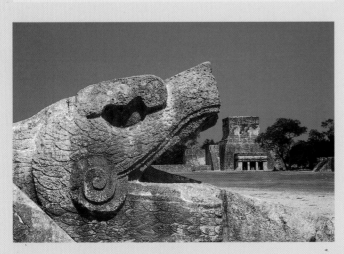

LEFT *A serpent's head lying at the base of the great pyramid of El Castillo (The Castle). The carving represents the god Kukulcan, the Mayan counterpart of the Aztec Quetzalcóatl. The use of sunlight to render an illusion of the serpent "coming to life" was probably seen as a hierophany, or manifestation, of the god.*

Mansions of the Gods

To express the divine in the solid materials utilized in architecture is an astonishing feat of human creativity. Yet the construction of buildings for sacred purposes is a truly universal human endeavor. Throughout the world, and in many forms, buildings give visible and tangible shape to a concept of the divine and provide a focus for worship.

A sacred building does not depend for its holiness on brick or stone, but on the concentration of sacredness that it embodies or makes possible. Rites of consecration and purification make the building a suitable point of contact between humanity and the realm of the divine.

Within this space, the meeting is generally enacted through the religious act of sacrifice (whether literal or symbolic), or else by prayer and dancing. These human deeds are matched by actions of the gods, who grant favors to those within the building. This two-way communication intensifies the sacred power of a site, sometimes attracting pilgrims who seek a transformation in their lives at this proven gateway to the gods.

RIGHT *The enormous 12th-century temple of Angkor Wat was built by King Suryavarman II of Cambodia as a vast sacred microcosm, with towers symbolizing mountains of the gods and a ritual purification pool representing the waters surrounding the world.*

DWELLINGS OF DIVINE POWER

The sacred building expresses a fundamental paradox. The gods are the living force within everything on Earth, yet they are not of this Earth. They are both *in* their cult objects and icons (immanent) and *beyond* them (transcendent). They can be encountered in the sacred building, but although they may leave behind holy relics as objects of veneration and tokens of their presence, their everyday attendance cannot be taken for granted. Sacred architecture is in part an attempt to capture a divine presence that by its very nature cannot be fully secured.

In monotheistic religions there is an emphasis on the formless, transcendent nature of God. This is most marked in Islam and Judaism, where the mosque and synagogue do not contain a representation of God, but instead focus people's worship on his cosmic law as written in a holy book (see pages 186–187 and 190–191).

In Christianity, although the building may be the "house of God," this is widely viewed as meaning not that God resides in a church, but that He can best be encountered there. Synagogues, mosques, and churches are not houses for a god, like the shrines and temples of many other religions, but houses for God's people as communities of worshipers. Early Christians used existing secular buildings for their humble meeting places, reacting against the pagan temple and the power of state religion, in which emperors and deities were worshiped side by side. Even as the Church establishment grew, and specific architecture developed, the ideal of spirituality manifest in a prayer meeting of believers was retained.

In polytheistic world-views, such as the Hindu or ancient Greek religions, temples accommodate different gods and serve in part to distinguish them from each other. Some religions combine notions of the gods' transcendence with more literal ideas of dwelling. Priests in ancient Egypt used to give the statue of the god in the inner sanctum a daily bath and feeding. In Japan, while the Buddhist temple is built to enclose a congregation, the Shinto shrine houses *kami* deities and often is not entered by the worshiper. But to the extent that they are present in this world, the gods are not equally present at all times or in all places. Even when they dwell in a sacred building, gods may visit it more intensely on special days and during rituals. The idea of a literal indwelling may be underscored by a ceremonial procession of a statue or holy relic around the temple, city, or territory. This idea seems particularly strong when the temple is likened to a palace, from which the god emerges like a king or queen to tour his or

Hindu Temple Shrines

In several Hindu traditions deities such as Krishna and his wife Radha are represented in human form and consequently the temple becomes their house. The images are placed in shrines with doors and curtains to give them privacy at night and during their times of rest, with a miniature couch provided. Rituals represent each daily activity of waking, dressing, bathing, and feeding the god, and the temple will keep an elaborate array of clothes and ornaments.

In larger temples the deities share their residence with their servants—the ascetics and priests—so there are dormitories within the compound, ranging from decoratively carved and painted wooden buildings in earlier centuries to modern apartment complexes. Guest-houses are set aside for visitors, and provision is made for the multitudes who come for major festivals. Thus many temples have kitchens, dining rooms and storerooms, and some have stalls for the cows that produce milk for the temple. All food is first offered to the deities in small symbolic amounts; the rest may then be eaten by the devotees as *prasad* (holy leftovers). The temple becomes a microcosm of sanctified human life.

ABOVE *The 14th-century marble structures of the Jain temple of Chaumukha in Ranakpur. The elaborate adornment of this area is explained by its function as a celestial assembly hall of the* tirthankaras, *the worthiest idealized beings. Jainism does not glorify an absolute god but seeks to attain self-perfection for its adherents by abandonment of the material world.*

her domain. Sometimes—for example, during a siege—a statue may even be chained to its place in a temple to prevent the god from deserting the city.

Egyptian temples

As the Nile River retreated each year from the height of its flooding, it gradually revealed islands of mud. In the same way, according to Egyptian myth, a mound of dry land arose from the Waters of Chaos, providing a place where the first god, Atum, could come into existence.

Many Egyptian temples were actually representations in architecture of this primordial island: the visitor was drawn up steps or a ramp at every stage from the entrance through to the inner sanctum. The primeval mound, as the locus of creation, may also symbolize potential for rebirth, an idea illustrated by the cenotaph of Sety I (*c.*1290–1279BCE) at Abydos, where the coffin of the Nineteenth-Dynasty pharaoh was placed on an island surrounded by a channel of water.

The Egyptian temple was trabeate (beamed) in construction—that is, made from upright posts and crossbeams. Roofs were simply flat lids. Wooden beams in the earliest temples were held up by stiff bundles of papyrus reeds, symbolizing the vegetation on the primordial island. Later, stone pillars replicated these papyrus bundles, even down to the vertically ridged effect of the multiple stems. From the Third Dynasty onward, papyrus flowers were portrayed open, and from the Fifth Dynasty they were also shown in bud. Sometimes capitals depicted the lotus (waterlily). The papyrus represented the delta area of Lower Egypt, the lotus represented Upper Egypt. These two species were often later combined in the same building to symbolize the unification of the two kingdoms.

The temple is essentially a long straight upward path, which in the most elaborate examples passes through an alternation of open sun-drenched courts and the cool dark interiors of gateways and halls, and finally reaches the inner sanctum. The entrance to the temple was formed by a monumental gateway, or pylon, adorned with flags, multicolored carvings and colossal statues. The pillared hall, representing the island of mud, was like a forest of gigantic reeds and was often paved to resemble water; the ceiling was frequently painted with stars. The inner sanctum

The Importance of the Nile

Egypt is a narrow strip of land on the banks of a long river, with desert beyond. The Blue Nile, bringing fertile silt from the mountains of Ethiopia, made Egyptian civilization possible. In ancient Egypt the river rose rapidly from June to October, then fell gradually again. Agriculture was possible only from October, as the waters started to recede, and this left a great labor force available for monumental building during the flood period. The Nile was also the main avenue for transport—stone blocks weighing up to 15 tons were floated down it.

At Thebes, in Upper Egypt, the City of the Dead was built on the western bank (like the setting Sun, the dead entered the underworld in the west); causeways led from the river to a necropolis of funerary temples and cliff-tombs. Also on the west bank was the royal palace. The "city of the living," with workers' housing, lay on the east bank. The temple, with its long path, may be modeled on the Nile as a central axis with banks and fields on each side. Space itself may have been conceived of as long and narrow—an idea made physical in the temple's shape.

The Nile also played its part in the cult of Amun. Once a year, when the river was in flood, his statue at Karnak was hidden in a cloth and taken upstream on a barge to Luxor where the pharaoh and his wife were secluded with it in a room to perform a ritual.

LEFT *Fifth-century* BCE *Greek historian Herodotus called Egypt "the gift of the Nile." This image of Beni Hasan, sited just above the former high-water mark, makes clear the effect of the river on what would otherwise be desert. Prior to the modern era—before dams controlled waterflow—the Nile flooded every year and deposited a fertile layer of rich, dark silt. The name Kemet ("black land") was given by the people to these riverbanks bounded by the arid Deshret ("red land").*

The Temple of Creation

Karnak, Egypt

Thebes (modern Luxor) was the royal capital of Egypt during the New Kingdom (*c.*1539–1075BCE), and at its heart was the vast temple complex of Karnak on the east bank of the Nile, dedicated to the worship of the creator god Amun. After the monarchy, the temple of Amun was the most powerful institution in Egypt, and the high priests there wielded wealth and power that rivaled—at times even surpassed—that of the pharaoh himself.

From the bank of the Nile an avenue of sphinxes (far right) forms the approach to the massive First Pylon or gateway—the westernmost entrance to the complex. In spite of its name this gateway was in fact the last to be built, by the pharaoh Nectanebo I (382–362BCE), who left it unfinished. Beyond this is an open courtyard before the Second Pylon, with two massive statues of the pharaoh Ramesses II (*c.*1279–1213BCE) in front. This pylon leads to the Hypostyle Hall, built by Sety I, with its colonnades of columns 70 ft. (21 m) high and 12 ft. (3.6 m) across, each carved in the form of a huge papyrus plant and therefore creating a stylized grove. The great hall, which was originally roofed, gives the impression of being a passageway rather than a chamber, a stage on the journey through the temple. This feeling is highlighted by the fact that the 134 huge columns that form a central avenue through the hall are taller than, and out of alignment with, the pillars of the low-ceilinged space on either side. These "side" aisles would have been dim and fragmented by the pillars, while the central path was higher, sharply defined, and lit from window-slits just below the roof.

The path leads on through a succession of inner halls and three more pylons, some originally with gold doors and silver floors, to the inner sanctuary of Amun, which was built by Thutmose I (ruled *c.*1493–1482BCE). This chamber, the sacred nucleus of the temple, contained a statue of Amun within a shrine of gold and gems. Today both shrine and statue are lost. The god was believed to reside in his image, and he was tended by shaven-headed priests who ritually washed him, "fed" him, and dressed him in fine linen thrice daily. Only the pharaoh and his priests were allowed to enter this dark inner space.

In the grounds of the main temple is the sacred lake, which was used by the priests to purify themselves before they carried out their rituals.

LEFT *The rectangular, stone-lined sacred lake at Karnak served a variety of cultic purposes, providing water for ritual ablutions and a home for sacred aquatic creatures such as crocodiles. The site is adorned with imagery evoking the Egyptian creation myth.*

The temple was extended by successive pharaohs from the inner sanctum outward, with entrance pylons—ten in total —constructed to the west and south. The Seventh to Tenth pylons connect to another grand processional avenue of human-headed sphinxes that leads to the Temple of Luxor, some two miles (3 km) to the southwest, which is also dedicated to Amun. It was from here that the cult statue was ferried on a barque upriver.

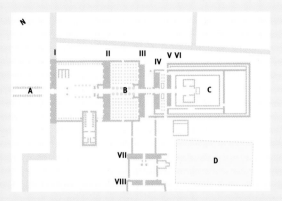

ABOVE *The temple complex. A: Avenue of Sphinxes; B: Hypostyle Hall; C: Inner Sanctuary; D: Sacred Lake. Pylons are indicated by Roman numerals (pylons IX and X are not shown).*

LEFT *Pillars at Karnak bear lotus and papyrus imagery, representing the heraldic plants of Upper and Lower Egypt and symbolizing the unity of the two lands.*

BELOW *Ram-headed sphinxes sacred to Amun and carved with the royal cartouche line the processional way leading from the First Pylon of the temple to the ceremonial quay on the Nile River where the barque for the cult statue of Amun was moored.*

housed the statue of the god and was the god's dwelling-place, sometimes surrounded by other inner rooms containing model boats and priests' offices. As the path led toward the ultimate small enclosure, the ceilings became progressively lower, adding to the impression of depth and mystery.

During the course of some 3,000 years a number of temples became enormous and complex. At Luxor and Karnak (see pages 150–151) the sense of a path was extended over centuries by adding a chain of further courts, each fronted by a pylon.

Shinto shrines and temples

The Japanese religion Shinto (Way of the Gods) emerged from ancient folk ideas of dynamic divinity manifest in all things, animate and inanimate. There are believed to be an infinite number of deities, or *kami*, and these reside in great people, in ancestors, in trees, mountains, rocks, waterfalls, and other features of the environment, as well as in phenomena such as birth and decay.

Reflecting a concept of nature permeated with divinity, Shinto shrines are often found at places of outstanding natural beauty or sites with an air of grandeur or mystery about them. Shrines are frequently places for the worship of nature itself. As befits this outlook there is a profound respect for both the quality and type of natural materials used in the buildings.

Four prototypical shapes are found in Shinto shrines, according to the historian Nitschke: the hut, pillar, mountain, and funnel. Most, however, contain more than one of these elements. All shrines are essentially movable and renewable, reflecting the idea that each is a temporary abode (*yorishiro*) of a deity who periodically visits the people. All four models derive from the notion of the archetypal bundle of grass (*shime*) tied with the sacred straw rope, which was originally used in ancient times to signify occupation or ownership of land. Over time, such marks of the humanization of the world were sacralized.

As Shinto evolved, so did its shrines. The very early simple outdoor altars had become temples by the seventh century CE, their style bearing an architectural resemblance to older raised-floor wooden dwellings and rice-stores. From around the same time, after the arrival of Buddhism, Shinto temples also imitated the look of Chinese Buddhist temples. In a departure from the simple early style, these were brightly colored and elaborately ornamented.

Modern shrines are built in a diversity of styles, but most are situated within a garden or amid trees, reflecting the significance of nature, and most have a similar layout. At the entrance is a gateway or *torii*. This originally consisted of two posts set in the ground with a straw rope stretched between them; the rope was later replaced by a wooden crosspiece extending past the posts and a second crosspiece just below, connecting them. Eventually the *torii* became an elaborate architectural form in its own right—sometimes it stands alone in the landscape, denoting a sacred place beyond. When a *torii* serving as a shrine entranceway is passed through, the devotee crosses the threshold separating the secular from the sacred world. Preparing to enter the presence of the gods, the worshiper cleanses himself or herself with a scoop of pure water from a stone trough.

The shrine itself will typically consist of one or more halls, and an inner sanctuary—the domain of the priest—containing the image of the *kami*. Some shrines are very small, while others are great temple complexes dedicated to several Shinto deities. The larger ones may contain many subsidiary buildings in their precincts, including stalls where good-luck charms are sold, to be hung up later for the attention of the *kami*.

RIGHT *Akino Miyajima Great Torii rises out of the sea, marking the entrance to the precinct of the sacred place. The torii is seen here from the window of Itsukushima Shrine on Miyajima Island, a shrine dedicated to the divine daughters of Japan's storm god Susano.*

The Grand Shrine at Ise

Honshu, Japan

SEA OF JAPAN

SOUTH
KOREA

JAPAN

Tokyo

Ise

PACIFIC OCEAN

The Grand Shrine at Ise is the most sacred shrine in Japan, dating back to the third or fourth century CE. In a ritual that first took place in the eighth century, its buildings are destroyed every twenty years and new ones built on a carefully prepared adjacent site. The new shrines, although identical to the old ones, are not considered a replica, but are Ise created afresh once again. The process reveals the Shinto understanding of nature as constantly renewed. The spirits are ritually transferred to the new site during the Shikinen Sengu celebration, the sixty-first of which was held in 1993 when the shrines were last rebuilt.

Set amid ancient and lofty cryptomeria trees, the Grand Shrine—better known as Jingu—consists of two similar complexes about four miles (6 km) apart, dedicated to two major goddesses. Naiku, the name given to the Inner Shrine and the holiest part of the entire site, is dedicated to the Sun goddess Amaterasu. She is the *kami* from whom the imperial family is believed to descend, and only the emperor, his family, and his priests may enter the precinct. Geku, the Outer Shrine, is dedicated to Toyuke, the rice or harvest goddess.

The shrines express the Shinto spiritual ideals of purity and simplicity. The buildings are raised on posts above the ground, in a style that may have been based on the raised-floor dwellings of ancient Japan. The structures themselves are made of timber from the hinoki tree, a species of white cypress whose wood is particularly treasured.

RIGHT *This 18th-century woodblock print shows crowds of visitors attending the site of the Ise shrines. From the Middle Ages pilgrims were encouraged by the emperor's agents to come to Ise and pay their respects. The atmosphere was carnival-like, and on several occasions more than a million pilgrims descended on the area. Today the site attracts in excess of five million devotees a year.*

ABOVE *Harmony of structure is evident everywhere in Ise's buildings of wood and thatch, which, being torn down and reconstructed every two decades, are at once both ancient and new. They embody the renewal of nature and enhance the sacredness of the entire site. Before entering any shrine, a pilgrim must pass through a simple* torii *(gateway), to step from profane into sacred space. Only Shinto priests and members of the royal family, however, can enter the sacred precincts of Amaterasu's inner shrine. As the direct descendant of Amaterasu, the emperor still presides over the annual rituals at Ise to this day.*

LEFT *A detail from the roof of one of the buildings. The roofs have to shed Japan's heavy rainfall; some are pitched in wood planking, others are thatched in a delicate curve from strips of* hinoki *(Japanese cypress) bark and then trimmed.*

Just as the god is mobile, so, too, is its humanly constructed vessel. This receptacle often takes the form of a float—a "mountain" marking the descent of a deity. Those used in Kyoto's 1,100-year-old Gion Festival consist of a wonderful assortment of four-wheeled square chariots, sometimes with a small roofed shrine for the deity, sometimes with a hemispherical mound representing the mountain.

Most ritual floats are topped with pine or cedar branches. The spiky leaves act as a conduit for a deity residing in the High Plain of Heaven, who is called down to the summit of a "divinely selected fire mountain," then guided down to the festival site via the branches of the tree. The floats have evolved and diversified over the centuries and many signify particular mountains without now bearing any visual resemblance to them.

Hindu temples

The Hindu temple is essentially a house for the deity (*deva-sthanam*), and it usually has an inner sanctum where the god's image is kept (an image in which the deity is believed to be present). The temple reproduces the form of the Hindu cosmos through a mandala (see pages 120–122) used as its ground-plan.

Hinduism is not a single unified religion but combines numerous spiritual traditions, elements of which are also found in Buddhism and Jainism. In all these religions the temples and forms of worship have continually influenced one another. The earliest surviving Hindu shrines, the temples of Udayagiri in Orissa, are hewn entirely out of the living rock, in imitation of Buddhist models. Such cave-temples embody the idea of an inner sanctum or *garbhagriha* (womb-house). Later, free-standing temples opened out the sanctum in the four cardinal directions by adding projecting alcoves to the exterior to house representations of deities.

The classic form of the great Hindu temple developed during the same period in which the great cathedrals were built in Europe (*c*.500–1500). Under many elaborations and additions, these follow the same basic structure as the early temples. The womb-house contains a central sanctum (*vimana*) where the main statue or image of the god is enshrined. Directly above this rises a tower (*shikhara*) that represents Mount Meru as center of the universe. The temple is encircled by a path or veranda for sanctifying or protective circumambulation, and there is usually an adjoining assembly-hall (*mandapa*).

The *shikhara* is generally built up out of repetitions of the same shape or motif, as if it were constructed out of repeating cells. The surface of the temple gives the effect of concentrated devotional

LEFT *Offerings of flower garlands adorn this marble statue of Nandi, the faithful bull of Shiva. Every village and city in India has shrines that serve local concerns. Some are grand, while others consist of a platform on which are placed images of spirits, ancestors, and heroes.*

ornamentation, being often entirely covered with carvings of deities, mythical figures, and heroes from the Hindu epics.

There are two main traditions of the Hindu temple —the Nagara (northern) and the Dravida (southern). The northern tradition is notable for its development of the image of the ribbed seed of a medicinal plant, *amala*, symbolizing fertility, health, and fruitful life-processes. Originally used to top the head of the free-standing pillar, this seed, in greatly expanded style, came to provide the main roof-form of the temple, surmounting its central axis. Other towers and shrines were grouped below it, giving architectural support to this image of fertility and the eternal

ABOVE *The 13th-century Hindu Temple of the Sun at Konarak in Orissa, India, was designed as a massive chariot flanked by two dozen carved stone wheels and pulled by seven stone horses, enabling the gods to embark on a procession around their domain.*

cycles of life. In the southern tradition the primary form is a pillared pavilion with barrel-roof. Small pavilions cluster round a taller one, forming the tiers of a pyramidal structure.

Communal services and festivals take place in Hindu temples on auspicious dates, but worshipers may also enter to make offerings at any time. The deities on the exterior are protectors of the locality

Minakshi Temple

Madurai, India

The Minakshi Temple at Madurai in Tamil Nadu does more than merely accommodate the god's shrine and priests. Like many temples in southern India, it provides for both individual and community worship, with complex groupings of sanctums and courtyards. Indeed, the outer part of the Minakshi Temple is filled with a tremendous sense of life, bustle, and energy, perhaps more reminiscent of a market than of a temple. This is where pilgrims buy the offerings for use in their *puja* (worship) in the deeper, more sacred areas of the temple. *Puja* items include coconuts, *ghee* (clarified butter), garlands of flowers, milk, and incense. These areas are linked by nine magnificent tower gateways (*gopurams*), which become smaller as they near the central shrines. Their surfaces teem with colorful statues of deities and mythological figures.

The Minakshi Temple dates from the seventeenth century (the original was destroyed in the fourteenth century) and is typical of an architectural style that successfully blends together northern and southern traditions. The temple is dedicated to Shiva (in his local incarnation, Sundareshwarar) and his consort Minakshi—it is she who, unusually, is the presiding deity. A sculpture celebrating their divine marriage stands outside the Sundareshwarar shrine.

The temple compound is surrounded by an outer wall with four massive, nine-storied *gopurams*. Inside, the temple has long corridors and roofed quadrangles, supported by some 2,000 carved columns and decorated with painted murals depicting episodes from the lives of the gods.

Pilgrims wind their way along processional paths, past images of great heroes from the Hindu epic, the *Mahabharata*, halting frequently to make offerings to minor deities. The progression toward the innermost sanctum is measured by the length of the passages, which seems to be exaggerated by the many turns made on the way. Before entering the inner shrines, devotees must ritually bathe in the sacred Golden Lotus tank. Reputedly it was here that Indra the storm god once gathered this flower to offer to Shiva, the creator and destoyer. The lotus is a potent motif in India; among many meanings, it symbolizes the manifested form of the universe, arising from the chaos of the cosmic waters.

LEFT *The Golden Lotus tank, where pilgrims purify themselves in the waters before they enter the inner sanctum of the temple complex. The lotus is one of the most popular of Indian artistic motifs, symbolizing water, creativity, fertility, and perfection.*

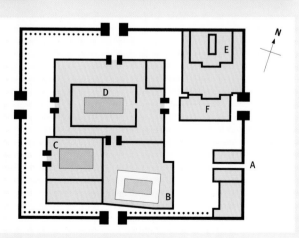

ABOVE *A view of the Minakshi Temple showing the* gopurams. *It has been estimated that there are more than 30 million carvings on these gateways. The larger* gopurams *indicate the external boundary of the temple, while the smaller ones are inside the compound. The golden cupola is the central shrine (C in the plan below) toward which all worshipers progress.*

LEFT *One of the long corridors inside the Minakshi Temple. The pillars are ornamented with a variety of carved subjects, including lions, galloping horses, deities, and mythical creatures.*

LEFT *A simplified plan of the temple showing its main elements. (A) the main entrance; (B) the Golden Lotus tank; (C) the Minakshi shrine; (D) the Shiva shrine; (E) the hall of the thousand pillars; and (F) the pavilion of Nandi (Shiva's mount, the bull). The nine* gopurams *(gateways) in the outer walls and leading to the inner shrines are shown as heavy-black pairs of rectangles.*

The Stupa

The dome-shaped *stupa* is the primary Buddhist monument. Deriving from ancient kingly funeral mounds, the *stupa* was adopted by Buddhists as a reliquary (relic container). After the Buddha died and had been cremated (leaving no ashes according to one legend), his remains were divided up between ten places, and a consecrated mound or *stupa* was erected over each relic. Later, *stupas* were constructed for the relics of other holy figures such as monks and saints.

The *stupa* embodies a complex symbolism. Intimately linked to the death of the Buddha, it is the ultimate monument to his *parinirvana*—his final transcendence. The dome itself represents *nirvana* (enlightenment and liberation from worldly desire and suffering), and is also a symbolic mountain (see page 180). As well as the cosmic axis, the pole or spire and the parasol on top of the dome refer to the bodhi tree under which the Buddha attained enlightenment, and therefore signify the Buddha's compassion. The square base represents moral restraint.

The *stupa* has varying features. In Nepal some *stupas*, such as Svayambhunath in Kathmandu, have a thirteen-tiered steeple surmounting the dome, representing the thirteen Buddhist heavens, and a gilded square base, on each side of which is a pair of huge eyes, possibly representing the all-seeing Buddha. At Pagan in Myanmar (Burma) bell- or drum-shaped *stupas* form part of *cetiya* (*chaitya*) temples, with a stepped pyramidal base and a spire. In Thailand the *stupa* is often shaped like a lotus bud and topped with a gold finial.

The Sri Lankan *stupa* (*dagoba*), breast-shaped and painted white, is associated locally with mother's milk. The Singhalese for relic, *dhatu*, is also the word for semen. The *stupa* therefore represents regenerative power through both male and female imagery.

and are more accessible than those inside. The building demarcates ever more sacred space, culminating in the sanctum, often behind doors or a grille. Here the worshipers make their offerings of flowers, rice, fruit, or sweets, and the priest hands back some of these offerings as *prasad*, the blessing of the god in the form of his leftover food (see page 146).

Buddhist temples

The historical Buddha, Siddhartha Gautama, lived in north India in the sixth century BCE, and it was there that Buddhism first took root. After his death the religion spread throughout Asia, adapting to new conditions and giving rise to a huge diversity of Buddhist art and architecture.

BELOW *This portal and* stupa *at Sanchi in eastern India were built in the second century* BCE. *The dome-shaped monument is believed to symbolize the Buddhist path to liberation and to house bodily relics of the Buddha and prominent disciples. The square balcony indicates the Heaven of the thirty-three gods. The panels on the posts and lintels depict events from the Buddha's past lives but the Buddha is represented only indirectly.*

Wat Arun

Bangkok, Thailand

Until the mid-thirteenth century, Thailand was dominated by the Khmer people, who were Hindu, and although Buddhism gained the ascendancy, much Thai architecture still bore the influence of the Khmers. Brick and wood replaced much of the stone, reflecting Buddhist concern with the impermanence of matter and also giving to their temples the ethereal fairytale effect for which they are famous. Although Wat Arun (Temple of the Dawn), on the Chao Phraya River, was not completed until the mid-nineteenth century, it is an elegant example of the Khmer temple style that was adopted in the Ayutthaya period (1350–1767).

The temple complex is situated on the banks of the river partly because Thai Buddhist architectural convention has it that the *viharn* (or *vihara*, the worship- or assembly-hall) of the monks should face water. This is not only an echo of the primordial ocean encircling Mount Meru but also a reflection of the fact that the bodhi tree, beneath which the Buddha sat when he achieved enlightenment, faced a river.

Surrounding the monks' assembly-hall is a colonnaded cloister, lined with a row of gilded statues of the Buddha, which offers a tranquil place of meditation for the monks. To the west of the main tower is an elegant hall traditionally reserved—here as at many other Thai temples—for worship by the Thai royal family.

At Wat Arun's center is a *prang*—a tall, tower-like monument, rounded at the top, containing niches that hold relics or images of the Buddha or holy men. It represents the thirty-three heavens or stages that must be lived through in order to reach perfection; its shape is also an allusion to Mount Meru, the cosmic axis. A steep stairway climbs each side of the tower at the cardinal points. Three terraces, representing the three worlds of Buddhist cosmology, allow circumambulation at each level. At the corners of the temple complex are four smaller *prangs* with niches containing statues of the god of the wind.

LEFT *At the foot of each of the stairways is a* mandapa *(porch or pavilion). Each of these structures contains an image portraying an important event in the life of the Buddha: his birth, a scene of meditation, the Buddha preaching, and his death.*

ABOVE *The central* prang *soars 225 ft. (70 m) into the sky in seven progressively diminishing levels. The tower is topped with a pronged* vajra, *the indestructible scepter-shaped thunderbolt of Hindu mythology that came to symbolize—to Buddhists—ultimate reality. The upper section of the* prang *is circled by a ring of demon guardians.*

LEFT *The surface of Wat Arun is decorated throughout with multicolored ceramics—pieces of broken Chinese tiles that were donated by devotees—serving to evoke the mythical world of Mount Meru. Such elaborate decoration has its basis in the Hindu (Khmer) belief that the elements of the temple should be a reflection of the beauties of Heaven.*

The cult of the *stupa* had begun to proliferate in the third century BCE, under the Mauryan emperor Ashoka, who had converted to Buddhism after the carnage he experienced in a battle led him to understand the Buddha's teaching on suffering. With the zeal typical of a convert, Ashoka is reported to have built between 1,000 and 84,000 *stupas* but few, if any, have survived.

Many *stupas* were covered in carvings of significant events in the Buddha's life and previous lives, although the very early *stupas* depicted his presence only in symbolic form (a wheel, a bodhi tree, or a miniature *stupa*). The first groups of monks congregated around the domed *stupas* containing relics of the Buddha (see box, page 160). Over the years *chaityas* ("temples" or "assembly-halls") and *viharas* ("monasteries") were constructed alongside them.

A Forest of World Trees

Whereas the pyramids built by the Toltec and Aztec civilizations in central Mexico give an effect of massive solidity, further south in the region of the Yucatán peninsula the Maya developed a more slender vertical thrust, and the pitch of the Mayan pyramid and its staircase is particularly steep. The pyramid often rose over a tomb, and its inscriptions detailed events from ancestral history.

Representations of the *wakah-chan or* World Tree are rare in Mayan art, but there are depictions of it at both Izapa and Palenque; the latter contains a panel showing King Pacal standing alongside the tree, locating the ruler and the temple at the center of the cosmos. The temple was itself a cosmic axis where the trunk of the World Tree rose out from Xibalba, the underworld. Together, the hundreds of pyramids that rose skyward from their jungle clearings made the Mayan landscape a forest of World Trees.

The temple is the main Buddhist sanctuary, in which the laity attend services and make offerings. It is often part of a larger complex such as a monastery, where monks concentrate on meditation and self-enlightenment. An important part of Buddhist doctrine is generosity or the giving of *dana* ("donations") by which the donor accrues the spiritual merit that leads to ever-better births in the cycle of reincarnation. Temples contain an altar where devotees make offerings of food, incense, or flowers, usually accompanied by chanting and prayer.

As discussed earlier, many temples are built on a mandala plan so that the Buddhist cosmos is mapped out by the building. For example, at Angkor Thom in Cambodia the tall central temple represents Mount Meru, the cosmic axis, while a surrounding moat recalls the primordial ocean.

A Buddhist temple usually contains a wealth of images, for both worship and instruction. Many ancient temples, such as Ajanta in India and Luoyang in China, existed in the form of caves hewn out of rock and containing large carvings of the Buddha or murals depicting scenes from his life. In the Theravada tradition (the conservative southern school of Buddhism) the statues and paintings are of the Buddha in conventional postures—typically teaching, meditating, or reclining. Devotees recognize these as stages on the Buddha's path to *nirvana* ("enlightenment"). The more devotional of the two major Buddhist traditions, Mahayana, emphasizes *bodhisattvas*, enlightened beings who strive to lead others to *nirvana*. The Mahayana temples contain images of such figures, together with a pantheon of saints and benign or fierce deities.

Mesoamerican temples

For well over 2,000 years, until the Spanish destruction of the Aztec capital city of Tenochtitlán in 1525, the general form and setting of a Mesoamerican temple remained unchanged. It stood on a platform at the top of a high pyramid, which rose up in a

number of terraces or stages. At the foot of the pyramid lay a sacrificial altar, a plaza, and other open spaces such as ball-courts.

The pyramid itself was usually square or rectangular in plan, and the temple was approached up one or more sides of the construction by a centrally positioned monumental flight of stairs. Originally these stairs were set into the mass of the pyramid, but later they came to stand out and were elaborately ornamented. The grand staircases were used mainly by priests, while the congregation gathered below around the altar where most sacrifices were performed. A few pyramids featured an additional altar in front of the temple at the top.

The main pyramid in the Aztec capital of Tenochtitlán was the Templo Mayor or Great Temple (see page 176). The platform at the very top of the pyramid supported twin temples, each representing a

ABOVE *The Maya temple ruins at the city of Palenque in the southern Mexican state of Chiapas, dating from c.500–c.900CE. The Temple of the Inscriptions (center, right) contains the tomb of the king, Pacal, and has nine levels reflecting the nine layers of the underworld. The tomb connects to the upper galleries via thirteen corbels, equating to the number of levels in the Maya Heaven. The other buildings visible here are the three-story tower and the great palace (far left).*

mountain. One temple was dedicated to Tlaloc, the rain and Earth god, and represented the Mountain of Sustenance; the other temple was dedicated to Huitzilopochtli, the god of the Sun and war, and represented the mountain where the newborn god had fought and destroyed his 400 half-brothers as they came to kill him and his mother. This may have been a metaphor for the daily battle between the Sun and the Moon as leader of 400 stars.

Teotihuacan

Central Mexico

This vast and mysterious site lies northeast of modern Mexico City in the Valley of Mexico. It was built (begun *c.*100CE) by an unknown people believed to be related to the Nahua, and the city once housed 200,000 inhabitants. Its economy was based on the control of trade routes, and the population was supported by irrigated agriculture. The city had no fortifications and no warlike motifs in its art, and the reasons for its collapse remain a mystery.

In the seventh and eighth centuries the monumental temples on top of the pyramids were systematically burned. Later, the abandoned city was regarded with awe by the Aztecs, who believed it to be where their pantheon of gods was brought into being (they named it "birthplace of the gods") and where two—humble, disfigured Nanahuatzin and vain, handsome Tecuciztécatl—had sacrificed themselves to become the Sun and Moon, and bring into being the Fifth Sun (meaning the present world).

The town of plazas, palaces, and pyramids once contained some 100 religious buildings and is planned along a central thoroughfare (Miccaotli or the Avenue of the Dead), which runs for two miles (3.2 km) north to south and changes elevation several times. Archaeologists have so far identified 2,600 major structures laid out in a tight grid, each containing its own temple. Among them are numerous pyramids that were faced with roughly jointed stone blocks and finished with painted plaster rendering. The Aztecs named the most prominent of these the Pyramid of the Sun, and the next largest the Pyramid of the Moon (*c.*150CE), and these may be thought to have been the mounds on which Nanahuatzin and Tecuciztécatl did penance before throwing themselves into the flames.

The Pyramid of the Sun (*c.*225CE) used 2.5 million tons of material and marked the culmination of an increasing concern with permanence in architecture. Early Olmec mounds (1200–900BCE) were built of compressed soil or sun-dried brick, but the vast new pyramids were meant to last; the large stone retaining walls contain huge amounts of earth and rubble.

LEFT *A carved head of Quetzalcóatl, the plumed serpent god, mounted on a wall of the temple dedicated to him. These heads alternate with those of the rain god Tlaloc. Teotihuacan's builders regarded Quetzalcóatl as a god of nature, but later the Aztecs recognized him as a culture hero (a being who assists humans in their primeval struggles), strongly identifying him with Venus.*

RIGHT *Teotihuacan stretches into the distance, as seen from the top of the Pyramid of the Moon looking along the Avenue of the Dead. Although the Pyramid of the Sun (seen at the left) is a taller structure at 210 ft. (63 m) in height, the summits of the two pyramids are level because the Pyramid of the Moon has been built on higher ground.*

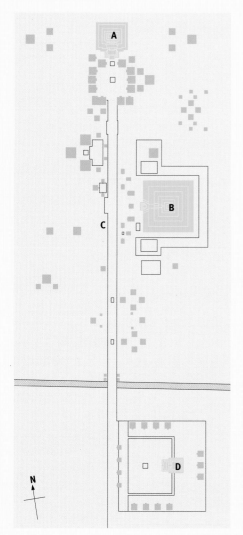

LEFT *A plan of the main temples and pyramids of Teotihuacan. The Pyramid of the Moon (A) stands at one end of the long Avenue of the Dead (C), giving on to a plaza that would have been surrounded by smaller pyramids. The Pyramid of the Sun (B) is situated on the eastern side of the avenue, while toward the southern end is the Temple of Quetzalcóatl (D).*

BELOW *Lined with the remains of smaller structures, the Avenue of the Dead leads up to the Pyramid of the Moon, which, like many of Teotihuacan's pyramids, deliberately echoes the shape of nearby mountains, including the dead volcano, Cerro Gordo, behind it.*

The Three Orders of Greek Architecture

The styles of building in classical architecture, distinguished by the capitals at the top of their columns, are known as orders. The three principal orders of Greek architecture—Doric, Ionic, and Corinthian—show an increasing ornamentation. Each was named after its region of origin, but they spread across the classical world and became elements in the overall repertoire of architecture, so that temples may contain elements of more than one order.

The Doric order is the oldest and simplest, originating between 1000 and 600BCE. Doric columns are rooted directly in the earth and are topped by a capital shaped like a bowl. Some scholars think that the fluting imitates the bundle of papyrus reeds that supported the early Egyptian temple, with the capital as the block of wood that held the bundle together; others believe the fluting represents the strokes of the adze in stripping the trunk of a tree.

Doric columns are often stout and the resultant effect is heavy or massive. In the horizontal beam, square panels known as metopes alternate with triglyphs—panels with three vertical grooves, representing the ends of the crossbeams from the early period of wooden temples. Notable Doric temples are the Parthenon and the Theseum at Athens; the Temple of Poseidon at Paestum in southern Italy; and

the Temple of Athena in Syracuse, Sicily, which is now the Roman Catholic cathedral.

Ionic temples appeared in the mid-fifth century BCE. They have more slender columns than the Doric, topped with a capital resembling tendrils, ram's horns, or a swirl of water, and suggesting an upward energy. The columns are placed on a base and the fluting is narrow. The metopes and triglyphs have disappeared, often replaced by a marble frieze so that the Ionic temple is conceived as well as executed entirely in stone. Examples are the Erechtheum in Athens and temples in coastal Turkey (the main Ionian region), such as that of Artemis at Ephesus.

The Corinthian column, topped with a spray of carved acanthus leaves, is the most treelike of the columns. According to legend, its inventor, Kallimakhos (late fifth century BCE), saw these leaves twined around a basket of funeral offerings. Kallimakhos was a bronzesmith and the capital does indeed give the effect of metalwork. Unlike the Ionic capital, it can be viewed equally from all directions and it therefore allows more elaborate patterns of symmetry. The Corinthian column was used in the Temple of Olympian Zeus at Athens. It later became widespread and because of its exuberance was especially popular with the Romans.

At sunrise and sunset a priest on the platform of the Templo Mayor would beat a loud drum to signal the start and end of the day's work throughout the city. The gap between the twin temples was aligned precisely to sunrise at the equinox when viewed from the circular temple of the serpent god Quetzalcóatl.

Some Mesoamerican pyramids—mainly in the Mayan area—were built over an underground burial chamber. Like those of the Egyptians, these pyramids were sometimes dedicated to the glorification of deceased rulers. The Temple of the Inscriptions (seventh century CE) built by the Maya at Palenque,

Mexico (see page 165), contains a vaulted burial chamber in which the great king Pacal was buried wearing a mosaic portrait-mask made of jade, which symbolized life. Important burial chambers have been found elsewhere, including at Tikal in modern-day Guatemala.

Most Mesoamerican architecture has a strong frontal aspect and is designed to be viewed from outside. But at Chichén Itzá (see pages 142–143), architects developed the colonnade, allowing them to span a room with several vaults and to use wooden lintels to create large internal spaces. The result was a new conception of architecture as interior space, exemplified by the Temple of the Warriors—a pyramidal temple surrounded at ground level by colonnaded halls where many people could be received.

Mayan civilization was at its peak *c.*300–*c.*900CE, and the Maya carried Mesoamerican sacred architecture to its most elaborate and refined extent, as can be seen in the delicate sculpture of Copán and the painted stucco-work of Palenque. The Maya developed the corbel vault, in which stepped brickwork was built up to form an arch. In Mayan pyramids all effort was concentrated on the upward thrust of the architecture. The temples, which were entered only by priests, were often very small and the sense of height was increased by a distinctive "roof-comb."

Greek temples

Against a rugged landscape of browns and greens, Greek temples stood out as white sharp-edged geometrical shapes highlighted with red and blue. Buildings devoted to a single deity appeared around 800BCE, in many shapes but already tending toward a rectangular hall (*megaron*). The great classical rectangular temples were mostly built between 600 and 300BCE, after the invention of roof-tiles and the replacement of earlier wooden material with stone. The god came increasingly to "dwell" in the temple in the form of a large statue, so that temple architecture evolved side by side with sculpture.

The god's statue stood in the hall or the sanctum and faced outward, usually east, so that it was lit by the rays of the rising Sun. The congregation did not enter the sanctum but remained outside around the sacrificial altar, their activities watched by the statue of the god looking out through the entrance.

Rather than having arches, the Greek temple was trabeate (beamed) like the Egyptian temple, piling weight upon weight while avoiding outward thrust. The original *megaron* came to be surrounded on all four sides by a continuous row of columns (a peristyle). While the inner hall retained a solid wall breached only by one door, the columns of the surrounding peristyle provided a permeable and inviting boundary between inside and outside. The temple was thus not an inward path like the Egyptian

RIGHT *A Corinthian capital from the Odeion of Agrippa in Athens, with the pronounced carved acanthus leaf decor. The Romans were particularly appreciative of this classical column design because of its flamboyance.*

The Parthenon

Athens, Greece

The Parthenon temple was dedicated to Athena (patron goddess of Athens) in her form as Athena Parthenos, the virgin. Commissioned by Pericles, the Athenian leader, it was constructed *c*.447–432BCE in the flush of victory over the Persians. It is widely revered as perhaps the most harmoniously perfect building in Europe. In the *naos* ("inner chamber") there once stood a vast statue of Athena in her form as warrior maiden with a helmet, shield, and spear, sculpted by Phidias in ivory and gold.

The Parthenon crowns the Acropolis, the summit of the city and the site of the amphitheater where classical drama was first performed. The geometrically regular buildings are set irregularly over the uneven rock—a sense of unity comes not from a single glance but from walking around the site.

The facade of the Parthenon is eight columns wide instead of the more usual six, so that the eye can never take in its whole width at once and must move across it repeatedly. Like the quick-witted goddess Athena whom it embodies, the nature of the Parthenon can never be grasped all at once.

Although the columns are Doric, the effect is light. Using sophisticated mathematics, the architects created deliberate irregularities in the columns' profile in order to produce the overall effect of evenness. These devices reinforce the feeling of an upward movement, and the entire temple seems to follow and complete the upward thrust of the hill itself.

The Parthenon survived largely intact until 1687, when it was severely damaged during bombardment by Venetian forces, leaving the ruins we see today.

LEFT *In many Greek temples the columns swell slightly around the middle to correct the optical illusion that they are pinched inward, but the columns in the Parthenon also tilt slightly inward to avoid the illusion that they are falling outward. Moreover, all the temple's horizontal lines are made to rise slightly toward the middle to counteract the impression of sagging.*

ABOVE *The Parthenon still dominates the hill of the Acropolis looming above Athens. The remains of the Propylaea are visible to the left: this was the gateway that led to the whole ceremonial precinct. Beginning at sunrise, the processions in honor of Athena would wind their way up the rocky hill, through the Propylaea, and into the sacred area, where as well as the Parthenon there were smaller temples and free-standing altars.*

LEFT *A battlescene from the Parthenon's frieze. The architects were subordinate to the master sculptor Phidias, and the building served, in effect, to display his craft. Carvings on the outer colonnade depicted, for example, battles among Titans, Amazons, and centaurs, and between the Greeks and the Trojans.*

temple, nor a container of space like the mosque. Rather, the building encouraged movement around itself. With its triangles, rectangles, and cylinders, it was designed to be seen from outside at all angles, and may be considered a work of sculpture. In fact, the architects were often supervised by sculptors, whose artistic visions they were realizing.

Roman temples

Early Roman temples were influenced by the local Etruscans (eighth to third centuries BCE), who had placed their temples on a very high base, so that they were approachable only up steps at the front. Even when the Romans came into direct contact with Greece, their temples retained this emphasis on a high and imposing frontage. While the Greek temple was designed to be viewed from all sides, many Roman temples seem almost two-dimensional, with steps and columns only at the front. Along the sides,

columns may be attached to or even inset into the walls of an inner chamber (*cella*) taking up the entire width of the platform on which the temple stands. The front porch was often built several rows of columns deep, giving a high dominating aspect appropriate to the imperial period.

The Roman temple usually followed the basic Greek design of a rectangular building with an open-air altar in front, where burnt offerings were made and worshipers stood outside the front door. But resemblance to the Greek temple is superficial. For the skills of Roman engineers allowed architects

BELOW *The Temple of Bacchus at Baalbeck, Lebanon, c.150–200BCE. It stands on a high Roman platform but it has an unusual Greek peristyle of freestanding columns. Bacchus (the Greek Dionysus) was the god of the vine, as well as of altered states. Members of the mystical cult dedicated to him practiced rituals in which they became frenzied and liberated from self-control.*

to develop new techniques, so that they no longer thought only in rectangles and triangles. The invention of concrete and curved arches made it possible to construct an apse (arched semicircular recess) to hold a statue of a god, and large interiors crowned with a dome. These features would be carried over into the Christian basilica (see pages 194–195). Such interiors did not require supporting pillars; Corinthian pillars were retained—free-standing or embedded in walls— more for decoration than structural need.

The Roman temple therefore turned the Greek temple inside-out, as temples came to be conceived and designed primarily as interior spaces rather than as sculptures facing outward. While some interiors became very large, worship in any formal sense remained outside at the altar; the size of the buildings, meanwhile, meant they were used for political and administrative meetings. The interior itself became the Roman architect's main art-form, which reached its apotheosis in the Pantheon in Rome.

The Pantheon was built during the reign of the emperor Hadrian around 117–128CE. As its name indicates, it was dedicated to "all the gods," which, by Hadrian's time, encompassed a very wide range of deities. As well as deified former emperors, the Roman religion now included Middle Eastern figures such as the Persian Mithra and the Judean Christ. The Pantheon's enormous scale and its circular form emphasized the all-embracing nature of its theological and political symbolism. The building embodied a wholly new vision of a vast, multiracial empire, unified in the centralized Roman state and watched over by every conceivable divinity.

A conventional classical temple porch with Corinthian pillars leads to a circular hall, or rotunda, surmounted by an immense dome. This dome is a perfect half-sphere, its radius exactly equal to its height. In its center there is a large circular hole, the oculus ("eye"), open to the sky and allowing sunlight, rain, or snow to fall on to the marble floor beneath. The sky god Jupiter was thought to be present in the slowly arcing shaft of sunlight.

Round Temples

The Temple of Vesta, one of the oldest temples in Rome, was a small circular building surrounded by a ring of Corinthian columns. Inside, this goddess of hearth and home had no statue but her sacred flame was kept burning by six Vestal Virgins under a domed ceiling symbolizing the heavens. Near the temple stood an oak tree, on which the virgins hung their hair when it was cut off at their initiation. Thereafter they lived a life of strict chastity. Even in the grandest imperial time the state cult of the domestic hearth took place in this tiny temple, which survives today only as a ruin.

Another round temple in the city is the marble Temple of Hercules Victor, converted in the Middle Ages into a church that is now dedicated to Santa Maria del Sole. This temple has often been confused with the more famous Temple of Vesta because of its unusual shape.

Rome's hemispherically domed Pantheon remains a tremendous feat of design and engineering (if the dome continued as a sphere it would just touch the floor). In 609 it became the first temple in Rome to be converted to Christian use. Still a church, it is probably the world's oldest religious building in continuous use.

While the Greek temple was designed in relation to the landscape, the Roman one was often part of a planned townscape. The Forum at Rome, built under Augustus (ruled 27BCE–14CE), used the form of a temple facade to enclose a series of contrived views conceived as a unified expression of state power. To the left and right were colonnades of shops, while the vista ahead was closed by the temple of Mars Ultor (Mars the Avenger) on a massive podium. The whole area was enclosed by a 100 ft. (30 m) high wall that disguised the built and natural surroundings beyond and created an interior space outdoors.

WORSHIP AND RITUAL

A sacred building comes into a relationship with human worshipers through ritual action. Rites of consecration and purification turn the building into a suitable point for a meeting between humanity and divinity. Within this space the meeting is generally enacted through the central religious act of sacrifice (whether literal or symbolic), which is also developed and elaborated in other kinds of action such as praying and dancing. These human deeds are matched by actions of the gods, who grant favors and bless worshipers within the arena of the building. This two-way communication intensifies the sacred power of a site, sometimes turning it into a magnet for pilgrims who come, often at enormous personal cost, to seek a transformation in their lives at this proven gateway to the gods.

Consecration

The consecration of a building is the creative or ritual act that transforms a mere material structure into a functioning link with the divine.

The rite of consecration may symbolically repeat the creation of the cosmos, as can be seen in many societies from ancient Sumeria onward, or it may be a form of taking possession. This is the case with the consecration of a Roman Catholic church, where each phase of the ceremony isolates the building further from the secular world and brings it into the realm of Christ. The bishop processes round the church three times, stands on the threshold, and makes the sign of the Cross, and then after entering banishes evil with holy water and sanctifies the building with prayer. As a final act of possession, a relic of the saint to whom the church is dedicated is installed in the altar, establishing a direct historical as well as spiritual link to Christ.

In numerous cultures, temples and houses are purified by the burning of aromatic herbs—these are considered

LEFT *A Coptic priest at the church of the Holy Sepulchre in Jerusalem waves a censer containing purificatory incense during a ritual. This site is the rock cave where tradition dictates that Christ was buried and rose from the dead; under its dome the so-called Angel's Chapel contains the stone that the angel is said to have moved from the tomb entrance.*

to please the gods and to drive away demons. Frankincense (the resin of the Boswellia tree) was utilized widely in Greek, Roman, and Jewish temples. Early Christians condemned the use of incense as a pagan custom. During the Christians' persecution by the Romans they were ordered to burn incense before a statue of the emperor as a test of loyalty, and many were martyred for refusing. But its use in the Church grew from the fifth century onward and among non-Protestant denominations incense still plays a major role in purification.

In Hindu temples the physical repositories of spiritual power are not relics but images such as statues, which are treated as if they were the gods themselves. Images, like buildings, require consecration to convert them from the product of an artisan into a divine reality. Hindu statues may be consecrated by prayer, and by offering them food and sprinkling them with water. In Sri Lanka and Thailand statues of the Buddha are consecrated by painting on the eyes. This is when the spirit enters in, a moment considered so dangerous that the painter uses a mirror so as not to be caught in the spirit's direct gaze.

Animal sacrifices (see page 176) are often made in the course of construction. In Yoruba regions of West Africa before the central housepole is erected an animal is ritually slain, its blood poured around the site and its body placed in the posthole. This consecrates the foundations by ensuring the benign presence of the spirits and by repelling any evil powers that may be at the site.

Once a building has been consecrated it must be protected from pollution, and this is often achieved by regular rites of purification. Some Mesoamerican temples were rebuilt at every renewal of a fifty-two-year calendrical cycle. Many Hindu temples are purified and rededicated every year.

Such rites may be echoed on a small scale in daily worship. Worshipers should be in a pure state of body and mind, and mosques and Shinto shrines in particular provide areas for washing before entering. A Shinto shrine's purity is often further protected by

ABOVE *The festival of Pooram is held annually in the town of Trichur in Kerala, southern India, in April or May, to honor the town's two principal goddesses. The two temples—Thiruvambady and Parammekkavu— each have their main deity carried by the central elephant in separate parties of fifteen animals, all richly adorned and carrying ceremonial umbrellas. During the evening's festivities the elephants of the Parammekkavu temple line up outside the town's most famous temple, the Vadakkumnathan, which is dedicated to Shiva.*

three bridges over three streams, which the worshiper must cross in a progressive purification.

The act of consecration can be reversed or annulled. Conquerors desecrate the temples of their

Mine Devils of Bolivia

Tin-miners in Bolivia believe that the ore they seek moves around underground and can conceal itself or yield itself to the miner at will. The ore is controlled by powerful spirits which resemble the Christian Devil and are the true owners of the mountains where the ore is found.

As with the harvesting of animals in hunting societies, the extraction of the ore is a privilege that must be paid for in a form of exchange. If the spirits are not properly appeased by regular offerings they can cause catastrophe and death underground. Effigies of the mine devils are placed at specially constructed shrines in the mine, and it is to these that offerings are made, typically consisting of coca leaves, cigarettes, and alcohol. Some shrines are simply excavated out of the rock, others echo the styles of the religious architecture of the area in an amalgam of Roman Catholic and pre-Christian pagan traditions.

enemies through impure or insulting actions. Redundant churches are deconsecrated before being turned over to secular use, and it is very possible that the great temples at Teotihuacan in Mexico were deconsecrated by being burned down (see pages 166–167).

Consecration and purification reveal very clearly the analogy between a building and the human body (see pages 122–126). The consecration of a priest is similar to that of a building, and in monastic traditions the consecration of the individual and maintenance of a state of purity become a way of life.

Sacrifice and offerings

Sacrifice is a religious ritual in which an object or a life is offered to a divinity in order to establish a desired relationship between humanity and the sacred order. It has been found in the earliest-known forms of worship and in all parts of the world, with self-sacrifice often featuring in creation myths. Many bloodless symbolic rituals refer to an archetypal sacrifice involving killing—the offering of a physical life in return for a life-sustaining blessing. Just as sacrifice itself is a complex phenomenon, the architecture connected with it takes many forms.

In some societies that have no separate temples, sacrifices are conducted in every home. In West Africa an altar may be built in each family's compound, frequently in the shape of a dome, which is sprinkled with the blood of chickens sacrificed to the ancestors. These altars are a point of contact with the ancestors, fulfilling the same basic function as a temple or church elsewhere.

This basic similarity is not always appreciated when different religions come into contact. When the Catholic Spanish invaded Mexico in the sixteenth century they found a powerful Aztec civilization based on large-scale human sacrifice. The solar deity Huitzilopochtli required a constant supply of human hearts in order to allow the life-giving Sun to cross the sky. At the complex of the Templo Mayor in Tenochtitlán priests dragged their human victims up steep steps to the top of the pyramid where Huitzilopochtli's temple stood. The victims were stretched backwards over a sacrificial stone and their hearts, still beating, were cut out. The priests then flung the bodies down the steps—thus reenacting a mythical victory of the Sun over his sister the Moon, whose dismembered body was depicted in a carving at the base of the pyramid. The consecration of the Templo Mayor in 1487 is said to have involved 20,000 victims, although such figures were probably exaggerations by the Spanish to defend their moral right to the Americas.

In Asia sacrifice played an integral part in the rulers' exercise of divine power. In China complex sacrifices to Heaven and Earth were offered by the emperor. They took place in Beijing on the Altar of Heaven, three marble terraces surmounted by the round triple-roofed Temple of Heaven, built in 1420 on the site of an earlier sacrificial mound. These imperial sacrifices set in train the seasonal processes of the weather and fertility that would ensure the harmony and success of the empire. In southern China a different kind of sacrifice was practiced, connected with the cult of ancestors. Upon the death of an emperor, hundreds of his subjects were killed and their bodies placed in or near his tomb (see page 226). The blessing of imperial ancestors would be forthcoming only if they were properly accompanied by servants, in death as in life.

Hindu sacrifice in present-day Nepal unites all citizens in defeating demonic forces. In Bhaktapur the whole city acts as an arena for the drama of sacrifice in an annual ritual in which intoxicated water-buffalo (they are given alcohol to drink) are chased through the streets to the temple of Taleju, where they are slaughtered. The city comes to a halt and police hold up traffic for the stampede. Facing the entrance to the temple is a statue of its founding king, seated on a pillar.

Taleju is the goddess of the regional royal lineage, and although the kings of Bhaktapur no longer reign, their representatives (priests or officials) must still chop off the heads of the buffalo in front of the public. The twenty-four buffalo—one for each part of the city—symbolize the demonic armies. By killing them the priests demonstrate victory over evil and celebrate the divine-kingly rule that preserves both the natural and the moral order. This sacrifice also reflects the idea of the scapegoat. The buffalo represent not only external evil but the sins committed by the citizens, which must be expiated. Similar sacrifices take place all over Nepal.

In many religions blood sacrifice is transformed into a symbolic form or is replaced by other offerings. In early Judaism rites of atonement on the day of Yom Kippur involved animal sacrifice at the Temple in Jerusalem and the sprinkling of sacrificial blood in the inner sanctum by priests in order to annul the Jewish nation's sins and obtain divine forgiveness. This rite now takes the form of a day of repentance, with rituals and prayers in the synagogue. In Christianity the complex theology of Christ's sacrifice—the shedding of his blood to atone for the sins of all humanity—is reflected in elements of church architecture. While the rite of Communion is central to Christian worship, only the Roman Catholic Church retains its sacrificial terminology—the doctrine of transubstantiation asserts that the bread and wine are literally the body and blood of Christ. In Roman Catholic churches, therefore, the altar (where Communion takes place) is prominent. The Orthodox Church, on the other hand, views Communion as a life-giving encounter with the

The Altar

An altar is a structure on which sacrifices are offered. Originally probably no more than a mound of earth, a rock, or a heap of stones, altars became more ornate with the development of sacrifice as an element of worship in temples. In the book of Genesis, Abraham builds an altar on a mountain, on which he lays his young son Isaac as he prepares to make the burnt offering by which he is to be tested by God. Biblical sources mention different altars covered with goatskins and cloth.

In the Christian tradition altars notably take the form of a table, contrasting with the solid block of pagan altars. Often covered with cloth, the Christian altar also evokes the table of the Last Supper. Many such altars have become elaborate, incorporating an altarpiece (a structure above the altar table adorned with holy images) or a reredos (a screen fixed to the wall behind the altar). Although the altar itself is usually plain, the altarpiece and reredos have inspired some of the greatest painting and sculpture in the Christian tradition.

Ball-courts of the Maya

Yucatán, Central America

Mayan cities, like those of other Mesoamerican civilizations, had a ball-court (*tlatchtli*), an open-air space dedicated to the acting out of a cosmic myth in the form of the "ball-game." This game was intimately associated with the belief (shared by other Mesoamerican peoples) that the sacrifice of human hearts and blood was necessary in order to sustain the movements of the heavenly bodies.

In Mayan myth the Hero Twins, the world's best ball-players (whose father, the maize god, had been executed by the lords of Xibalba—the underworld—for playing noisily), themselves disturb the lords of death with the bouncing of their ball. They are summoned to Xibalba, where they play against the lords, lose, and are sacrificed. Returning to life, they outwit the lords consistently in a series of deadly trials. Finally they trick the lords into sacrificing themselves and thereby vanquish the underworld,

whereupon the twins ascend into the sky to become the Sun and the Moon, forever setting and rising again. In other versions the twins are associated with the planet Venus, which is both the morning and the evening star.

The ball-court was believed to serve as an entrance to the underworld. Many remain, but the largest one of all is at Chichén Itzá, to the west of the main buildings. The walls depict the sacrifices that were performed at the end of a game and there is a platform decorated with hundreds of carved human skulls, in a manner reminiscent of the Aztecs.

The game was played widely as a popular spectator sport, but on ceremonial occasions captives of war and foreign kings were forced to play and were decapitated when they lost. Two teams had to keep a rubber ball (of varying size) passing back and forth, never touching the ground. The rules and the number of players varied, although usually players were not allowed to touch the ball with their hands (except when pitching it into play) and had to bounce it off their shoulders, torso, hips, thighs, and knees.

LEFT *A relief from the wall of the ball-court at Chichén Itzá. A player (left) has been beheaded and his torso is spouting blood. Similar carvings all around the court depict warriors, skulls, and sacrifices. Players' heads were placed on a rack and then offered to the gods, and some images suggest that they may even have been used as "balls"—following the example of the Hero Twin Xbalanque, who was forced to use his brother's head as a ball.*

ABOVE *The Maya had two principal types of ball-court. That at Chichén Itzá (above)—the largest in Central America, nearly 500 ft. (150 m) in length—typifies the first of these, with its high vertical walls. The other type has gently sloping sides with markers set into the center of the floor; the ball-court at Copán is of this type. At Copán a carved roundel marker in the ground is decorated with a relief of the Hero Twins playing the game in the underworld.*

LEFT *Scoring was probably achieved in different ways at the two types of court. At Copán the ball was hit into a designated "end zone." At Chichén Itzá, however, huge stone hoops (left, carved with entwined serpents) protrude from the walls halfway down the court and 25 ft. (8 m) from the ground. The aim was probably to get the ball to hit or go through the hoop, but the small size difference between ball and hoop means that even expert players would have found it difficult to score.*

The Mountain and the Cave

The symbolism of the mountain in Buddhist and Hindu sacred architecture is often combined with that of the womb (*garbha*) or cave. The Buddhist *stupa* has an inner chamber, called the cosmic "egg," emphasizing the regenerative qualities of the holy relic inside, while the Hindu temple's icon is housed in the *garbhagriha* at the center. The Hindu temple of Parvati (*c.*465CE) at Nachna, Rajasthan, emphasizes the notion of a temple-mountain containing a cavelike space by having its outside walls ornamented to represent rockpiles and grottoes full of wild animals.

Examples of this hollow mountain-cave, with its connotations of the womb and promise of rebirth, are found throughout the world in the tomb, pyramid, and mausoleum (see pages 224–241). One such is the Pyramid of the Sun at Teotihuacan, Mexico (see pages 166–167), built on a mound beneath which is the sacred cave of an early people that has been extended or shaped into several lobes.

Central and South American mythology is full of creation and emergence tales set in caves. The Aztecs, who later acquired and revered the Teotihuacan site, told of their own coming to Tenochtitlán after their ancestors had emerged from the clover-leaf-shaped Chicomoztoc, or Seven Caves.

resurrected Christ; this is reflected in the celestial domes of the Russian tradition depicting the risen Christ. For Protestants, Christ's sacrifice was unique and all-sufficing; repeating it in ritual is unnecessary. Protestant churches are places not of cultic rite but of the commemoration of Christ's teaching.

Offerings are prominent in those religions that have rejected killing. In Buddhism and Jainism, for example, temples and shrines commonly have altars in front of the divine images for symbolic offerings, which include incense, money, fruit, and flowers. The offerings are made in a ritual, *puja*, in which gifts are combined with prayer, meditation, and chanting. *Puja* is also widespread in Hinduism, where it may include blood-sacrifice; in the non-violent traditions it is a "sacrifice," but one entailing the giving up of wealth. This mirrors the relinquishing of worldly things by the original ascetics. Thus, paradoxically, the temples of the Jains, who emphasize the spiritual merit of asceticism and poverty, contain the greatest heaps of offerings laid before the images by the devout.

The temple as sacred peak

Perceived in many faiths as the feature on Earth that aspires to reach Heaven, mountains are often held sacred and seen as the abode of the gods. Mount Kilimanjaro is to the Masai of East Africa what Olympus was to the ancient Greeks. Mount Kailash in the Himalayas is revered by Hindus, Buddhists, and the followers of Bon-Po, the old shamanic religion of Tibet, and the four faces of Kailash bear a distinct resemblance to the mythical Mount Meru, with its four faces aligned to the cardinal directions.

Even where mountains are not holy in themselves, they are potentially sites where gods may appear. In the Judaic tradition Yahweh appeared to Moses on Mount Sinai. Sites such as this often house a temple, as on the five sacred peaks of Daoism in China.

Just as the temple is a model of the cosmos on Earth, so it may mirror the mountain that is the center of that cosmos. In the irrigated desert landscapes of ancient Mesopotamia and Egypt the temple was often built to echo the mythical mound of earth rising out of the primal waters (see pages 147–148). The word ziggurat (a stepped pyramid) derives from the Babylonian word for mountain peak.

In some forms of the Hindu and Buddhist temple the idea of the cosmic mountain gradually came to be expressed more explicitly. While the simple altar alone could symbolize the mountain, it was often enhanced by the addition of an altar terrace and a shrine or a *stupa*, and ultimately by the repetition of these features in diminishing tiers to form a whole temple. Such temples, with their repetitive ornamentation, resemble a range of mountains. Similarly, in Mesoamerica several Mayan temples on one single platform represented a range of mountains towering over the forest below (see pages 164–165). At Angkor in Cambodia the architectural arrangement of the temple signifies the concentric rings of the Hindu universe, dominated by Mount Meru at the

BELOW *A reclining Toltec or Maya warrior figure made of stone and known as a* chacmool *forms an altar below the Temple of the Warriors at Chichén Itzá, Mexico. It is believed that the plate or bowl that the figure holds was once used as a receptacle for offerings, possibly of sacrificed human hearts, enabling it to serve almost as an altar. Gaping heads of rattlesnakes rest at the foot of the columns behind, indicating that this was a gateway representing the important Mesoamerican feathered serpent deity, known as Kukulcan along the Mayas. At the top of the columns the serpents' plumed rattles would once have supported lintels.*

Machu Picchu

Southeastern Peru

During the expansion of the Inca empire in the fifteenth century CE a number of small citadels were built high above the gorge of the Urubamba River 60 miles (100 km) to the northwest of Cuzco, the Inca capital, in Peru. One of these towns was Machu Picchu, a settlement of stone-built palaces, temples, plazas, and houses on a saddle-shaped ridge between the pinnacles of Huayna Picchu ("New Picchu") and Machu Picchu ("Old Picchu"). The town is surrounded on most sides by a steep drop.

The site consists of an outer and an inner sector; the latter is entered by a single gateway and appears to be the religious quarter, since it contains buildings that seem once to have had a sacred function. One such building stands on top of a granite outcrop that has been sculpted inside the building into a shrine or altar.

Beneath this outcrop is a grotto that is fashioned out of a natural overhang, within which a number of mummies have been found. The Incas believed in sacred geography and frequently selected places in the natural landscape—such as rocky outcrops, mountains, caves, or springs—to which they assigned great ritual importance. These sanctuaries, which were central to the Incas' religious beliefs and practices, were called *huacas*, and sacred power was believed to be permanently pervasive there. Sometimes farmers deliberately placed large stones in their fields to honor Pachamama, the Earth goddess.

Some authorities believe that Machu Picchu was simply a medium-sized fortified town remarkable chiefly for its state of preservation. But its isolation and the sacred sites within it have inspired other theories about its purpose. One suggestion is that it was a religious sanctuary for the Acclas (Chosen Women), an elite of female devotees of the Sun god Inti. Around 170 rich burials have been found at Machu Picchu, of which 150 were of women.

RIGHT *There is an abundance of perfectly fitted masonry, both spiritual (religious shrines) and practical, at Machu Picchu, such as this series of fountains and irrigation channels. The terraces themselves are linked by 3,000 steps carved in the rock.*

CENTER *The Inti Huatana, the ceremonial Sun stone, c.1500CE, is located at the heart of the town and echoes the shape of the mountain of Huayna Picchu (behind). In Inca belief stones often marked sites of events in myth, representing petrified ancestors or embodying sacred forces that were believed to reside in the Earth.*

ABOVE *The Incas' architecture normally embodied their vision of social order. The systematic nature of Machu Picchu's layout is captured in this view, which also shows the terracing—watered by masterful irrigation channels—used to make marginal land productive.*

LEFT *A view of the main plaza from the Temple of Three Windows, whose stones are hewn to fit without mortar in typical Inca style. When American explorer Hiram Bingham's expedition discovered the site in 1911, he thought at first that he had found the Inca place of origin, for stories told how Manco Capac, the first leader of the Incas, had built a masonry wall with three windows—an unusual feature for Inca structures.*

OVERLEAF *The mountain-ringed setting of Machu Picchu is stunning, and a magnificent place from where to view the night sky—of great importance to Inca religious practice, which included astronomical observations. It is noteworthy that of the 140 or so buildings, more than half were ceremonial.*

center. The base of the Baphuon temple at Angkor is concealed underground—as if, like the cosmic axis, the temple were simply passing through this world on its way from the lower world to the upper.

As a means for the soul's ascent toward the realm of the gods, the mountain may serve as the base for a further ladder, and even a small rock may be revealed as the platform for the thrust toward Heaven. The foundation rock of the Temple of Solomon now lies at the heart of the Muslim shrine of the Dome of the Rock in Jerusalem. It was the base from which the Prophet Muhammad climbed a ladder of light through the seven heavens into the presence of Allah.

The mosque: place of divine unity

According to Islam, Allah is everywhere, and so the mosque is a prayer-hall rather than a building enshrining a deity. The interior of the prayer-hall is an expression in architecture of *tawhid*, the doctrine of divine unity. The mosque focuses not on mass or surface, but on space. Inside the prayer-hall there is no path, and the devotee is encouraged to linger and contemplate this open undivided space.

BELOW *The Friday Mosque at Djenne in Mali is the largest mud-built building in the world. Real ostrich eggs sit at the top of each tower to symbolize creation.*

The earliest mosques were based on the Prophet Muhammad's house in Medina. Later, each region developed its own style, usually keeping the early distinction between an outer courtyard and an inner sanctuary or prayer-hall. In India the mosque was influenced by the Hindu temple. In the eastern Mediterranean the influence of the Byzantine Church can be seen, notably in the seventeenth-century Blue Mosque in Istanbul, which consists of a square hall with a minimum of internal supports, covered with a dome and surrounded by a porch and minarets. In a typical mosque the prayer-hall is entered only after washing at a tap or a fountain outside, and in some courtyards the fountain becomes a major architectural feature in its own right.

Muhammad had sent his followers to the rooftops to call the faithful to prayer, and the minaret soon developed as a special tower, from which the muezzin or crier proclaims the hours of prayer five times a day. In Syria and North Africa minarets are square with several stories; in Iraq they are wide and spiral; and in Iran and Turkey they are slim and cylindrical, supporting high balconies.

The Arabic word for mosque, *masjid*, means a place where one prostrates oneself in obedience to the law of Allah, and the meaning of the word Islam refers to the sense of peace that comes from submission to this law. The sacred geography of Islam reaches from within the bounds of the mosque to encompass the whole world outside. Set into an inside wall of the prayer-hall is a niche called the *mihrab*, which is always oriented toward the city of Mecca (see pages 188–189), the *qiblah* ("center") of the Islamic universe. Thus in Britain, Algeria, or Canada, it will be oriented to the east or southeast, while in India, Indonesia, or Australia it will face the west or northwest.

The *mihrab* is often lavishly decorated and hung about with lights, and may also be surmounted by a dome—a symbol of paradise. The *mihrab* provides a focal point for each mosque's congregation and it orients all Islamic worshipers toward the center of the

"Anthill" Mosques

In much of West Africa, village mosques are often made of mud on a framework of sticks, supported by heavy buttresses. The pinnacles may be an enlarged form of the ancestral pillars placed at the entrance of many compounds of local houses, and the entire mosque may also be an imitation of the large termite hills that are found throughout the region. Like a termite hill, the mud mosque needs frequent repair, and the structural sticks assist this process by serving as scaffolding. Because of the limitations of the building material, the interior is small and dark. Larger mosques in the towns, despite being made of cement, often reproduce this vernacular shape.

faith. Five times a day congregations line up facing this niche behind the prayer-leader (*imam*) to pray to Allah. Women pray in a separate area from men, and where a congregation is all-female it is led by a female *imam*. In large collective mosques, known as Friday (*jami*) mosques, the congregation also listens on Fridays and holidays (*id*) to sermons from the raised pulpit (*minbar*) built alongside the *mihrab*.

Islam's reverence for the written word made the mosque also a center of literacy, and the building is often accompanied by an Islamic school (*madrase*). The ritual of prayer is the foundation for a way of life, so that religious leaders originally used the mosque also as the place from which to govern the community and administer the law.

The mosque contains no visual representation of Allah or of the human form—no statues or pictures. Instead, surfaces are covered with an elaborate geometrical ornamentation based on vibrant patterns of straight and flowing lines which interweave in a restless rhythm of vegetation and arabesques. The doctrine of *tawhid* teaches that Allah is both the

The Kaaba

Mecca, Saudi Arabia

The religion of Islam itself is conceived as a building, raised on five "pillars." The first four are profession of faith, prayer, almsgiving, and fasting during the month of Ramadan. The fifth, which takes place in the month of Dhu-al-Hijjah (twelfth in the Muslim calendar), is pilgrimage (*hajj*) to Mecca in Saudi Arabia, the center of the Islamic world, where Muhammad received God's word and law (later written down as the Koran). Every able-bodied Muslim man and woman should try to perform *hajj* at least once in a lifetime, and the event constitutes the world's largest annual pilgrimage.

Mecca is the point of intersection between the vertical axis reaching up to Heaven and the horizontal plane of human existence. For the *hajj*, pilgrims stream to Mecca from all over the world; some journeys can take years and use up a lifetime's savings. Upon drawing near, pilgrims change into special clothing made of simple, seamless white sheets.

This is done to symbolize purity of soul and to place all the ranks of participants at the same level. Over the course of several days the pilgrims will reenact central events in the life of Muhammad.

The goal of the several million pilgrims, or *hajjis* as they are called, is the Great Mosque, al-Masjid al-Haram. In the center of its vast courtyard, which is adorned at each corner by a pair of minarets, stands the massive black shrine called the Kaaba. Historically, Mecca was an oasis town drawing in crowds regularly for trading and the Kaaba stood as a shrine to pre-Islamic deities. Muhammad's act of clearing out the idols in 630CE was a key moment in the development of Islamic monotheism.

RIGHT *The Kaaba is a cube-shaped building built of gray stone with a door 7 ft. (2.1 m) above ground level on the east side. Framed in silver and inserted into the southeast corner of the building is a black stone, possibly a meteorite, said to have been received from the angel Gabriel. The exterior of the Kaaba is covered with a cloth, embroidered in gold and silver with a band of Koranic verses, which is renewed every year, while the interior is lined with marble and silver-gilt panels. On the first day the pilgrim performs the* tawaf, *circumambulating the Kaaba seven times in a counterclockwise direction.*

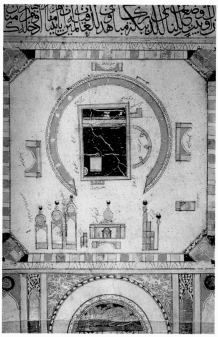

ABOVE *Hundreds of thousands of hajjis crowd into the tiered spaces of the Great Mosque. The Kaaba was built by Abraham (revered in Islam as a prophet) near the well of Zamzam, which had been revealed in the desert to Abraham's wife Hagar by an angel. Attached to the top level seen here is a wide walkway along which pilgrims run back and forth seven times to reenact Hagar's search for water to save her son Ishmael from dying of thirst. Pilgrims proceed from the causeway to the town of Mina and the Plain of Arafat, where the Prophet gave his farewell sermon. Pilgrims return to Mina for three days, where they stone three pillars representing Satan. An animal may be sacrificed, to commemorate Abraham's sacrifice of a lamb in place of his son. Lastly a* tawaf *around the Kaaba is performed.*

LEFT *A hajj certificate from 1432, commemorating a pilgrim's visit to Mecca. Today, notably in West Africa, hajjis often paint pictures of the journey on an outer wall of their house.*

source and the culmination of all diversity, and some of the patterns may incorporate the Arabic letters for his name. Allah himself is conceived as light and this belief explains the perforated grilles and pierced screens set into mosque walls, which serve to blur the distinction between light and solid substance.

The synagogue: place of prayer and study

The Temple, the House of God, was built in stone by King Solomon in Jerusalem in the tenth century BCE, on the site where the Hebrew patriarch Abraham had prepared to sacrifice his son Isaac. A main hall led to an inner sanctum containing the Ark of the Covenant. Rites were conducted by hereditary priests called *kohen* and, as with other types of temple in the ancient Near East and Mediterranean, ordinary worshipers remained outside, by the altar from which burnt offerings were sent up to God.

The Temple was the center of Jewish religious life. After its destruction by the Babylonians in 586BCE it was rebuilt, only to be destroyed again, once and for all, by the Romans under Titus in 70CE. Just one wall remains today—the Western or so-called "Wailing" Wall of the Jews.

The Evolving Synagogue

A synagogue that was excavated in 1932 at Dura-Europos, a Roman fortress in Syria, challenged assumptions about early Judaism and revealed how much the form of the synagogue had changed since 245CE. The inside walls are covered with paintings, with colorful images of animals and humans used freely. A nearby building, also excavated, was a Christian house-church and it is possible that the Jewish paintings of Bible stories and stylistic representations of the human figure were a strong influence on early Christian art.

RIGHT *It is not uncommon for synagogue design to reflect the architecture of the surrounding community. The local Islamic influence is unmistakable in the style of La Ghriba synagogue at Djerba, Tunisia, with its Arabic arches and decorative, tiled mosaics.*

The synagogue ("assembly") is based on a very different concept, and it became widespread only after the final destruction of the Temple, as part of a democratic movement based on rabbis ("teachers") rather than *kohens*. The synagogue is not a consecrated building, for God does not reside there as He did in the Temple. A living room or even a hired cinema can serve as a synagogue, but even a more permanent building does not have to adhere to a very formal structure and will probably follow the style of the local Christian or Muslim majority. A rabbinical school (*midrash*) may be attached to the building, as one of the main roles of the synagogue is the study of the Talmud (Jewish law and legend). Orthodox synagogues incorporate a separate room or gallery in which women are segregated, although this feature was abolished by the nineteenth-century Jewish Reform movement in its synagogues. The Reformers introduced the organ into their synagogues, as an addition to the tra-ditional unaccompanied singing.

The focus of ritual in all synagogues is the Ark, a cabinet containing the scrolls of the Torah (the first five books of the Bible given by God to Moses on Mount Sinai). The Torah is often richly ornamented in silver, but is not an object of worship. It is valued because it contains the word of God, who is the only true object of worship. This is reflected in the synagogue's orientation, for the Ark is set into the wall facing the Temple Mount in Jerusalem. Near to the Ark is a platform or pulpit (*bimah*) from which portions of the Torah are chanted.

As in Islam, God (Yahweh) is not portrayed—a practice that served in biblical times to highlight the contrast with neighboring idolatrous tribes. The decoration in a synagogue is often abstract, with geometric designs and Hebrew calligraphy.

The Temple Mount

Jerusalem

Jerusalem is holy to three of the world's greatest religions, Islam, Christianity and Judaism, but it is the latter that has the the longest association with the city.

After King David had united the tribes of Israel, he conquered Jerusalem and made it the Jewish capital (*c.*1000BCE). He decreed that the nation's greatest religious relic, the Ark of the Covenant, should be given a permanent home on an acropolis near the city, Mount Moriah, where Abraham had made the altar on which to sacrifice his son Isaac. Built under Moses, the Ark was said to contain the tablets God inscribed with His laws.

During the reign of David's son Solomon, the Temple of Jerusalem was built (*c.*957BCE), both as a permanent shrine for the Ark and to provide a place of community worship. This dictated the form of the complex, with a small room (the Holy of Holies) to house the relic, a porch, and a main room of religious

service, called the Holy Place. The Holy of Holies could be entered only by the High Priest, and then only on Yom Kippur, the Day of Atonement.

During the late sixth century BCE the Babylonian ruler Nebuchadrezzar II took treasures from the Temple, deported Jews, and then destroyed the building completely. In 538BCE, however, the Persian king Cyrus II liberated the exiles and allowed them to return and rebuild the Temple. Subsequently, the architecture was modest, until the rule of Herod in the first century CE when he sought to restore the glory of the original and its centrality to Jewish life.

This walled Temple Mount incorporated a series of courtyards from the consecrated area of the Holy of Holies outward. The outermost area was a meeting place open to gentiles and included sites for merchants and money-lenders (whose practices contributed to protests by Jesus and his followers), with a main southern entrance in the form of the Triple Huldah Gate. An eastern gate led to the Court of Women where females could observe the annual celebration of Sukkot. The western gate led to the Court of the Israelites, part of the Court of Priests that was open to all male Jews. Surrounding the inner sanctuary, the Court of Priests contained a sacrificial altar and a laver for priestly ablutions. The altar represented the mountain of the gods and the world center. After the Temple dedication ceremony the Ark was placed in the sanctuary and thenceforth God (Yahweh) was considered to be invisibly present.

LEFT *The entrance to the Dome of the Rock, 685–691CE, revered by Muslims as the place from where Muhammad ascended to Heaven on his "night journey." The Sacred Rock is the same site celebrated by Hebrew tradition as the spiritual center of creation, and where Abraham was asked to sacrifice his son. The foundation stone of Solomon's Temple once stood here.*

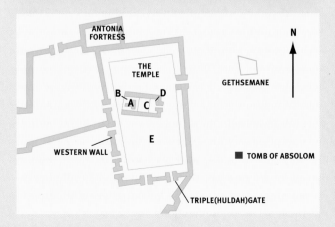

ABOVE *The Western, or Wailing, Wall is all that remains of Herod's lavishly reconstructed Temple of Jerusalem, and traditionally it is the place where Jews lament its loss. Following civil unrest the Romans demolished the building in 70CE.*

LEFT *The Dome of the Rock and the Al-Aqsa Mosque that occupy the modern Temple Mount area, known to Muslims as Haram esh Sharif or Noble Sanctuary.*

LEFT *A plan of the temple built under Herod—a series of connected courtyards, presided over by a High Priest descended from Aaron, brother of Moses. The central sanctuary was the Holy of Holies (A) where the Ark was kept and only entered on the Day of Atonement by the High Priest. A dynasty of priestly familes looked after the complex from the Court of Priests (B). The outer area, the Court of the Gentiles (E), was open to non-Jews, while the next area beyond was the Court of Women (D), then the Court of Israelites (C), where men could pray and watch the priestly rituals being performed in the next precinct. Part of the Roman garrison was housed in the Antonia Fortress (named after Herod's patron Mark Antony).*

Many medieval synagogues in Europe have been either destroyed or converted into churches, although a number of important synagogues have survived in Prague, Amsterdam, Toledo, Cracow, Regensburg, and Budapest. The twelfth-century synagogue at Worms in Germany was destroyed by the Nazis but has been faithfully reconstructed.

The transition from Temple worship to synagogue assembly was directly linked to a change in the use of architecture. Communication with God through animal sacrifice in the Temple courtyard was replaced by an emphasis on righteous actions in front of the Torah inside the synagogue. But the Temple remains a powerful symbol and serves by its very absence as a focus for a Jewish sense of longing and exile. The

liturgy in the Orthodox synagogue still looks forward to the time when the Messiah will return, the Temple will be rebuilt, and its ritual will begin again.

The church: The Word on Earth

The early Christians met in ordinary private houses, where their principal rite was a shared meal—the Eucharist—in commemoration of Christ's last supper. This rite has remained central to the design of most later churches. After Christianity became the official religion of the Roman empire in 313CE, the basilica, a Roman public hall, was adopted by Christians. The royal connotations of this word (from *basileus*, "king") were reflected in the use of the building, in which God was worshiped as emperor of Heaven. The path of the nave led to the altar, but also beyond it to a throne, where the bishop sat—a practice that was abandoned only in the Middle Ages.

In western Europe the basic plan was the Latin cross, representing the Cross of Christ. A long nave led from the west toward a shorter chancel in the east, where the altar was situated. The arms of the Cross were formed by a transept. Large churches and cathedrals developed side chapels, ambulatories, and areas for monks and pilgrims.

An elaborate symbolism grew around the basic design. The northern arm of the transept, associated with darkness, cold and evil, was decorated

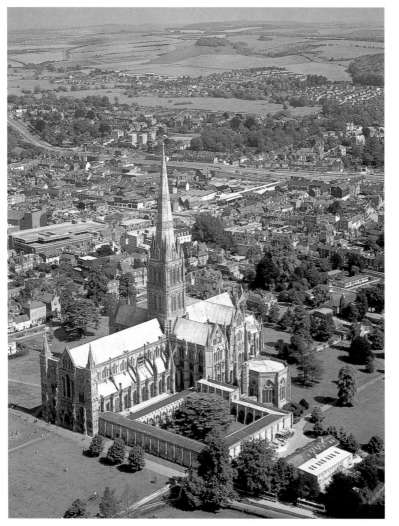

LEFT *Large churches were typically built in the shape of the Latin cross, with the altar at the eastern end in the direction of the Holy Land. This view of Salisbury Cathedral, England, demonstrates the cruciform layout, as well as showing how the spire dominates the landscape.*

Christ Pantocrator in his Dome

The central dome of an Orthodox church has been deliberately conceived as a baldachin, a hemispherical ceremonial canopy that represents a model of the heavens. The dome dominates and defines the interior space; the walls become insubstantial and space seems to project itself downward, just as in Christian theology Heaven descends to Earth.

The dome is usually occupied by the figure of Christ Pantocrator, Ruler of All, who has his right hand raised in a gesture of blessing; the hand is turned toward the heart, indicating the inner knowledge that is given outward expression in an open book, containing quotations from the Gospels, in his left hand.

The Pantocrator emphasizes Christ's cosmic role rather than his incarnation, and his halo therefore contains the three Greek letters that mean "The One Who Is." The Pantocrator also represents the Byzantine concept of Christ as the universal judge to whom all must render account, and his features are often stern.

While painting in the West after the Renaissance uses perspective to open a window on to a world behind the foreground figures, Byzantine figures are presented without depth and look out on to the space in front of them. The worshiper who looks up into the dome is not a spectator but a servant confronted directly with the Lord.

with scenes from the Hebrew Scriptures (Old Testament); the southern arm, associated with light and warmth, depicted scenes from the New Testament. The path of the nave from west to east, culminating in the altar—the symbol of Christ's life—represented the passage from less to more sacred space, or from death to eternal life (see pages 218–219). This imagery was reinforced by the location of the baptismal font, site of the symbolic beginning of a Christian life, at the west (less sacred) end by the entrance to the nave.

In the eastern Mediterranean the architecture of the Byzantine church focused the attention of the worshiper on the dome, which represented the vault of Heaven. The dome was often centrally placed, typically in a Greek-cross plan in which the four arms are of equal length. The eye of the visitor was led down the nave and upward into the majestic dome, floating skylike above. The altar remained important, but came to be placed behind a screen or iconostasis. Much mystical symbolism was attached to its hidden position, inaccessible to lay worshipers.

A tension in Christianity between ritual and teaching is directly reflected in architecture. Many modern Protestant sects emphasize pulpits and lecterns rather than the altar, and abandon the sense of a path given by the nave in favor of a plan that is more like an auditorium. Some modern Roman Catholic churches also follow this plan, but retain the focus on the altar.

Christian architecture reflects the opposition between grandiosity and humility, between the wealth of the now-established Church and the private humble rooms of the early Christians (see page 146). The unassuming simplicity of the Society of Friends (Quaker) meeting house, with its lack of ritual, is similarly found in Protestant mission huts in New Guinea and Africa today. Yet the royal imagery of the basilica continues to surface: in a simple Baptist meeting house in India, while men and women sit separately on the floor, the pastor preaches from a wooden chair set behind a table covered with a cloth and holy books. It is an unmistakable echo of the early basilica plan, in which Christ's earthly deputies sat on thrones behind the altar.

Sacred Living Space

Religion concerns not only the relationship between humans and the divine, but also that of humans with one another. Sacred buildings often reflect the social distinctions between priests and laypeople, men and women, or even the dominant and subordinate political groups in society—frequently, buildings even help to create and reinforce such distinctions. Through the way they are constructed, ornamented, and used, sacred buildings also teach and reinforce religious beliefs and understanding.

The concept of sacredness is not limited to specially designed buildings. In many societies the domestic house is also sacred, being the locus of family life around the hearth and the focus from which important values are transmitted down the generations. Indeed, many societies have no separate temples, so that all their architecture is equally hallowed, reflecting a sanctity that is inherent in the world itself.

RIGHT *The watchful eyes of the Buddha are a common protective motif painted on the outer walls of Tibetan buildings. This example is a doorway in the 15th-century Kumbum complex at Gyantse, which celebrates the Buddha as a supreme, cosmic deity who is ubiquitously present.*

THE HOME AS SANCTUARY

The extent to which the home is considered sacred varies greatly among cultures. Modern Western society with its broadly secular outlook tends to focus ideas of sacredness on a specified area, usually outside the home, and on an established priesthood: religion is not generally considered to embrace all areas of life. In many traditional cultures, however, the distinction between secular and sacred is either blurred or does not exist at all. But in any culture a dwelling is a visible, material demonstration of an ongoing way of life, and as this is often felt to be the "right" way to live, so the dwelling may embody an order and ethical values that are deemed sacred.

In this way, even the domestic home can be used imaginatively to give shape to ideas. The house may be a physical model of another structure, such as the human body (see pages 122–123) or the cosmos (see pages 120–122). In other instances, more than just copying the structure of a living thing, the house is thought actually to *become* a body during rituals, when it is made to perform like one. For the Barasana Indians of Colombia the longhouse is an ordinary dwelling-place most of the time. At each end is a door, for the menfolk at one end, for women

at the other, and a central corridor runs between the two. Each family has its hearth along the edges of the longhouse, and communal activities take place in the center. But in rituals to convey mythic truths the house is personified as a mythical figure, an enormous bird called Roofing Father. The palm leaves used for roofing are his feathers. His head is at the male end of the house, his anus at the female end, and the roof-struts are his ribcage. The central male–female axis is his digestive tract, and the two doors represent the bodily openings for eating and defecation. Variants of the same idea can be found among many peoples worldwide, from Brazil and

Central America to Indonesia and the Pacific region. By using their houses in ritualized ways—such as the acting out of the Roofing Father myth by the Barasana—human beings believe they can control or change the processes of the cosmos.

People may build a house to reflect the structure of the cosmos, as in the Inuit igloo, a temporary hunting shelter made of ice blocks and found in certain regions of the Canadian Arctic. It reproduces a more widespread form of circular Inuit house, often underground, with a long narrow entrance passage for protection from the weather. In this society without separate temples, every element of the home has sacred meaning. For ritual purposes the igloo is likened to the womb and the entrance passage to the vagina. The domed roof represents the sky, the ice window the Sun and the doorway the Moon.

Similarly, the Navajo people of the Southwestern United States build their traditional earth and timber home (the hogan) in imitation of that built by the gods for the First Man and First Woman. The circular single-room structure has a doorway facing east to receive the blessing rays of the Sun as it rises at dawn. The building's timber framework consists of a trio of interconnecting forked poles positioned to the south, west, and north. The interior divides into a southern male half and a northern female half, with the hearth at the center. Movement within is around the hearth in a clockwise direction, in imitation of the Sun as it travels from east to west. The entire structure is consecrated with corn pollen.

In Southeast Asia the house is held to be "alive." In part this arises from the presence of a vital force suffusing everything: trees are thought to have their

LEFT *A Central Asian yurt provides an everyday space as well as a hallowed one—its circular shape is symbolic of the cosmos. The yurt's central feature is the hearth, which is positioned at the vertical axis that ascends upward through the smoke-hole to the heavens above. During cooking, rituals of purification and propitiation are performed that ascend skyward to the deities.*

own wild power, which must be domesticated when they are felled for house-timbers. Among the Bugis of Indonesia each house has a "navel-post" where life-energy concentrates, and this post is dressed up to make it, as the Bugi say, "look like a king." The Malays follow the principle of "one house, one tree." The nine major house- posts are taken from a single treetrunk and erected in the same order as they were cut, so as not to annihilate the tree's "life." Thus, the vitality of the tree continues in the house, and at the same time the ritual process of construction confers vital energy on the dwelling.

Given these beliefs, carvings are made as much for protection as for decoration. In Southeast Asia the house is a both a home and a shrine. Its inhabitants are its soul, and its structure and carvings serve to protect that soul. Carvings must consist of flowing lines; a broken line may bring misfortune. If angered,

Remote and Rocky Sanctuaries

Fortified sanctuaries are found in many monastic traditions, such those of Tibetan Buddhism or Greek Orthodoxy. In Europe the fortified sanctuary combined monastic retreat from the world with the seat of a knightly order.

The most notable examples are those sanctuaries dedicated to St. Michael (see page 141). The Christian associations of Michael as archangel and friend to pilgrims were combined with earlier pagan legends of him as dragon-slayer and guide to the underworld. St. Michael's sanctuaries are almost all on rocky peaks or islets. The remoteness of these locations—such as Skerrig Michael, off the west coast of Ireland; St. Michael's Mount in Cornwall, southwest England; and Sangra di San Michele in Piedmont, Italy—relates to the mystic revelation to be found in outer realms, where it is thought that the divine may be spontaneously contacted.

a house can make someone ill, and there are healing ceremonies to deal with offended houses. If a dwelling is destroyed by fire and "dies," mourning rituals are conducted.

Inner and outer realms

In sacred architecture, humans arrange the materials provided by nature to create a special space within which they can encounter the divine. This space is marked off from the "ordinary" space outside, echoing the way in which, in religious thought, the problems of evil and human suffering are widely seen as being due to the separation of humanity from divinity or wisdom. The goal of religion—to reunite oneself with the godhead—is mirrored in the structure of sacred buildings as they invite worshipers to advance inside them from a secular outer realm, through gateways and along paths, in a movement towards the center—usually the most sacred part of the building. The approach may be guarded by barriers and monsters, in an architectural representation of the difficulty of the spiritual journey from separation to unity.

Marking off an enclosed space sets up a distinction between what lies within and what lies without, and combines the human need for shelter with a powerful and widespread cosmological principle. In the home a boundary may separate private from public space; at the edge of a jungle village it may separate the human from the wild. The temple boundary marks off a holy, pure and powerful space from an outer space that is ordinary and unclean. This inner space is often so sacred that it can be reached only by degrees, as the visitor passes through successive barriers before reaching the innermost, and most sacred, point. Individuals must be purified before entering this space (see pages 174–176) and entry to the inner area is often limited to special categories of people.

A distinction between inner and outer realms is evident from the smallest to the largest scale. In one of the most basic forms of sacred architecture,

RIGHT *Adorning the exterior of this West African mud building are fetish niches containing spirit effigies and charms. It is common in areas where animism still holds sway for spiritual symbolism to be associated with parts of the home. In such places monumental temples are rare and arrangements such as this are the nearest equivalent.*

common to very many West African peoples, a diviner sits in a circle of stones that no one else may enter. Similarly, village huts are often arranged in a circle with their entrances facing inward and the gaps between them closed by a fence that controls the inward and outward movement of people, animals, and spirits. The Cheyenne of North America expressed their cosmology not only in the inner structure of the *tipis* but also in the arrangement of the camp in a circle with an opening to the east, the side from which new life entered, in the form of the Sun. In large empires, it was often not the house or temple, or even the city, that was bounded, but the empire itself. The traditional Chinese city was built in a series of concentric rectangles, with the imperial residence occupying the innermost "box"—a city within a city. Far outside, the Great Wall marked the outer boundary, between civilization and the barbarian tribes.

Outer realms represent or contain a form of power that can be dangerous but can sometimes be harnessed. A densely populated and urbanized inner realm can seem sordid and unclean, as opposed to the freshness of the countryside beyond. A sense of this underlies the modern Western appreciation of "nature" and is also seen in the widespread idea of the wilderness as a place of simplicity and spiritual

OVERLEAF *The Potala Palace dominates the holy city of Lhasa in Tibet. The 17th-century building was built as a monastery and fortress, home to both the Dalai Lamas and the government of Tibet. "Potala" derives from Mount Potalaka, celestial abode of Avalokiteshvara, the* bodhisattva (one who selflessly delays nirvana to help others attain it) *of compassion and the patron deity of Tibet. It is believed that Avalokiteshvara is reincarnated in the form of the person who becomes Dalai Lama. The outer White Palace envelops the inner upper section known as the Red Palace, which contains a series of temples. A labyrinth of shrines occupies the top of the palace, their golden roofs emulating a celestial mansion.*

Ninstints

Queen Charlotte Islands, Canada

The abandoned village of Ninstints lies in a sheltered bay on Anthony Island, in the Queen Charlotte Islands group off the Pacific coast of Canada. The sea-going Haida people have occupied these islands for at least 7,000 years, living off ocean creatures, from killer-whales to sea-urchins, and hunting and gathering in the coastal forests. They call them the Gwaii Haanas or Islands of Wonder.

Ninstints was the main village of the Kunghit Haida, who occupied the southernmost part of the territory. The Haida called it Sqa'ngwa-i lnaga'i (Red Cod Island Town) after the abundant supply of red snapper caught locally. Its present name is a corruption of the name of Chief Nanstins (He Who Is Two), who was the last to rule the village before it was abandoned in the late nineteenth century.

The Kunghit Haida were divided into two large groups, the Eagles and the Ravens. Each group had several clans, with their own traditions, myths, and symbols, many of which are represented on the distinctive totem poles. For example, the first clan encountered by Europeans was called Those Born At Songs Of Victory Town and its heraldic crests were the Moon and the thunderbird.

At that point in the nineteenth century Ninstints was just one of thirty to forty villages on the islands. However, within ten years smallpox had decimated the population, while missionary activity and government interference caused severe cultural disruption. By 1880 Ninstints, and all but two of the other towns, had been abandoned by the Haida.

RIGHT AND CENTER *Weathered totem poles bearing their clan emblems still stand among the trees and in front of the broken remains of houses at Ninstints. The many poles that remain there feature carvings of mythical beings and totemic animals such as bears, ravens, and eagles. In addition, the Haida also erected mortuary poles upon which they placed the remains of the dead in cedar boxes. The soft aromatic wood of the red cedar tree provided the Haida with an ideal carving and construction material, resistant to weathering but easily cut and shaped with adzes and other tools. The posts, beams, and planks for the communal houses were all produced from cedar.*

ABOVE *Ninstints today is abandoned and a ghostly atmosphere pervades. The one-time population of more than 300 people lived in perhaps twenty, cedar-plank houses. Each house had a name: the house farthest south was called People Think Of This House Even When They Sleep Because The Master Feeds Everyone Who Calls. Outside the buildings stood totem, mortuary, and memorial poles, many of which are still there.*

BELOW *A reconstruction of the plan of the village, showing the location of houses and their associated poles. Memorial poles bore the emblematic crests of people who had died while absent from the village.*

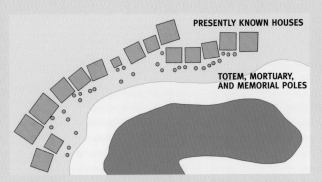

PRESENTLY KNOWN HOUSES

TOTEM, MORTUARY, AND MEMORIAL POLES

purification, where nothing more elaborate than the hermit's hut or the makeshift initiation lodge is built. In this view the wilderness is a source of power and strength, which may be symbolically brought back into the community—for example, in India, the hut of the forest hermit may be reproduced in the finial of a temple tower.

The most extreme Western idea of wilderness requires it to be uninhabited, with no buildings. More commonly points of special spiritual power are marked architecturally by shrines and pilgrimage sites. Here, within the wider outer realm, small areas of inner space are set up, and the shrines may reproduce in miniature the boundaries of the city.

Retreat and isolation

Certain religious traditions exalt the spirit and place an intense value on contemplation of the other world, often at the expense of the material substance of this world. In architecture this has contradictory consequences. The withdrawal from this world by the hermit or monk seems to imply a disengagement from architecture altogether. Yet monasteries may be large institutions and are often centers of wealth and power—a fact that is demonstrated by their magnificent architecture.

The hermit's shelter may be deliberately more basic than even the poorest ordinary dwelling—the Greek sage Diogenes lived in a barrel, and for millennia Christian, Buddhist, and Hindu hermits have dwelt in caves. Such isolation may be combined with an exaltation, or rising, toward God. St. Simeon Stylites spent most of his life on top of a pillar that supported a small platform just large enough for him

to be able to sleep. In early Christian Britain, isolated hermits' cells and chapels were built on inhospitable islands in the sea.

In many cultures, from Native America through East Africa to New Guinea, almost everyone experiences a period of temporary isolation. Adolescents are isolated singly or in a group in a special hut to reflect on spiritual truths. While ordinary houses are often divided into male and female, senior and junior, spaces, the simple structure of the initiation hut

RIGHT *The isolated Hindu shrine of Matanga Parvatam is set on a rock promonotory above the ruins of India's Achyutaraya Temple, overlooking what is now the city of Hampi. Ascetics throughout the subcontinent have practiced their beliefs in remote places for centuries, as part of the discipline of rejecting worldly distractions.*

reflects the removal of all previous social status. Since initiates are in the process of becoming a new social entity, the hut often resembles a womb, from which they will be reborn as adults. In parts of India or the Amazon girls are secluded during their first menstrual period; among the Dyak of Borneo they are isolated for a year in a white hut where they are dressed in white and allowed to eat white food only.

As a lifelong vocation, monasticism is especially highly developed in Christianity and Buddhism. Large numbers of men and women withdraw from the life of sexuality, family, and mundane economics, to pray for a world that will not pray for itself. In both religions this is linked to a theology in which salvation or *nirvana* is hindered by the distractions of the material world and of the flesh. Early monasteries grew to become the major social institutions of their society. The Buddhist monastery began as a retreat for contemplation, and evolved into a large center of learning, as in the early Buddhist university

Ajanta Caves

Central India

The complex of the twenty-nine cave temples of Ajanta in central India were carved into the sheer cliff-face of a meandering and horseshoe-shaped gorge on the River Waghora. They are the work of Buddhists, who used them as retreats from the second century BCE to the fifth century CE. Many of the caves have carved, pillared entrances, and interior sculptures, but their most striking features are the frescoes that cover almost all the walls and ceilings.

The paintings were all made with the same pigments and have complementary themes. Different subjects were painted in different parts of the chambers: images of the Buddha near the antechambers and shrines; and *jatakas* (popular tales of the Buddha's previous incarnations) in the principal halls. Ceilings were painted in geometric patterns with intertwined animal and plant motifs suggesting the gardens of paradise. This unified conception suggests a profoundly holistic view of the cosmos.

One scene, painted in the first century BCE, shows a prince and his entourage walking toward a sacred tree where musicians accompany two lively dancers; another, in a late fifth-century *vihara*—a cave in which monks both lived and worshipped—shows a prince called Mahajanaka surrounded by beautiful women. The initial impression of both of these narratives is strongly secular, although the first depicts a sacred ritual and the second shows the prince at the moment of renouncing his worldly life for that of a religious recluse.

RIGHT *A view that shows a Buddha-flanked temple facade cut into the solid rock of the cliff-face. The temples in the cave complex are elaborate architectural designs that stretch back a considerable way inside the rock. The buildings were discovered in 1824, some 1,500 years after they had been abandoned. By then the brightly painted retreats had deteriorated into dark and damp caves—overgrown, vandalized, and inhabited only by animals. This is the entrance to cave nine, which leads through into one of the large temples lining the gorge.*

ABOVE *The twenty-nine caves sweep around the wooded ravine at Ajanta. Among the European discoverers in 1824 was British army officer Lieutenant James Alexander, who noted: "On the floor of many of the lower caves I observed the prints of the feet of tigers, jackals, bears, monkeys, peacocks, etc.; these were impressed upon the dust, formed by the plaster of the fresco paintings which had fallen from the ceilings."*

CENTER *The jambs and lintel of the door to cave six, intricately carved with figures, leaves, and animals. The door opens into the lower shrine. The painters at Ajanta used natural earth ochers and the blue of lapis lazuli in their work. Scenes of the Buddha preaching are relatively restrained, but those depicting events from his previous lives and from the* jataka *folktales are often sensual and worldly.*

LEFT *The caves extend around the semicircular cliff-face of a scarp above the Waghora River. Caves were excavated roughly side by side, varying in elevation from 35 ft. (10 m) to 100 ft. (30 m) above the river. The numbering is consecutive from right to left for archaeological purposes.*

at Nalanda in Bihar, India. In Tibet, Buddhist monasteries became landowners and administrative and economic centers, as did Christian monasteries in medieval Europe.

The Christian orders built up into vast economic enterprises that rivaled the power of kings and emperors, their thriving, independent communities becoming pioneers of a succession of architectural styles, from the Romanesque of the Cistercians and Cluniacs to the Gothic of the Franciscans and Dominicans. This marked one noticeable difference between western European Catholicism and eastern Orthodoxy: the latter retained familiar, unchanging building forms.

The first of what were to be many monasteries on Mount Athos, northern Greece (also called *aghios oros* or "holy mountain"), was founded in 961CE by Athanasius. About twenty are still inhabited by monks of the Greek Orthodox Church. No female is allowed on the Halkidiki peninsula—it is considered the exclusive territory of the Virgin Mary. The monasteries are built as fortresses, with massive wooden gates that are locked at sunset. Inside are extensive courtyards, each with its own church.

In a cenobitic ("life in common") monastery the monks hand over all property and eat together in a collective refectory. In an idiorrhythmic monastery they retain their own property and the architecture enables them to live and eat separately. Outside the monasteries are *sketes* and *kellia*—small huts lived in

BELOW *Buddhist figures adorn a cliff at the Longmen caves near Luoyang, northern China. This is one of three major rock-cut sites in the area, constituting China's earliest Buddhist sculpture. Nearly 200 figures can be seen in 1,000 caves or recesses carved out of the stone more than 400ft (120m) above the ground. The figures glorified Buddha and honored the ancestors.*

Niketas the Stylite

In the late eighteenth century a French explorer wrote of the strange "pyramidical houses" he had seen in a remote part of the Mediterranean, inhabited by troglodytes. But more remarkable still were the rock-cut places of worship.

The arched entrance to a hollowed cone on the slopes of Güllü Dere (the Rose-Pink Valley) in Cappadocia leads to a small chapel lit by a single square window. The walls of the chapel are covered with images of saints and apostles, the Virgin and Child, and the Crucifixion. Also in the chapel is a dedication to a monk called Niketas. Like St Simeon, whose image is near by, Niketas was a stylite—a Christian ascetic who lived on top of a pillar (*stylos* in Greek,).

Above the chapel, near the top of the cone, rock has fallen away to reveal a small cramped chamber in which it is thought Niketas lived on his pillar a millennium ago. The chamber would have been accessible only by ladder or by precarious footholds carved in the outside wall leading up to an opening at the top of the cone.

by two or three monks. Beyond these are the cells of the strict hermits, who live outside of the system altogether. A hermit's dwelling may be just a ledge or a hole in the cliff-face. Other monks lower food to them in a basket but never see them or exchange a word. If one day the basket is not emptied they know the ledge is available for another inhabitant.

Worlds in living rock

Well-watered but infertile valleys in the Anatolian region of Cappadocia have been eroded into an eerie wasteland of strange conical formations (see pages 66–67). The first outsiders to describe this unearthly place in the late eighteenth century noted the houses hollowed out of the cones, but more fascinating still was the region's great quantity of rock-cut churches, small chapels, and stark cramped cells where a millennium ago monks and other Christian hermits devoted their lives to solitary prayer.

Rock-cut caves express the desire for unity between the human spirit and the ancient body of the Earth. At Ajanta in India, between the second century BCE and the fifth century CE, generations of devout Buddhists created sacred space in solid rock by carving out temples and filling them with scenes of the life of the Buddha (see pages 208–209).

In the late sixth century Hindus created a great cave temple to the god Shiva on Elephant Island in Bombay harbor. The main temple has a pillared nave that leads to a *lingam*, a phallus-shaped symbol of the god (see page 59). Adjoining this central area of worship are smaller cave shrines with sculptures illustrating scenes from the god's life. In remoter areas of northern China the Buddhist fervor that swept the countryside from the fourth century CE inspired similar complexes. Near Maijishan (or Corn Rick Mountain) a cave temple developed at the site of a naturally formed *stupa*, an earthen mound or hill regarded as a mortuary shrine to the Buddha. Over centuries the cliff-face has become honeycombed with chambers, from simple niches to pillared shrines with vaulted ceilings. Earthquakes and the weathering of friable rock have caused some shrines to collapse, but many still contain clay statues of the Buddha and his attendants as well as those of other Buddhist divinities and of worshipers.

OVERLEAF *El-Deir, the "Monastery," was carved out within the pink sandstone city of Petra by the ancient Nabateans, c.150BCE–c.150CE, and is one of the world's most remarkable cave churches. The valley, in modern Jordan, is home to hundreds of sacred buildings, all magnificent in setting and execution. The two other places of worship are the temple of Dhu-Shara and that of the Winged Lions. The frontage of El-Deir conceals a large chamber behind, and it is likely that the present structure replaced an earlier temple building.*

ENCOUNTERS WITH THE SACRED

People may define territory broadly in terms of the Earth's own boundaries (oceans, seas, lakes, mountain chains, plateaux, and rivers); and, more specifically, within these natural confines, in terms of predominant vegetation, fauna, climate, soils, or rock type. The borders between areas may be centuries old and undisputed, but when human groups define territory in terms of the cultures that have emerged there, competing claims almost inevitably occur at some stage between neighboring groups. Conflict over the precise determination of frontiers occurs frequently, and national myths have very often arisen as

In Search of a Sacred Vision

The vision quest of *hanbleceya* or "crying for a vision" was a sacred rite said to have been given to the Oglala Lakota people of the North American Plains by a supernatural being called White Buffalo Calf Woman. The vision-seeker is taken to a sacred hill by his spiritual advisor who digs a pit and covers it with brush, marking the four sacred directions with decorated poles and tobacco offerings. The advisor instructs the seeker to take no food or water and to leave the pit only at dawn in order to pray to the Morning Star. During the ordeal supernatural beings may visit the pit and talk with the seeker, who will experience visions that will be an influence on him in the future. If an animal or bird comes to him, he may hunt and kill its kind and carry it as war medicine. But if he dreams of thunder and lightning he must act out his dream in a ceremony called *heyoka kaga* or "clown making," in which he shows his new role as a divine fool: his function within the tribe from now on is to do everything idiotically, or backward.

part of the process of territorial definition. In such a way the occupation and extent of a group's territories is justified and the special bond between people and the land is strengthened.

In many societies concern about land ownership has tended to focus on the areas associated with small kinship groups or communities. For example, among the Native American peoples living along the northwest coast of Canada individual family groups traditionally owned rights to the area of land that provided them with sufficient shellfish, fish, and other food resources. By contrast, foraging rights among Australian Aboriginal tribes are much more loosely defined, and their clan estates are based rather on the guardianship of sacred places and the myths, songs, and ceremonies that go with them.

Recent land disputes, such as those in Australia and North America, in which indigenous peoples have confronted the modern political state, demonstrate the difficulty of reconciling the Western concept of land as a commodity, which may be owned and traded, with ancient, more sacred, tribal notions. The Aborigines, for example, believe that the land was formed by mythological beings during the creation period or Dreaming; as such it is not merely a geological phenomenon but a spiritual one. Human beings may be entrusted with guardianship of ancestral sites associated with the Dreaming, but the idea of land "ownership" is alien: it would mean placing oneself above the sacred spirits of the Dreaming who had created both land and people.

At the heart of the contest are different interpretations of humankind's relationship with the world around it, but the different visions at least share a belief in some form of profound relationship. Societies even draw consciously on the natural world for emblems of nationhood, using them to express aspects of collective identity. For example, the former Yugoslav republic of Slovenia adopted a stylized view of the Alps as a national symbol after it achieved independence in 1991; this was felt to express the Slovenes' self-reliance as a mountain

people. Elsewhere historical monuments may be claimed by nations far removed in culture or time from the peoples originally concerned with them. In Africa the one-time European colonies of Dahomey, Gold Coast, and French Sudan adopted after independence the names Benin, Ghana, and Mali, respectively—all once powerful precolonial empires—and Zimbabwe in southern Africa is named after the ruined medieval city of Great Zimbabwe. Such names helped to instill a sense of unity within culturally disparate states whose artificially drawn frontiers rarely took account of pre-existing ethnic, cultural, or linguistic boundaries.

ABOVE *A men's spirit house in the Sepik River region of New Guinea. A meeting house is often more than a place of assembly: it may have a sacred purpose, as a forum in which initiates can encounter the gods. Such a use might also define the people inside it in relation to those outside. The uninitiated are kept out by taboos that stop them violating the building's sanctity and the house becomes an instrument of tradition and identity.*

Vision quests

Just as a nation might seek to find and define itself, so, too, may individuals; one method is the "vision quest," an ancient yet common practice found worldwide, including Native Americans, Siberian shamanistic societies, and Australian Aborigines. An individual seeking self-knowledge or spiritual power will enter upon a deliberate ordeal of seclusion, fasting, and prayer with the aim of self-purification and in the hope of receiving an ecstatic vision that will reveal to him or her the true path to follow in life.

Once in the "vision state," it is claimed that an individual becomes a disembodied traveler who flies into the heavens and looks back at the Earth and the universe. In the quest for truth he or she is said to journey beyond the frontiers of the known world,

experience a landscape alive with spirits, and return bringing supernatural knowledge and power. (In other societies, notably those of South American shamans, the path to the spirit world is found by the taking of hallucinogenic potions.)

As well as the apparent ascent to Heaven (or altered state of consciousness), there are other themes common to the vision quests of different cultures. Before returning to the everyday world, the visionary traveler will usually descend to the underworld, confront demonic forces, and communicate both with the spirits of the dead and with birds and animals.

Prior to entering the state of ecstasy, visionary travelers may have to go alone into the outside world, away from their group, in order to find a secret place where they can prepare for the vision. The choice of site is important because it must have easy access to the spirit world. Among the Algonquin people of northeastern North America high cliffs, rock shelters, or unusual rock formations are often favored, as being places imbued with spiritual power (see page 81).

The vision quest often begins at puberty when a boy, or sometimes a girl, asks an elder or medicine man for help in obtaining

LEFT *A doorway to one of the shrines at the Ladakh monastery, at Alchi in the upper Indus Valley, one of the oldest temples in the western Himalayas. The door jambs are carved with auspicious motifs and Buddhist figures; the most prominent, though, is the figure of Garuda (top, center), the magical eagle of Vishnu, offering to protect against the forces of evil.*

visions. The seekers receive religious instruction and may participate in rituals in a "sweatlodge," a hut filled with steam inside which they retire for purification and healing. They are then taken to an isolated spot to await the vision. The site may be a cleft in a rock, the summit of a hill, or a nest of branches and leaves in a tree. Once there, the initiate must go without food or sleep for a day or more until visited by a spirit, often in a dream. The initiates must never divulge the exact details of their dreams, but they may adopt the symbols of their spirit helper and use them in face paints and decorations, thereby tacitly revealing the helper's identity.

Vision quests may go on throughout life. The Comanche people of the southern Great Plains of North America believed that a warrior must continue seeking visionary guidance into old age. Pursuing the same visionary path as he did as a youth, he would climb up to a sacred hill with his robe, pipe, and tobacco, to smoke, pray, and fast in order to be close to the spirit world.

Gateways, thresholds, and openings

Gateways, thresholds, and openings mark the transition between one kind of space and another. Crossing them can mark an individual's transition between different kinds of sacred or social state. The Hindu god of thresholds is the elephant-headed Ganesh, and his statue or picture is often placed at doorways. But he is also the god of beginnings in a broader sense, and is worshiped at the start of any important undertaking, whether it be a wedding, a journey, or a new business venture.

Openings such as doors and windows are a basic necessity, but they are also the most vulnerable parts of a building. The door represents the point at which entry is invited and can be controlled. Thresholds are often symbolic barriers at these openings, and they may be marked with prayers, spells, and blessings meant to ensure that such entry is benign and to protect the space within. The Chinese use spirit

Entrances of Light

Light is perhaps the most fundamental metaphor in Islamic scripture. The Koran states: "God is the light of the heavens and the Earth." Encoded in the "abstract" designs in Islamic architecture are figures representing sources of spiritual light —such as stars, lamps, and rays—often entwined together with verses from the Koran, and located at doors, windows, and prayer-alcoves.

The Kabylie Berbers of Algeria (see page 223) feel that the door should remain open all day, so that sunlight can enter and bring prosperity. A closed door signifies sterility; to sit upon the threshold, obstructing the Sun, is to shut out happiness and fertility. To say, "May your door always be open" is a way to wish someone well.

screens—short walls built just inside the gate—to repel demons. Or demonlike images can perform this function: in Buddhist temples, fearsome masks above the door are used to repel evil.

In central Nepal the *thelo* (threshold) separates the veranda from the interior. Special spikes are hammered into the threshold and into window-ledges, to guard magically against the entry of witches. Supposedly impure "castes" (for example, butchers, Muslims, or Christians) are only allowed to cross the *thelo* as an exceptional favor, after which the house needs to be purified. In some Arab cultures the threshold (*atabe*) takes the form of a long stone that forms an upward step: different levels mark a qualitative hierarchy between outer and inner space (see pages 200–201). The *atabe* is where the shoes are left and where the visitor should wash. An identification may be made between the threshold and the household itself—in Mongolia if anyone kicks the wooden threshold of the tent, even inadvertently, it is considered a symbolically aggressive act directed at the family within.

ABOVE *Kneeling camels and other animals line the avenue leading to the imperial tombs of the Ming Dynasty emperors at Nanjing, China's capital during the early Ming period. The animals offer positive and respectful symbols for the afterlife. Such a site would have been chosen by a feng shui master to ensure that it possessed an auspicious balance of Earth-energy forces.*

Gateways make the most elaborate and explicit statements about controlling who may or may not enter a sacred space. From the Christian cathedral door on which the archbishop must knock, to the house of the Indian Sora people where the shaman's assistants break down the door to bring in an ancestral name for a baby, to the gates of the monasteries of Mount Athos that are barricaded from dusk until dawn, gateways control the identity and the timing of those who are allowed to enter.

Reflecting or proclaiming the perceived importance of what is inside the building, the door is often given exaggerated significance, marked by features such as arches, pillars, or porticos. Many doors are fortified even when they have no military purpose – this can be seen in Europe where massive church doors are reinforced with iron. In China the gateway was often the main element of the building and was protected by moats and towers. The head of a conquered enemy was buried beneath the gate, imbuing it with magical power; the decapitated victim was said to become its spirit guardian.

A door opens outward into the world as well as inward, and functions as an exit. The front step of the Arab threshold is also the place over which a corpse is laid for a while as the dead person leaves the house for the last time. In many parts of the world a house's garbage is taken out through the back door, which is explicitly likened to the house's anus.

Pathways of the spirit

In architecture the pathway is the means by which people move in or between buildings. Its particular meaning—whether it is intended to lead to a focal point, encircle a holy site, or meander along natural lines—is provided by the whole structure of which it is an element. The pathway is therefore not merely an incidental means of traveling from one place to another. It is an intrinsic part of the architecture, even when it is not itself "built."

The simplest constructions may contain implicit pathways, and to move along these is often to enact symbolic or mythical meanings. The circle of Stonehenge in England (see pages 132–135), with its astronomical markers, formed several paths, as did the parallel passageways between the lines of stones at Carnac in France (see pages 130–131). The symbolic connotations of even a simple circular movement can be complex. The round hogan dwelling (see page 199) of the Native American Navajo is consecrated with a chant from the Blessingway ceremony, a ritual that involves participants moving round the "sunwise path" and symbolically encircling the world. With the concave floor representing the earth (female) and the rounded roof the sky (male), the participants circle the hearth clockwise; this movement also represents the passage from sunrise to sunset.

The sacred pathway is also significant in the great temple complexes and cities of ancient civilizations. Many Mayan cities were linked by processional routes, or *sacbes*, used by priests and pilgrims. One such route on the Yucatán peninsula connected the cities of Izamal, Uci, Uxmal, Kabáh, and Cobá. The Aztec capital, Tenochtitlán, built on an island in a lake, used canals as pathways to structure the city according to a divine ideogram. Four concentric pathways—representing the four main deities—

RIGHT *The nave of Canterbury Cathedral, England. The sense of pathway derives from the dominating lines of the tall columns, which reach up into the roof vault and lead the eyes and the steps of the worshipper toward the altar straight ahead.*

demarcated the city's districts (or *barrios*), with the ceremonial precinct at the center. In this way the city replicated universal space.

In some cases the pathway demonstrated imperial divinity. In ancient Egypt during the New Kingdom (*c*.1539–1075BCE) temples were linked by avenues of sphinxes, or Ways of God. Ram-headed sphinxes joined the temples of Amun and Khonsu at the complex of Karnak (see pages 150–151)—a symbol of generative power, the ram was sacred to the god Amun. The processional avenues of the New Kingdom, with their pylon gateways, colossal statues of the pharaohs, and towering obelisks of red granite celebrated the alliance of divine and earthly power.

In similar fashion, from the early dynasties of China the tombs of emperors and generals were approached by avenues lined with stone guardians on either side. The earliest images are those of the Han Dynasty (second to first centuries BCE). The intrinsic qualities and shape of the stone were left evident, to evoke the permanence of stone itself. The carvings were a substitute for the living guard of honor that lined the way for the emperor during his life and provided an eternal guard for him in death. The avenue often followed the landscape's contours to tap the sacred energies of nature. Featuring mythical creatures and auspicious beasts, it was also a symbolic link with the next world.

The Southern Dynasties (420–589CE) developed lively sculptures of pacing, grimacing, and often winged beasts, and seem to have been primarily concerned with the supernatural power of such creatures. In the Tang and Song Dynasties (seventh to thirteenth centuries CE), the avenues incorporated figures from the living world, such as high bureaucrats and military officials. Sacred creatures also occur, including the lion and the kneeling elephant (symbols of power) and the ram (filial piety). Tang and Song avenues create an image of the entire world to accompany the imperial ancestor in his afterlife.

Early Christians designed the church building to embody the spiritual path of the believer. This is evident in the nave (see page 219), the approach to the altar taken by the faithful, which represents a gradation from less sacred space at the west end to sanctified space at the east. Lines of pillars on either side evoke the sense of a path, and the depth given by the aisles beyond them makes the pillars stand in the round like treetrunks in an avenue. The shape of the nave seems to draw the devotee forward, and floor mosaics may also present patterns indicating forward movement. All these features come together at the east and focus the eye on the destination: the altar.

The divine enclosure

The significance of the courtyard varies greatly from society to society. For example, it can close off a community from the outer world for the sake of spiritual purity; it can be a space of historically sanctified power; or it can be the source of domestic vitality.

The Christian cloister (see box opposite), consisting of an arcaded walkway surrounding a garden, is often thought to have been foreshadowed in the Islamic East. But the rationale for the mosque courtyard (*sahn*) is quite different from that of the cloister. A dark corridor opens into the sunlight of the *sahn*, whose four walls symbolize the four columns that carry the celestial dome. The courtyard is thus linked architecturally to the sky or heavens. In the center of the *sahn* is an eight-sided fountain, echoing the octagonal shape of God's throne according to the Koran. The floor may be decorated with marble representations of fruit trees watered by rivers and streams. The whole courtyard represents paradise.

Moscow's Kremlin is a citadel courtyard; its walls are interspersed with towers and gates. It gained its sanctity by virtue of being the seat of the holy tsars, absolute rulers who were regarded almost as gods by many of their subjects. The Kremlin reflects a rejection of European modernization: its massive walls were erected in the seventeenth century, at a time when movements against autocracy resulted in the dismantling of city walls in the rest of Europe.

Cloisters for Contemplation

The Christian cloister was designed as a place of meditation for monks, consisting of a quadrilateral enclosure surrounded by covered walkways or ambulatories. The cloister was usually open-arcaded, although windowed versions were developed in northern Europe. Its central area and walkways provided the customary places of burial, with tombs set into the floors.

In the eleventh century at the Benedictine monastery of Cluny, France, the cloister became the chief architectural feature, owing to expanding numbers and to the wish of each monk to have his own cell. The common dormitory had been abandoned almost everywhere by the late fourteenth century; individual cells were built around three sides of the cloister and joined in an integrated complex with the other buildings. Gradually the significance of the cloister changed, as the urge to give expression to communal meditation gave way to the need to create spaces for individual work. From their cells monks were often active in public life (from his cloister cell at San Marco the fifteenth-century Dominican friar Savonarola roused Florence to revolt).

Containing cathedrals, armories, tombs, stables, and gardens, the Kremlin constitutes a separate historical zone that is out of step with the rest of Moscow. Perhaps for this reason a statue of Lenin was never erected there, although such statues once peppered the rest of the city. As such a Lenin statue was intended to symbolize the timeless future of the communist ideal, planners may have realized that it could not withstand the weight of historically legitimized sanctity represented by the Kremlin.

In West Africa the courtyard is the well-spring of life and fertility. Among the Ashante of Ghana it is the fundamental form of all traditional architecture, from palaces to shrines and houses. The courtyard

house reflects the central role of the family in Ashante society. The yards are semiprivate areas, used for the communal activities of a household. A sacred bush symbolizing life is planted in the center. The temple shrine echoes this pattern: the single entrance leads to a sacred courtyard, surrounded by rooms with diverse functions, including the main shrine room and a drum room. Significantly, the Ashante tomb, the realm of death, is the architectural opposite of the courtyard, being open on all sides under a hanging roof.

The concept of the enclosed courtyard can also be applied to sites that would seem to be open by their very nature. The Zapotec city of Monte Albán in Mexico was built at the top of a steep hill, yet the artificially leveled plaza (mid- to first millennium CE) creates an immense enclosed area in defiance of its topographical setting. The many temples at the edge of the plaza, separating it from the precipitous slopes of the hill, allow virtually no view of the surrounding valleys but concentrate attention inward to the group of three temples at the plaza's centre.

Space and gender

As has been touched upon, a distinction between male and female spaces is often found in sacred architecture. Sometimes this reflects only one among a number of social differences evidenced in the building. For example, Anglican churches in northern India assign women to one side of the nave and men to the other, but they also place low castes at the back. Gender distinctions can also indicate different roles for the sexes in religion itself. In Orthodox Judaism women are allocated a separate gallery in the synagogue, reflecting the idea that men uphold ritual tradition while women's sacred duty is to ensure the continuity of the nation. In Islam, while the Prophet Muhammad had declared that women were equal to men in the sight of God, by the Middle Ages women were seen as impure and were discouraged from attending the mosque; when they did

LEFT *The 18th-century Indian city of Jaipur in east Rajasthan is famed for its many pink-colored buildings. The Hawa Mahal, or Palace of the Winds, was purpose-built to house only women—a segregated structure known as a zenana. It comprises five stories of lattice-like carved casements designed, much like a veil, to allow palace women to look out without being seen.*

attend they had to stand behind men in their own rows. Today women still generally pray in a separate area of the mosque from men. In Christianity early patriarchal images of God the Father and raised separated spaces for male priests are being challenged by a more egalitarian use of space in some churches and, in some places, by the introduction of women priests.

Gender distinctions may also be seen in domestic sacred architecture. Among the Kazakhs in Xinjiang, China, the *yurt* is divided into male and female space; if a woman needs a utensil from the male side she will ask a child to fetch it. Because the *yurt* is a single open space, gender divisions appear in gestures, postures, and the placement of one sex in relation to the other. By contrast, in certain Hindu and Islamic cultures, women's quarters are built structures. Women are secluded in a special part of the house, the *zenana*, which forms a complete world. Yet it is not entirely separate: grilles and tiny windows allow women to see without being seen, in an architectural analogy of the veil.

More rarely, it is the male who has restricted access to space. Among the Bororo of Amazonia women inhabit and inherit the houses in which they were born. Bororo society is divided into two halves or moieties, and an individual must marry someone from the other group. The layout of villages reflects this convention. It is men who go to live with their wives and who cross the ideal line separating the two halves of humanity.

Structures themselves may be gendered. Tamil houses in southern India resemble the "living house" of Southeast Asia (see pages 199–200): the house is "conceived" when its corner post, which signifies the male tree, is implanted in the female earth. This rite of implantation is symbolic of sexual union.

Gender and the Wall of Light

Light, as we have seen, is an important decorative element in Islamic culture, featuring prominently in architecture—most notably to produce patterns of light and shadow. In North Africa the houses traditionally built by the Berber people relate the symbolism associated with light to the typical activities of each sex.

The simple rectangular dwelling of the Kabylie Berbers represents several complex and interlocking ideas of the sacred. The main door, symbolically male, is in the long eastern wall and is faced by the smaller female door, set into the western wall. Lit by the Sun coming through the male door, the western wall, called the "wall of light," is where women grind corn and do their weaving. Areas of darkness are considered female, and are associated with *haram* (taboo), animality, and nature (also located at the dark end of the house is a stable), as well as with sexuality, birth, and death. Areas of light are deemed to be male and are associated with the creative parts of the house.

According to the Kabylie, men are the light of the outside, public world, while women are the light of the interior. Men are expected to protect the domestic, creative activities of women, but they themselves must leave the house at dawn. Ridicule follows the man who spends time at home. To be inside, with their labor hidden, is the destiny of women. "A woman has only two dwellings," the Berbers say, "her house and her tomb."

Architecture of the Afterlife

Sacred architecture enlists society's greatest material and human resources to express the transcendent and the eternal through substantial materials, symbolic form, and meaningful ornamentation. In traditional cultures where all other buildings are small and humble, such visions of immensity and permanence are overwhelming and present a vivid contrast with the frailty of humans.

Mortals can share a little in this evocation of permanence, and even aspire to divine status, through the construction of tombs. While sacred buildings are often modeled on the living human body, the tomb suggests that the person continues to exist after death, either in another world or in the minds of those left behind. But even tombs, like temples, will eventually crumble, leaving enigmatic ruins only partly understood by future generations.

RIGHT *The "City of the Dead" in Cairo is a series of tomb-mosques and mausolea built during the rule of the Mamluks. The sultans were renowed for the beauty of their religious buildings. Note how the massive, stone domes are offset by distinctive geometric patterning.*

RESTING PLACES FOR THE SOUL

Tombs are the oldest-known form of architecture, and some of the earliest art ever produced was buried inside them. It seems that a main function of the early architect, as of the artist, was to provide for the needs of the deceased. This was based on the almost universal human belief that the dead continue to exist in some realm or dimension, and that communication and mutual support are possible between the dead and the living.

Much funeral architecture emphasizes the support that the dead will continue to need from this world. In many ancient civilizations the houses of the dead were more splendid than those of the living, which were built of mud and straw. Models or representations of useful everyday objects were buried with the corpse and much of our knowledge of ancient ways of life comes from such burials and the items retrieved from them. Egyptian tombs were decorated with scenes from everyday life and contain models of houses and food, while Han and Tang tombs in China are filled with terracotta models of soldiers, animals, servants, houses, granaries, and wells.

In many traditions live people and animals were sacrificed, and some tombs were large and many-chambered to accommodate these offerings. In China, in the sixth-century BCE, Confucius condemned this practice, and subsequently models replaced living creatures. A recently excavated burial platform of the Moche people in Peru revealed a

chamber with a sumptuously dressed warrior-priest in a coffin, while in coffins alongside lay two presumed concubines, a dog, and two guardians. Above in a separate chamber lay a further guardian. Several of the warrior-priest's attendants had had their feet amputated, as if to commit them to his service for eternity. At Pazyryk in Siberia the 2,400-year-old tomb of a woman was excavated from the permafrost in 1993. The burial chamber, oriented from west to east, resembled an underground log cabin; the woman was buried in a coffin, with a meal laid

RIGHT *The Mughal masterpiece the Taj Mahal was built on the southern bank of the Yamuna River, outside Agra, on the instruction of the emperor Shah Jehan as a huge mausoleum in memory of his beloved wife, Arjumand Banu Begam (also called Mumtaz Mahal or Chosen One of the Palace), who had died in childbirth. Designed by Indian, Persian, and Central Asian architects, it took two decades and the work of 20,000 laborers to build. The rectangular complex is aligned north to south with a garden at the center.*

beside her. The chamber was roofed over and several finely harnessed horses had been sacrificed and lowered down before the tomb was filled in. In this semi-nomadic society, the tomb was the only permanent building—one in which time was frozen.

Funerary architecture aims to meet the needs of the dead, but also meets the emotional needs of the living. A photograph, death mask, or lock of hair may be built into a tomb or memorial. Tombs may also be ornamented with statues of weeping figures. In Roman Egypt this led to a tradition of lifelike mourners painted on wood. In medieval Europe wax effigies of the deceased gave way to recumbent stone sculptures on tombs, giving the ephemeral human person a permanent architectural form.

In India, Hindus had generally cast ashes into sacred rivers, and early Islam had prohibited the building of monuments for the dead. But from the thirteenth century CE onward a new type of structure developed: the Muslim tomb. Muslim royal tombs were housed in spectacular buildings, surrounded by exquisite formal gardens representing paradise. The

southern suburbs of Delhi are sprinkled with large and small domes of various dynasties in differing styles. Around the ruins of Golconda near Hyderabad in southern India rise numerous royal tombs. The bases of the domes were constricted, giving a bubble shape, with a second, lower ceiling inside the main chamber. Today the rock-strewn landscape is virtually deserted.

In its most elaborate form the main chamber (*huzrah* or *estanah*) resembled the prayer-hall of a mosque. It was raised on a huge platform and contained a stone cenotaph in the center of the floor, while the body was placed in a crypt (*maqbarah* or *takhana*) below at garden level. The Taj Mahal (c.1632–c.1654) at Agra built by Shah Jehan for his dead wife is widely regarded as the most perfect of all Muslim tombs. The main hall is square in plan and the building's width is equal to its height. The height of the facade equals that of the dome, which swells outward from its base and is capped with a finial. The effect of absolute tranquility induced by the perfect proportions is emphasized by the symmetry of surrounding buildings and gardens. Islamic architecture in India generally replaced the glazed-tile finish of Persian models with materials such as marble and red sandstone. The Taj Mahal is faced in pure white Makrana marble that takes on different tones of light according to the time of day, sometimes seeming as translucent as pearl. Shah Jehan planned a similar tomb in black marble for himself across the river, but this was never built and he was buried alongside his beloved consort.

BELOW *At Malinalco, southwest of Tenochtitlán, the Aztecs carved into the mountainside and set womblike temples into the rock. This inner chamber was created as part of a temple specifically for soldiers—men who were expected to kill and be killed for the gods.*

Gateways to another realm

The hope of an afterlife is clearly expressed in the design and location of some burial chambers. Oval burial mounds built 2,000 years ago in central Africa, and topped by standing stones, are sited near springs so that the dead would never be far from water. At Newgrange, a great tomb constructed near the Boyne River in Ireland during the third millennium BCE (see pages 234–235), rays from the rising Sun at the winter solstice find their way through an opening above the entrance for a brief moment—perhaps intended to provide light for the dead on the darkest day of the year.

The choice of burial in the ground in most of the world's cultures is perhaps significant as well as practical. A number of cultures believed that humans originally emerged from within the earth, so to return there on the first stage of a voyage to the afterlife appeared to reflect the same recurring cycle evident in nature. In the ancient world the cult of Mithra celebrated this notion that the end of human life was but the beginning of another journey, in step with the rhythms of the natural world.

The Romans who were cult-followers of Mithra, the ancient Persian god of light, performed their rituals in dark caves and subterranean chambers, some of which still survive. This setting was determined by their belief that Mithra had slain a great ox in a cave after emerging from a rock with a sword and a flaming torch, and then making peace with the Sun. The slaughter of the bull symbolized how life emerged from death in the womblike darkness of the earth, for the blood and body of the beast were believed to be the source of all animals and plants. Every Mithraeum, or temple of Mithra, was a gloomy refuge that brought together images of life and death, darkness and light, Earth and sky: the bull was carved on the altar, and on the ceiling appeared imagery of the Sun, Moon, and planets. Worshipers gathered in the Mithraeum consumed the blood and flesh of a sacrificial bull in the hope of gaining immortality.

Megaliths for the Departed

The standing stone is perhaps the simplest form of funerary architecture, but its meaning may be highly complex. The Sora people of India use architecture to express the continuity of lineage. The main housepost symbolizes the link from ancestors to descendants, and offerings are made at its foot. Immediately after cremation a person's ashes are covered by a thatched roof on model houseposts. People are afraid to approach this temporary house, as the deceased is still a dangerous ghost.

The deceased becomes a full ancestor only after a series of rites, beginning with the "planting" of an upright memorial stone among the lineage's group of standing stones. Fed at this stone with wine and the blood of sacrificed buffalo, the dead person gives his or her name to a new baby in return. The stone summarizes the full range of the dead person's needs; the buffalo are not only food but are also used for ploughing in the underworld. Sometimes the buffalo and the stone would be anointed and addressed as though they were the dead person.

An early expression of the Christian cult of the dead was the catacomb (subterranean cemetery) in which funeral feasts (with a Eucharist) were held on the burial day and on anniversaries. The greatest network of catacombs in the Mediterranean area is that of the Christian cemeteries dug out of the soft volcanic tufa under Rome. These form a maze of underground galleries on many levels, lined with rows of rectangular niches, in which bodies were laid wrapped in shrouds and coated with lime. Occasional larger recesses served as family vaults.

The earliest catacombs date back to the second century CE. Although the persecution of Christians continued until the early fourth century, the pagan

Toraja Rock Tombs

Sulawesi, Indonesia

Among the Toraja people of Sulawesi in Indonesia a series of rites must be held before a deceased person can become a benign ancestor who protects the rice crop. Although the Toraja community is today predominantly of Christian religion, traditional funerals are still the usual custom.

The corpse is carefully clothed, and sacrificed buffalo are offered. A menhir (standing stone) is erected for each person who dies, and is placed with the other such menhirs that have accumulated over the generations, forming rows or circles reminiscent of the ancient megaliths of northwestern Europe. The body is kept near the menhirs in a "corpse-tower" constructed out of wood and bamboo in the form of a Toraja house, with a saddle-shaped roof and upswept gable ends. The corpse-tower is built on several levels and the corpse is laid on the first floor. During the funeral rites the death-priest and his female attendants sit on the second floor. Ritual dances are performed in front of the tower.

RIGHT *Standing stones of deceased Toraja people stand sentinel near a corpse-tower of a recently departed villager. The tower imitates the form of the traditional Toraja house.*

OPPOSITE BELOW *A funeral procession winds its way in front of the houses. The women are bearing gifts for the family of the deceased. The exchange of gifts at funerals creates endless cycles of social obligation, thus reinforcing the continuation of traditional customs. Funeral parties often last for days and are lavish affairs, frequently involving hundreds of people. During the rituals animals are sacrificed, so that their souls may accompany the deceased into the afterlife.*

The corpse is then interred in a family tomb that has been cut into a cliff-face. These chambers have square entrances sealed with wooden doors and are reached by means of bamboo ladders. The cutting of the rock is carried out by specialists. The family places an effigy of the deceased, called a *tau-tau*, outside the tomb—this joins the other *tau-taus* leaning on a balustrade and surveying the rice fields that stretch into the distance. The tomb is referred to as the "house from which no smoke climbs." In Toraja cosmology, ascending smoke is associated with the east and with auspicious rituals of fertility, while descending smoke is associated with the west and with the recently dead.

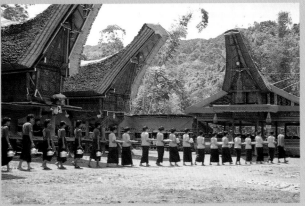

ABOVE *The corpse is eventually interred in a chamber cut in a sheer cliff-face, and an almost-life-size effigy or tau-tau is placed nearby. The tau-tau represents the deceased and is fed with offerings of food and betel-nut. The chambers are sealed with wooden doors, some of which are ornately carved or painted; after the corpse has been interred the doors are often hung with the deceased person's belongings. These burial chambers are family graves, and cutting them out of the rock can take months. The bamboo ladder by which the graves are reached is later removed, leaving them inaccessible once more.*

Ship Burials

According to many cultures, the dead had to travel at least part of the journey to their home in the afterlife by boat, sometimes encountering a figure such as Charon, the grim-faced boatman who, according to ancient Greek mythology, would ferry them across the Styx River and into the underworld.

In a number of cultures the boats needed by the dead were provided as part of the burial goods. Egyptian kings and noblemen sometimes had cedar boats buried alongside their tombs in the hope that this would enable them to accompany the Sun god on his daily journey across the sky (thought to be composed of water). In northern Europe it was commonly believed that an afterlife existed across the sea. In Viking belief, the world of humans, Midgard, was surrounded by oceans, separating it from Niflheim, the land of the dead, below, and Asgard, the realm of the gods, above. Valhalla, Odin's great hall for slain warrior heroes, was in Asgard.

Anglo-Saxon and Viking kings and chieftains often chose to be buried inside the boats that they believed would carry them to eternity. In the late 1930s archaeologists excavated a low mound at Sutton Hoo on the coast of Suffolk in eastern England, and discovered a ship-grave of the Anglo-Saxon period. The ship (only the impression of which remained) had been more than 25 ft. (82 m) long, with a hull of overlapping planks. Although no visible trace of a body was found, the burial yielded a fabulous treasure of gold, silver, bronze, iron, and precious stones (all of which had been used to decorate weaponry), armor, clothing, a lyre, drinking flasks and other utensils, coins, and jewelry. This was clearly the grave of an individual of high status, probably royal. It is widely held to be that of Rædwald, a king of the East Angles who died *c.*624CE.

Romans seem to have avoided desecrating them even when their location was known. Modern exploration of the catacombs dates from the sixteenth century, and new ones are still sometimes discovered during excavations for the foundations of buildings and underground railroads.

The need to preserve the body was motivated by the Christian expectation of bodily resurrection at the Last Judgment. Catacombs were also used for secret prayer-meetings, memorial services, and the celebration of the Eucharist. Believers tended the bodies of their own dead, while the community paid particular care to the bodies of saints and martyrs. Painted decorations often depict the raising of the dead Lazarus from his cave, and one of the many graffiti states, "There is light in this darkness, there is music in these tombs."

Burial and worship

Sacred buildings are seen in many traditions as being the means of salvation or rebirth for the dead. Thus the tomb and the temple are often combined: in India, Muslim tombs often have a *mihrab* (prayerniche) built into the western wall of the main hall, just as in a mosque.

The shape of tombs may express a belief in rebirth, as in the megalithic passage-grave (see page 136). The sarcophagus, as container of the body, can resemble both a womb and the entire cosmos. To emphasize such cosmic significance, Egyptian coffins often had an image of the sky goddess Nut painted on the inside of the lid.

In Mesoamerican architecture the sarcophagus of the seventh-century Mayan king Pacal was shaped like a uterus. The pyramidal Temple of the Inscriptions (see pages 165–168) beneath which Pacal's tomb is situated reflects the Mayan conception of the cosmos, with nine outer terraces symbolizing the nine layers of the underworld, and thirteen internal strata corresponding to the thirteen levels of the heavens.

A belief in the continuing power, as well as the needs, of the dead person underlies much tomb architecture. Christian shrines often contain sculpted effigies of saints, and the embalmed body of a saint may even be enshrined inside an altar.

Some of the most spectacular tombs ever constructed are Egypt's pyramids. The early tombs were merely pits in the earth, enclosed open-air courtyards beneath which lay the chambers of the dead; any superstructure above ground has disappeared. From the First Dynasty (*c*.3000–*c*.2800BCE) this chamber began to be covered with a long, low mud-brick platform, now called a mastaba. Many of these are found at Saqqara, the necropolis of Memphis, the site of the best-preserved example of the next stage of development, the step pyramid of Djoser. The greatest of the later "true" pyramids are those built at Giza in the Fourth Dynasty (*c*.2625–*c*.2500BCE) by pharaohs Khufu, Khafre, and Menkaure (Cheops, Chephren, and Mycerinus). Pyramids were sealed after burial, and worship of the dead pharaoh took place in a temple at the foot of the pyramid. The mastaba tombs of other royalty and courtiers were near by, sometimes laid out in rows like streets.

Although the pyramids remain mysterious, the evidence suggests that the buildings bring together ideas of permanence and rebirth by using astronomy to support the idea of a divine kingship. The Great Pyramid's square base is set accurately to the cardinal directions, as is the inner burial chamber holding the mummified body of the pharaoh. The nearby Sphinx to the southwest is also precisely oriented and its eyes gaze out at the equinox sunrise. The pharaoh was thought to travel to the underworld in a boat and, like the Sun god, to be reborn. Deliberately located near the pyramids were pits designed to hold boats for this purpose.

Ancient Egypt's pharaohs appear to have practiced a religion oriented to the stars' cycles of disappearance and reappearance. Two narrow shafts lead out at angles from the burial chamber of Khufu's Great Pyramid; the northern one was aligned to the star

ABOVE *A group of stones arranged to form a Viking longship forms part of an ancient necropolis of so-called boat graves in Sweden. In many of the Scandinavian sites such as this, a good proportion of the graves are shaped like boats, with most aligned north to south. These "stone boats" were normally for the lesser ranks of warriors—chiefs tended to be cremated in their own, magnificently appointed, sea-going wooden vessels.*

Thuban in its uppermost arc, while the southern one was oriented to Zeta Orionis, one of the three stars of Orion's belt which were linked to the god Osiris, who symbolized the cycle of birth, life, death, and resurrection. Thuban was the Pole Star of its day—continually visible and thus "imperishable." The pyramid thus served to allow the pharaoh's soul to travel to the heavens and perform its duties.

In the modern era, burial has become increasingly secularized. The problem of where to bury the new mass urban population led to one proposal, in 1829, to build a pyramid for the people in London which would be four times higher than St Paul's Cathedral and hold ten million coffins. This pyramid was not built, but the need for more space, together with new ideas of hygiene, led by the late nineteenth century to landscaped suburban cemeteries with only a small

Newgrange

Ireland

Newgrange is a massive chambered edifice built more than 5,000 years ago on a bend of the Boyne River in County Meath, Ireland. It shares its landscape with two large passage-graves at Dowth to the east and Knowth to the west, as well as a number of smaller earthen enclosures, and it is thought that Newgrange also served as a tomb or passage-grave.

Inside Newgrange a narrow passage leads to the main chamber, which opens up into a corbeled, or beehive-shaped, vault containing three flat-roofed chambers, which together with the passage itself form a cross plan. Bone fragments of at least four people have been found in the tomb floor.

In 1972 Professor M. O'Kelly discovered a "roof-box" above the entrance—that is, a structure positioned so as to allow a beam of sunlight at sunrise on midwinter day to fall on the triple-spiral design in the burial chamber, more than 60 ft. (18 m) inside. Newgrange is just one of a number of Neolithic chambered mounds whose interiors can become illuminated at particular times of the year, and this feature lends weight to arguments that the structure has inbuilt astronomical aspects.

Newgrange must have remained significant in Celtic times, because objects inspired by or imported from Roman Britain, and coins, have been found in the tomb. They were probably offerings to the spirits of the place. These prehistoric mounds entered Irish myth and folklore as *sidhe* or fairy-mounds, the dwellings of fairies and divinities. Newgrange was said to be the home of Oenghus, the god of love.

LEFT *Many stones in and around the mound bear geometric patterns. The entrance (seen here) is behind a large kerbstone covered in spirals and lozenges, which were pecked into the surface of the stones with flint tools. The spiral has been interpreted as the soul progressing through death to ultimate peace and rebirth; it might also be the Sun or Moon, or the Sun's rays during a year.*

RIGHT *Newgrange is one of the few megalithic monuments with a clear astronomical connection. At the end of the passage—60 ft. (18 m) long— shown here the central chamber is lit up at dawn at the winter solstice by a shaft of sunlight that penetrates through a gap—the "roof-box"— above the entranceway.*

ABOVE *The mound of turf and stones comprising the tomb at Newgrange rises almost 34 ft. (11 m) above its surroundings and is nearly 300 ft. (90 m) across. Skirting the base are nearly 100 rough-hewn stones laid end to end, the largest being 16 ft. (5 m) long.*

BELOW *As the plan shows, Newgrange is surrounded by a circle of standing stones. Thirty-five stones once made up the circle, but less than half have survived, the largest being 8 ft. (2.4 m) high. It is not known whether this circle was built at the same time as the mound.*

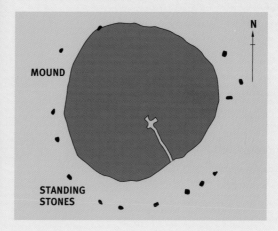

MOUND

N

STANDING
STONES

chapel attached. Today these cemeteries are being replaced by the even more hygienic crematoria—a minimalist approach to funeral architecture.

Stairways to the heavens

The middle of the third millennium BCE was an Egyptian golden age, reflected in the mass of royal pyramids built on the west bank of the Nile. Some of these buildings were the places from which the pharaohs, whose mummified corpses were laid inside them, began their journey into the afterlife. Egyptian texts suggest the reason for the form and scale of the pyramids: the spirits of the deceased kings would use the rays of the Sun, whose geometry the pyramids echo, as a ramp whereby to reach the sky.

Powers of the Pyramid

In the Middle Ages star-worshiping cults conducted rituals in cavernous chambers deep in the heart of the Great Pyramid of Giza, seeing the vast monument as a source of wisdom. In the 1970s and 1980s many Westerners became intrigued by esoteric theories and attempted to harness the allegedly mystical power of the pyramid by building their own pyramids, usually from cardboard, plastic, or some other easily obtainable modern material. Believing that the shape of the space inside the pyramid contained the secret of its power, they would sit under the pyramids while meditating, praying, or undergoing therapy. A Czech radio engineer, Karel Drbal, claimed that storing razor blades under a cardboard pyramid kept them sharp for up to 200 shaves, and took out a Czech patent for his "Cheops Pyramid Razor Blade Sharpener." Others were convinced that vegetables would stay fresh longer, or dehydrate without spoiling, if stored inside a pyramid-shaped box.

In the thirteenth century BCE the impact of these monuments was compromised when the white polished limestone that originally covered their steep sides began to be quarried for building material. Yet today the pyramids are still hugely impressive, both for their engineering achievement and for their connotations of spiritual energy.

The architectural form that eventually gave rise to the Egyptian pyramids had its inception as the simple mastaba, an enclosed open-air courtyard beneath which lay the chambers of the dead. Almost 5,000 years ago, during the reign of Djoser in the Third Dynasty, a celebrated architect, Imhotep, designed a radically new tomb for the king at Saqqara: by piling a sequence of six successively smaller mastabas one on top of the other he created a step-pyramid. For the next 500 years step-pyramids grew in size and their steps got smaller, and therefore "smoother," until in the reign of Khufu, the greatest of all these monuments rose out of the sands at Giza. Khufu's Great Pyramid, the focal point of a huge funerary complex, rose to a commanding height of 481 ft. (147 m).

In Mesopotamia, from the late third to the first millennium BCE, millions of bricks were baked and cemented with bitumen in order to form pyramidic models of the cosmos called ziggurats. The ziggurat was a step-pyramid with corners set at the cardinal directions and a main staircase running from the base to a shrine at the top. It may have been seen as a symbol of the primeval mound that was believed to have existed before the Earth and sky were separated at the beginning of creation; if so, it may have been looked on as an abode of the gods.

After the Near Eastern sites, the world's best-known pyramids are those of Mesoamerica, which are usually built of earth and faced with stone. Typically they are stepped, with a platform or temple structure on the summit. At Chichén Itzá, a Maya city in Mexico that flourished from the late tenth to thirteenth centuries CE (see pages 142–143), the Castillo pyramid rises almost 82 ft. (25 m) in height. Its nine terraces, symbolizing the nine underground

worlds of the Mayan cosmos, lead up to a simple rectangular temple. Priests would ascend the pyramid's steep staircase to perform sacrifices to their gods. Bas-reliefs found here depict bearded men who are believed to be priests of the snake god Quetzalcóatl.

Solar orientations have been identified in many Egyptian and Mesoamerican pyramids, reflecting an interest in astronomy and the calendar. Similarities between pyramids from such different cultural contexts also underline crucial engineering requirements: the pyramid form combined great height with structural stability. Massive in scale, these monuments provided evidence of the great power of the elites who built them.

ABOVE *The 9th-century Pyramid of the Magician at Uxmal in Yucatan's Puuc region is so called because it was said to have been built overnight by a sorcerer. It has two temples at the top and is unusual because its base is oval in shape.*

OVERLEAF *The 8th-century Temple II at Tikal, in the lowland rainforest. The view from the central plaza shows how the buildings rise above the forest in imitation of mountain-tops, the dwelling places of the souls of the ancestors (the nearest real peaks were hundreds of miles away). Temple II has three layers, which correspond to the Three Stones of Creation— linked to the maize god, who was resurrected after being killed, and three of the stars of the belt in the constellation Orion.*

The Great Pyramid of Khufu

Giza, Egypt

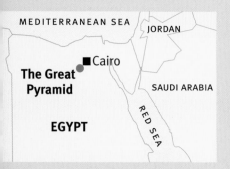

The Great Pyramid of Khufu (or Cheops) rises from the desert sands of a royal cemetery built during the Fourth Dynasty (*c.*2625–*c.*2500BCE) at Giza, on the outskirts of present-day Cairo.

The edifice is constructed out of massive blocks of limestone, each weighing more than two tons, which were chiseled into shape by gangs of stonemasons, then dragged from a local quarry to the pyramid site along great causeways and ramps. According to the Greek historian Herodotus (*c.*485–425BCE), the pyramid took thirty years to complete. Generations of workers laid more than two million blocks on a base 756 ft. (230 m) square to achieve the pyramid's original height of 481 ft. (147 m).

Little is known of the life of the pharaoh Khufu, but his name appears on monuments across Egypt, and members of his entourage erected their own temples and tombs around his pyramid. The second-largest of the three pyramids at Giza contained the remains of his son, Khafre (or Chephren).

Like all Egyptian kings, Khufu was revered as divine, and people wore amulets inscribed with his name. His reign was still recalled in the Ptolemaic period, more than 2,000 years after his death, but his pyramid received less respect. It was broken into and looted, probably during unrest that occurred when the Old Kingdom collapsed (*c.*2130BCE). In the Middle Ages the pyramids at Giza were quarried as a source of stone for new mosques in nearby Cairo.

LEFT *The passage leading from the entrance to the pharaoh Khufu's burial chamber is a massive gallery, 154 ft. (47 m) long and 30 ft. (9 m) high, with a corbeled roof. There are also several cramped passageways that lead to the burial chambers as well as a tunnel cut by the Muslim Caliph Mamun during the 9th century.*

RIGHT *The Great Sphinx, a statue of a human-headed lion, is thought to have been built in order to guard the pyramid of Khafre (c.2520BCE). It remains a mysterious figure and a byword for inscrutability. Both the Sphinx and the pyramids are incorporated into the Masonic emblem, and in their initiation ceremonies Masons call on the pyramids' sacred power. According to ancient occult lore, a pyramid represents life and spiritual resurrection. It unites the triangle (a symbol of cosmic trinities such as birth, life, and death) and the square (a symbol of the four quarters of the universe).*

ABOVE *The pyramids at Giza are the only one of the Seven Wonders of the Ancient World still extant. Plundering of limestone has left the Great Pyramid 30 ft. (9 m) shorter than it was originally. The image of Khufu's burial monument (center, above) and its perfect geometric shape have become worldwide symbols of the heroic defiance of death, the presumption of the living, the endurance of civilizations, the irretrievable nature of past faiths, and the psychic power of abstract geometry. The entrance to the pyramid gives way to a sloping passage, at the bottom of which is an unfinished chamber: the intended burial place. Before completing this chamber, the builders apparently changed their plans and built an ascending passage. They then built a third one, rising almost to the center of the pyramid. This was Khufu's final burial place.*

Time chart

The interval between the development of modern humans some 100,000 years ago and the present day is but a tiny fraction of the lifetime of the planet, but in that minuscule period of cosmic time humankind's influence on the Earth has been profound: in the past 10,000 years alone agriculture and cities have transformed the landscape. The chart plots some of the most significant strands of human culture.

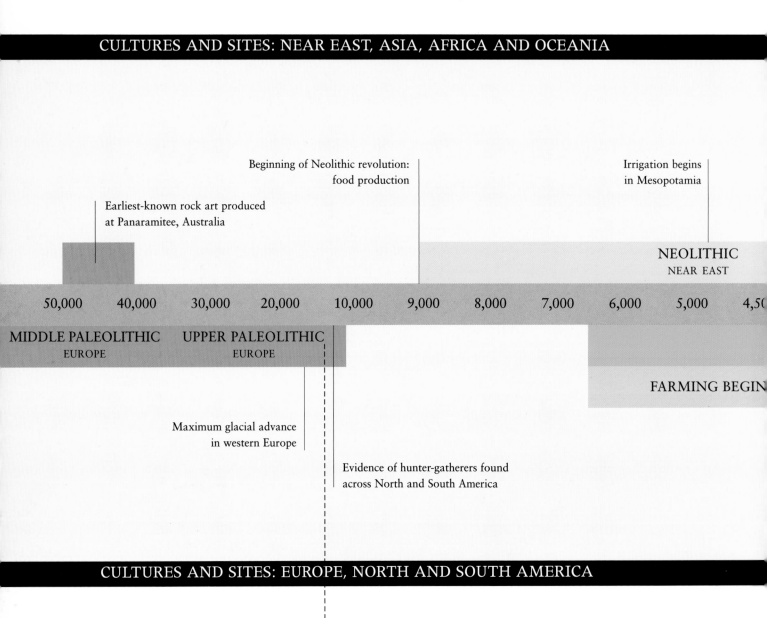

CULTURES AND SITES: NEAR EAST, ASIA, AFRICA AND OCEANIA

Beginning of Neolithic revolution: food production

Irrigation begins in Mesopotamia

Earliest-known rock art produced at Panaramitee, Australia

NEOLITHIC
NEAR EAST

| 50,000 | 40,000 | 30,000 | 20,000 | 10,000 | 9,000 | 8,000 | 7,000 | 6,000 | 5,000 | 4,50 |

MIDDLE PALEOLITHIC
EUROPE

UPPER PALEOLITHIC
EUROPE

FARMING BEGIN

Maximum glacial advance in western Europe

Evidence of hunter-gatherers found across North and South America

CULTURES AND SITES: EUROPE, NORTH AND SOUTH AMERICA

The cave paintings of Lascaux, southwestern France, c.15,000BCE (see pages 50–51)

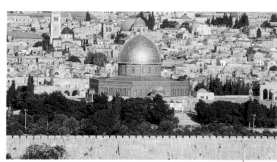

*The Great Pyramid
at Giza, Egypt,
c.2500BCE
(see pages 240–241)*

*The Dome of the
Rock, Jerusalem,
c.685–c.691CE
(see pages 192–193)*

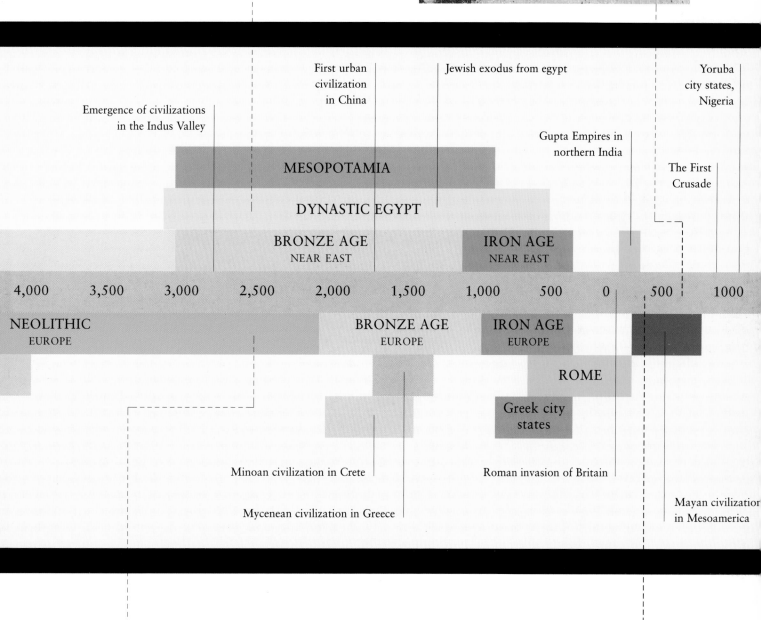

First urban
civilization
in China

Jewish exodus from egypt

Yoruba
city states,
Nigeria

Emergence of civilizations
in the Indus Valley

Gupta Empires in
northern India

The First
Crusade

MESOPOTAMIA

DYNASTIC EGYPT

BRONZE AGE
NEAR EAST

IRON AGE
NEAR EAST

| 4,000 | 3,500 | 3,000 | 2,500 | 2,000 | 1,500 | 1,000 | 500 | 0 | 500 | 1000 |

NEOLITHIC
EUROPE

BRONZE AGE
EUROPE

IRON AGE
EUROPE

ROME

Greek city
states

Minoan civilization in Crete

Roman invasion of Britain

Mycenean civilization in Greece

Mayan civilization
in Mesoamerica

*Stonehenge, England,
c.2500BCE
(see pages 134–135)*

*Nazca lines, Peru,
c.1–c.650CE
(see pages
106–107)*

Fact files

NATURAL PHENOMENA

Earthquakes and tidal waves

The scale of destruction caused by an earthquake can be awe-inspiring: a landscape unchanged in the history of a people may be broken up, lifted high above its accustomed level, or riven with cracks.

Striking suddenly and violently, earthquakes have often been attributed to the wrath of powerful gods. For example, for the Japanese, who inhabit an area of great seismic activity, tremors and quakes are traditionally said to be a manifestation of the storm god Susano. The ancient Greeks, who also lived in a region where earthquakes were commonplace, believed them to be the work of the brother of Zeus, the sea and storm god Poseidon, to whom they sometimes gave the title Enosicthon ("Earth-shaker").

The most famous earthquake of classical mythology destroyed the civilization of Atlantis, a great continent which, according to Plato, existed far to the west beyond the Strait of Gibraltar, 9,000 years before his time. Atlantis, whose rulers were of divine descent, flourished for centuries but fell into moral decay. Then "there occurred violent earthquakes and floods" that put an end to Atlantis "in one day and night of disaster."

Numerous theories have been proposed to account for Atlantis as a place that really existed. However, the story is probably best seen as belonging to a whole group of myths, in many cultures, that relate the rise, flowering, and decline of a world or race. Eventually the gods' anger at the degeneracy of the people can no longer be withheld, and the corruption is swept away in a divine cataclysm. In such stories natural phenomena frequently provide instruments of divine retribution.

Earthquakes, as omens, can also signify momentous change of a political or religious nature. At a fundamental level, whatever our religious inclinations, earthquakes remind us of planetary perspectives on human life, the infinitesimal speck made by human history on the geophysical timescale. They also provide a focus for meditations on chance, transience, and the value of life.

The Earth's surface is in a permanent state of flux caused by the slow but constant movement of tectonic plates, the individual sections that form the Earth's crust. According to the theory of "continental drift," first proposed by the German geophysicist Alfred Wegener (1880–1930) in 1912, there was originally one huge land mass or "supercontinent," which he called Pangaea (All Earth). In the course of 200 million years, Pangaea broke into several pieces along great geological faults (lines of weakness in the Earth's crust where the inner molten core can break through), and its components drifted apart. These faults are either divergent (pushing apart), characterized by deep trenches mainly in the ocean floor, or convergent (colliding so that one plate slides under another), characterized by "fold" mountain ranges where one plate has buckled under the pressure from another pushing against it.

Earthquakes occur when volcanoes erupt along fault lines or when adjacent plates shift suddenly along part of the fault that divides them. Most tremors are not detected, but others cause devastation, destroying human settlements, triggering avalanches, diverting rivers, and creating crevasses and new faults in the Earth's surface.

A ship at sea near the epicenter of an earthquake may experience little more than a sharp jolt, because the most powerful shock waves are far below the surface of the water. The deep ocean presents little resistance to seismic waves, which may travel thousands of miles without diminishing in power. As they approach land, they encounter greater resistance and slow down abruptly, but their tremendous momentum causes water to pile up to a great height: in 1993, a giant tidal wave or *tsunami* in the Sea of Japan rose nearly 100 ft. (30 m) above sea-level. The *tsunami* that struck the tip of the Kamchatka peninsula in Siberia in 1737 was 230 ft. (70 m) high.

Like earthquakes, *tsunamis* may also be triggered by a volcanic eruption. When the island of Krakatoa, to the west (not the east, as Hollywood would have it) of Java, blew up in August 1883, the explosion was heard 2,500 miles (4,000 km) away and set off a *tsunami* 115 ft. (35 m) high that devastated low-lying islands and coastal communities along the Sunda Strait, including one village 10 miles (16 km) inland.

Thunder and lightning

In many cultures thunderstorms have been associated with powerful male divinities. For example, among the Yoruba of West Africa it is said that the god of thunder, Shango, was the greatest of the Yoruba warrior-monarchs. In Hindu myth, thunder and lightning are weapons of the warrior god Indra, the chief of the Vedic (early Hindu) pantheon who was known as Vajri (Wielder of the Thunderbolt); the *Rig Veda* describes how he used his thunderbolts to kill the demon Vritra.

Similarly, thunderbolts were said to be the main weapons of Zeus (Jupiter), the supreme god of the Greco-Roman pantheon, for whom they were made in the underground forges of the smith-god Hephaistos (Vulcan) by the Cyclopes. One myth relates how Zeus used a thunderbolt to kill Asklepios, the demi-god of healing, because he raised a man from the dead; in revenge Apollo killed the Cyclopes.

In Native American myth the spirit of thunder and lightning is widely envisaged as a great bird, the Thunderbird, which resembles a giant eagle. Lightning is caused by the flashing of the Thunderbird's eyes, thunder by the beating of its wings. Like other thunder deities, the beast is fierce but also a protector of humanity against evil forces: just as Thor was said to have fought malevolent giants, in some areas of North America thunderstorms were believed to be the Thunderbird's battles against malign underworld beings.

Western scientists began to understand thunderstorms in the eighteenth century. In 1752, Benjamin Franklin in the USA and M. d'Alibard in France, working independently, flew kites in storms and demonstrated that thunder and lightning were electrical phenomena. Within a raincloud, warm, moist air rises, sometimes very rapidly. High in the clouds the air condenses, freezes, and falls to Earth as hail; in the lower reaches of the cloud, the hail melts and turns to rain. But as the prevailing winds grow stronger, the rain or hail may be blown up again with violence, freezing rapidly to create hailstones that may be quite large and fall with considerable force. This process generates vast amounts of electricity, giving the cloud an electrical charge. In a process not yet fully understood, this is released as lightning, a huge, negatively charged spark which seeks a positive contact elsewhere—most destructively, on the ground below.

In 55BCE the Roman author Lucretius proposed that thunder was the crashing of clouds, but modern science suggests that it is caused by the sudden, massive expansion of the air in the path of a lightning bolt, a single one of which may be several miles long. It is common to distinguish forked lightning from sheet lightning, but the sheet effect is simply the result of the bolt being obscured by clouds. The human eye can only detect a single flash of lightning, but high-speed photography has shown that a bolt in fact consists of a series of rapid descending and ascending strokes which occur in a few thousandths of a second. Lightning is most common in thunderstorms, but it can also accompany snowstorms, sandstorms, tornadoes, and waterspouts. It has even been reported in clear air: a literal "bolt from the blue."

Ash, pumice, and other material ejected from erupting volcanoes also generate enough electrical energy to cause lightning. When submarine volcanic eruptions created the island of Surtsey near Iceland in November 1963, violent explosions hurled clouds of ash into the sky at 200 mph (320 kph). These eruptions sometimes blazed with short, zig-zag bursts of lightning.

Lightning is also manifested as red, orange, or yellow balls of electricity lasting for a few seconds, which have been seen hanging in mid-air or falling from clouds to the ground, sometimes bouncing when they make contact. According to one theory, the location of some prehistoric stone circles in Britain and elsewhere may have been influenced by sightings of ball lightning. At such places the phenomenon may be connected with the local topography, geology, or geomagnetism.

Hurricanes and floods

Storms and floods are the most commonplace of all natural disasters, and feature prominently in the mythology of peoples on every continent.

The word "hurricane" comes from Mesoamerican myth: the name of the Maya storm god, Huracan, was adopted into Spanish as the word for a great storm, and passed thence into other European languages (English hurricane, French *ouragan*, and German *orkan*).

Storm divinities such as Poseidon and Susano are figures of awesome power who embody the forces of disorder and turmoil. However, as controllers of the rains they may also be bringers of fertility; an example of this dual role is the ancient Canaanite storm god Baal.

In myth, floods may appear as disasters of cosmic proportions which wipe out the human race, often as a divine punishment for people's transgressions. In the Jewish and Christian traditions, the most famous flood narrative is the Biblical story of Noah. The account in Genesis probably derives from the deluge myths of the ancient civilizations of Mesopotamia, a region prone to serious flooding where the great rivers Tigris and Euphrates meet. There are striking parallels in these accounts: the flood, caused by rainstorms, is divinely decreed to punish sinful humans, but one man—Noah in the Hebrew Scriptures; Atrahasis, Utnapishtim, and Ziusudra in the three older accounts that are extant—survives the disaster by building a ship and, after the waters have receded, begins repopulating the world.

The Middle Eastern stories may have influenced the Greek myth of Deucalion, the son of Prometheus, and his wife Pyrrha, who were the sole survivors of a cosmic deluge sent by Zeus. They may also have some connection with the Indian myth of Manu, the first man, who was forewarned by a great fish of an imminent cataclysmic storm and flood and survived by constructing a boat. But such stories are common anywhere that is prone to floods.

The idea of a new cosmos emerging after the destruction of the old by storm and flood is not confined to the Old World: according to the Aztec myth of the Five Suns (worlds), the second ended when its presiding deity, Quetzalc atl, was carried off by a hurricane. The (present) Fifth Sun arose after the fourth was annihilated by a flood and the people turned into fish.

In some cultures the flood may be caused by the misdemeanour of an individual. For example, the Chewong people of Malaya believe that disastrous inundations occur if a person mocks an animal, thereby provoking the anger of the primal underworld serpent, the controller of the floodwaters. The Aborigines of northern Australia also have numerous origin myths in which a great serpent identified or associated with the rainbow causes a storm and flood after being angered by the actions of an ancestral hero or heroine. The flood sweeps away the previous society and landscape. It is believed that such myths may be rooted in the rise in sea-levels after the last ice age.

Storms and hurricanes arise from the movements within the Earth's atmosphere as the Sun heats its surface, causing wind as hot air rises and cooler air sinks. Some of the strongest winds are generated in association with cyclones—powerful rotating wind systems. Cyclones occur worldwide but are particularly prominent in tropical regions during late summer and autumn, when very warm and moist areas of high pressure run into cold low-pressure areas coming from the north or south. At the point of collision between the two air masses, the Coriolis effect (a spinning motion caused by the rotation of the Earth) causes a cyclone. Cyclonic winds circulate counterclockwise in the northern hemisphere and clockwise in the southern hemisphere.

The lower the pressure at the center of the cyclone, the stronger the winds swirling into it. Around the focal point of the cyclone, a calm and cloudless low pressure area known as the "eye," the rotating winds are at their fiercest, forming a spinning cylinder of wind known as the "eye wall." The combination of violent rising winds and great humidity engenders the dense raincloud formation and precipitation characteristic of cyclonic systems.

A severe cyclone containing winds of at least 75 mph (120 kph) is described by various names, depending on location: in the Atlantic, the Caribbean, and Gulf of Mexico it is called a hurricane, in the Indian Ocean a cyclone, and in the China Sea and western Pacific a typhoon. These giant swirling storms may be up to 1,200 miles (1,920 km) wide, with winds averaging more than 100 mph (160 kph). In the strongest storms, sustained gusts may even exceed 200 mph (320 kph). Tornadoes may also accompany a hurricane.

When the eye of a hurricane, usually around 20–25 miles (30–40 km) in diameter, passes over, the violent winds and rain cease temporarily—only to return with equal force when the other side of the eye wall strikes.

Bangladesh is particularly vulnerable to cyclones from the Bay of Bengal, as most of the country is less than 52 ft. (16 m.) above sea-level. The worst destruction is the result of the "tidal surge" that is caused by fierce winds whipping up the sea to many feet above its normal level. On November 12 and 13, 1970, a devastating cyclone brought winds of over 150 mph (240 kph) and caused a tidal surge with waves up to 23 ft. (7 m) high. At least 300,000 people perished.

Whirlwinds and whirlpools

One of the most awe-inspiring of meteorological phenomena is the vortex: a tight, rotating funnel of water or wind.

In large bodies of water a vortex may form as a whirlpool, which develops when currents collide at sea, sometimes resulting in great swirling eddies or a maelstrom (from the Dutch, "whirling stream")—a giant whirlpool capable of sucking ships into the depths of the sea. In Greek myth this phenomenon is represented by the female monster Charybdis, the offspring of the Earth goddess Gaia and the sea god Poseidon. Charybdis, said to infest the Strait of Messina between Sicily and mainland Italy, sucked in water three times a day in a terrifying whirlpool with enough force to swallow any ships nearby. The hero Odysseus survived an encounter with Charybdis by clinging to a tree branch as his ship disappeared into the vortex.

Whirlpools pose a regular threat to ships in areas such as the Naruto Strait (between the Sea of Japan and the Pacific), the Hebrides and Orkney islands (Scotland), and the Lofoten Islands (northern Norway).

Vortices in the air arise as a result of the Coriolis effect, and the process of their formation is similar to that of the biggest storms and hurricanes. Heated surface air rises and may begin to spiral, especially when it has to flow around an obstacle. This movement creates a twisting column of air that develops a downdraft in the center. As the whirlwind moves, it picks up dirt and litter and becomes visible as a cloud of dust, from 3 ft. (1 m) to several hundred feet high. Such whirlwinds are especially common during dry seasons in tropical regions amid the heat of the day. They range from "dust devils" and other relatively gentle eddies to large towering tornadoes of immense destructive power. Dust devils are small whirlwinds that occur where the temperature of the Earth's surface is high, as in tropical regions.

A tornado (derived from the Spanish word *tronado*, "thunderstorm") forms beneath a thundercloud, in areas where high humidity combines with zones of warm and cool air. A fast, narrow updraft of air rises from the Earth's warm surface into a thundercloud where the temperature may be at 32°F (0°C). The Coriolis effect causes the updraft to spin, eventually giving rise to the funnel-shaped "twister." A tornado can also develop when a dust devil contacts a developing cumulus cloud overhead.

The conditions in which tornadoes form are typical of the northern hemisphere spring in general, and of the midwestern United States, northern India, northern Indochina, and China in particular. Smaller tornadoes also occur in southern Britain and mainland western Europe. Many of these tornadoes peter out before they develop fully, and about two-thirds of them exist for no more than three minutes.

When a tornado funnel touches ground it sucks most things lying in its path into the sky and scatters debris from its base. The exact speed of the winds inside one can only be estimated, as few measuring instruments will withstand a twister's onslaught.

Witnesses have described the noise of a tornado as resembling a giant swarm of bees or the roaring of jet engines. The few who have lived to tell of the interior of a tornado describe a whirling mass sparking constantly with lightning. The air pressure in the middle of the vortex is extremely low: buildings may explode with the rapid drop in pressure when a tornado strikes.

Twisters have been known to lift trains off railroads and to move entire houses some distance and set them down again. A tornado will also suck up water and fish from rivers and deposit them elsewhere.

The worst tornado on record hit Missouri on March 18, 1925, and traveled for 200 miles (350 km) through Missouri, Illinois, and Indiana, destroying towns and leaving 689 people dead. The parent cloud was so close to the ground that the funnel was not visible: one eyewitness described it as a strange fog rolling toward him under a boiling mass of cloud.

Tornadoes in mountain regions (so-called "mountainadoes") form when small vortices are magnified as they come into contact with cooler air flowing across the mountains. During one winter in Boulder, Colorado, a storm of these developed, each a huge spinning mass of snow about 100 ft. (30 m) across, generating winds of 90 mph (150 kph).

BUILDING TECHNIQUES

The sacred building

Until recent centuries, almost all large buildings had either a sacred or a royal purpose. To mobilize the wealth and labor necessary for construction required the authority of the state and of its divine king. In ancient civilizations the categories of secular and sacred, temple and palace were not as distinct as they are in the world today. The techniques of sacred architecture were thus those of any large-scale architecture, and the main challenges were in the struggle to achieve size and height in the face of the force of gravity.

Sacred architecture expresses ideas of the divine in material form, so that every aspect of style and structure tends to be intensely imbued with theological meaning. But a structure is constrained by the limitations of technology and materials and this is perhaps why many styles give a feeling, not simply of upward achievement, but of an effort behind this achievement which strains to the very limits of human capability. Not infrequently, architects overreached themselves and their towers collapsed.

The stylistic evolution of buildings is inseparable from their technical development. A dome, for example, will be supported in a way that reflects the integration of local styles and technology. Where there are no modern engineering models or computer simulations, each previous building serves as a model for the next and acts as a starting point from which to make minor adjustments and adaptations to local conditions and materials. However, style may lag behind technology: what was once a structural necessity often persists under a new technology as an element of ornamentation. The anthill shape of mud mosques is preserved in cement mosques, just as Greek architects continued to reproduce the ends of wooden beams in the triglyphs of the stone temple.

The plan

The ground-plan represents a building on a horizontal plane, showing its point of contact with the ground on which it stands. It is from here that the building's mass must thrust itself up against the forces of gravity. In sacred architecture, the plan is the god's-eye view, and indeed gods are often called architects, as if the universe itself were a huge building. Some plans, such as the mandala, are conceived as reproducing the shape of the universe.

But the plan is only two-dimensional. The third dimension—height—is indicated by elevation and section. The elevation shows an exterior facade from one particular point of view, while the section slices vertically through the interior of a building to show the sequence and proportions of the rooms inside. Many alternative elevations are possible for any given plan, as is shown by the greatly varied reconstructions proposed by archaeologists in cases where nothing has survived of a building except the foundations.

Plan, elevation, and section are related to the sense of sight, but they are primarily concepts. The full experience of a sacred building calls on all the senses as a person moves around through a series of rooms, corridors, courtyards, and halls or a succession of light and dark spaces, up into a dome or down into a crypt. Feelings of liberation or confinement can be enhanced by smells, the touch of stone, or the sounds of echoing footsteps and distant music.

So although the building is stationary it must be experienced in time, through a person's movement. Such movement is through two kinds of space, which the architectural historian J.G. Davies calls "paths" and "places." A path, exemplified by a nave, an aisle, or a labyrinth, has edges, direction, and destination, and suggests a journey or a quest. A place, by contrast, is a concentration or focal point, a non-directional point of rest, such as the interior of the prayer-hall of a mosque. The alternation of path and place is fundamental to the rhythm of a building— for example, movement along a path may lead the worshiper to a still center for contemplation.

Davies also explains how sacred buildings are "mass-positive", "surface-positive," and "space-positive", according to how far they stress these three aspects. Architectural traditions vary in their emphasis on each of these and buildings may combine mass, surface, and space in numerous ways. A building that emphasizes mass has a sculptural quality, as exemplified by a Greek temple such as the Parthenon, where it is the solid elements that are important rather than the voids in between. Such a mass-positive building invites experience through touch and its essence is revealed on a plan by the solid lines and dots which represent the walls and columns.

A surface-positive building accentuates the planes that bound the building's internal space, as in the solid facades of the Egyptian temple. The result may feel somewhat two-dimensional, but such surfaces often carry highly elaborate decoration with tiles or sculpted reliefs.

A space-positive building captures space or volume in a special way and makes effective use of all three dimensions. Perhaps the supreme example is the Byzantine dome, which can appear to hover almost weightlessly over the hall beneath. The essence of such a building lies not so much in the walls and columns, but in the gaps between them.

Height and light

A repeated theme in monumental sacred architecture is the struggle to create large internal spaces and give them height—to produce something similar to the archetypal cave, but reaching into the sky. This has traditionally been achieved according to two main technical principles, which may be called static and dynamic.

The static is based on the lintel, architrave, and corbel. Involving the use of uprights and crossbeams, this is the simplest technique, and the earliest in every tradition, especially where wood for beams was plentiful. It is found in the Egypt of the pharaohs, in classical Greece, in India before the Muslims, in the wooden temples of Japan and China, and in most Mesoamerican architecture. In the simplest trabeate, or post-and-beam system, horizontal beams with their downward force are held in place by the upward thrust of posts or columns. All architecture with columns is based on this principle, or imitates it. The width of an interior space is limited because a beam cannot stretch far without needing the support of a pillar.

The dynamic technique uses a principle of thrust and counter-thrust based on the arch, vault, or dome. It was sometimes used where timber was not available, as in the igloo of the Arctic regions or the mudbrick buildings of ancient Mesopotamia. But the large-scale arch and dome in stone originated in the Hellenistic (late Greek) and Roman periods, from where they later spread into most Christian and Islamic regions and styles. The arch can span a wider distance than a beam can because its rise generates horizontal as well as vertical forces, so that some of its weight is transferred to its central point and the two curves of the arch support each other.

Where the arch is continued for some depth, forming a ceiling, this is called a vault. Where it is rotated on itself through 360 degrees, the result is the dome, which resembles the way that humans perceive the sky. As well as representing a distinctive technical achievement, in the Mediterranean and Middle Eastern regions the dome is appropriate for the sacred architecture of those areas because both Christianity and Islam conceive of the sky as the residence of God.

In building a dome the technical problems of how to support it must be overcome, as must the theological challenge of how to emphasize its significance as a model of the heavens. For all its engineering accomplishment, the dome of the Pantheon in Rome was simply a lid on a cylindrical building. The later dome of

Byzantine churches was conceived in a more subtle way as a baldachin—a hemispherical canopy like an umbrella. It was supported on four columns, which linked the circular dome to the square base of the building beneath. The dome dominates and defines the shape of the interior space overall, so that the walls in between the four supports become insubstantial, almost like curtains—or even optional. The emphasis is not on mass or surface, but on space itself, which seems to radiate down from a hovering dome, just as in Christian theology Heaven descends to Earth.

The baldachin serves to show how ornamentation in a sacred building is not just decoration for its own sake, but grows out of the very form of the building. The Byzantine dome is often supported on four pendentives. The pendentive is a curved triangle at the point where the dome meets its supporting pillars. It appears to be caught up in the spherical movement of the dome above it, giving a smooth transition from the dome down into the square base of the space beneath. At the same time, the pendentive provides a tapering surface that is ideally suited to the display of painted or mosaic figures, and in the Byzantine church it became the conventional location for images of the four evangelists. The interior walls of the Byzantine church are largely covered with paintings or mosaics to fit the contours of the building, so that, as in the mosque, ornamentation is inseparable from structure.

The Gothic style, which developed in France in the twelfth century and spread through most of western Europe, strives toward a similar effect but achieves it in a very different way. Both Gothic and Byzantine aimed to make walls more insubstantial, so that the building would emphasize space more than mass or surface. In each case, the engineering solution gave a different twist to the architectural expression of Christian theology. In the Byzantine cathedral, Heaven descends from the dome; in the Gothic, the gaze is swept upward to the forest of peaks where all vertical lines seem to meet.

Whereas domes and circular arches are limited in size to their circumference, the pointed Gothic arch can reach any height, so that the sense of movement begins from the very bottom. Whereas the Byzantine overcomes the solidity of walls by using pendentives so that the dome appears to float in space, the Gothic makes walls thinner and breaks them up into bays through the use of buttresses. These remove part of the load-bearing mass to the exterior of the building and allow the height of the nave to reach more than three times its width.

In the Byzantine style, windows around the base of the dome are often used as the main source of light, to enhance the

heavenly effect. In the Gothic cathedral, however, the gaps that buttresses make possible in the outside wall are used for windows that flood the interior with colored light.

Building with huge stones

Some of the largest sacred monuments were constructed with the most basic technology. The details of the techniques often remain unknown, but the effort required to build them is testimony to the faith and determination of their builders.

At Stonehenge in England, sandstone boulders (known as sarsens) were brought from 20 miles (35 km) away, probably pulled on sledges or wooden rollers. Once arrived, they were prepared using stone hammers. The lintels were slightly curved on the inside so that when they were joined they formed a complete circle; each was fixed to its neighbor by a V-shaped groove. Owing to the slope of the site, the height of the uprights was graded so as to make the circle of lintels horizontal.

The raising of these massive stones suggests extensive previous experience. The uprights were probably maneuvered into place by ropes and levers, with the base of each stone levered into its hole and the whole stone hauled upright. Raising the lintels was much more difficult. They were probably moved gradually up a scaffolding, with logs used as levers underneath to raise them at alternate ends.

In Egypt the builders of the pyramids relied on similar techniques. Massive blocks of stone were floated downriver when the Nile was in flood and hauled on sledges for the remaining short distances. These sledges were pulled along either on top of log rollers, or over ground on which water had been poured to reduce friction.

The stones had to be raised to an enormous height, and this too was accomplished entirely by human muscle-power. The great pyramids at Giza were built from the bottom up and finished from the top down. The core of the pyramid was built in steps, like the earlier step pyramids. Stones were hauled from one step to the next up ramps of earth and brick. Each course of stones was laid on a square platform and itself provided the square base for the next course. The pyramid was finished with a granite capstone. The outer surface was made of gleaming white limestone, of which only a little survives today, at the top of Khafre's pyramid. The outer casing stones were held together by matching joints which seem to have been carved on the ground beforehand. The joints were coated in mortar before the sloping stones were maneuvered into position. Finally, the blocks were dressed layer by layer downward from the top and the ramps were dismantled.

Glossary

Akkadians Semitic people who were established in northern Sumer (in Mesopotamia) by the middle of the third millennium BCE and subsequently occupied the whole of Sumer.

ambulatory a walkway around the apse of a church or around a shrine; the covered walk of a cloister.

Animism the belief, especially in various non-Western cultures, that all objects, animate and inanimate, possess a living spirit essence.

apse a vaulted semicircular alcove, such as at the end of a Roman basilica or behind the sanctuary of a Christian church.

architrave a main beam laid across pillars, used in classical architecture.

Assyria an ancient empire in northern Mesopotamia that at its height reached Egypt and the Mediterranean; it fell in 612BCE.

axis a notional line, often vertical, about which parts of a building are arranged.

Babylonia the region of southern Mesopotamia, including Sumer and Akkad, of which Babylon was chief city between c.1850 and c.300BCE.

baldachin a hemispherical ceremonial canopy usually above an altar; a dome in the form of such.

barrel vault an arched ceiling or roof forming half a cylinder.

barrows earthen burial mounds constructed in a wide variety of shapes and sizes; they often contain stone passages and chambers.

basilica in Roman architecture, a large meeting-hall, usually rectangular, lit by a clerestory; the form was taken up in early Christian churches.

Bronze Age the period in which bronze was the primary material used to make tools and weapons (in Asia during the third and second millennia BCE and in Europe during the second and early first millennia BCE).

buttress a projecting structure, usually masonry, that strengthens or supports a wall or building.

capital the top part of a column.

cathedral the principal church in a bishop's diocese, containing his throne (cathedra).

ceques in Inca belief, sacred straight "lines" radiating from the Sun Temple at Cuzco, along which *huacas* were found.

chaitya an Indian Buddhist temple—often a cave-temple carved out of a cliff, with aisles, and decorated with sculpture.

chancel the area around the main altar in a church, often containing seats for the choir and reserved for the clergy and choir; see also sanctuary.

clerestory an upper section of a wall, containing windows that admit light to a hall; see also basilica.

cloister a covered, arcaded passage surrounding a courtyard, often linking a church and a monastery.

corbel a projection of wood or masonry (often stepped) from a vertical wall, supporting a weight.

cosmogram a diagram of the structure of the world or universe.

Cybele Anatolian Mother Goddess who was celebrated in Rome during fertility rites at the spring equinox.

Demeter ancient Greek nature goddess, responsible for the fruitfulness of the Earth, and agriculture; she and her daughter Persephone were grain goddesses.

Devi "the Goddess", the supreme female deity of Hinduism; her many aspects function as discrete goddesses, such as Parvati, the wife of Shiva, and the fierce and terrible Kali.

dolmen a prehistoric tomb made of large upright stones topped with a horizontal stone, and originally buried under a mound of earth.

flying buttress a sloping or arched buttress, typical Gothic architecture, in which the outward thrust of the upper part of a wall is transferred to the lower support of the buttress.

Gaia in Greek mythology, the primal goddess embodying the Earth.

gopuram in southern India, a tower-gateway of a temple.

henge large, upright stones or posts set in a circle, such as Stonehenge.

huaca in Inca belief, a land feature imbued with mythic significance and supernatural power.

hypostyle hall a large hall with a flat roof supported by pillars, especially in ancient Egyptian architecture.

Ishtar in Babylonian and Assyrian mythology, the goddess of love, sexuality and fertility; associated with many earth goddesses.

Isis in Egyptian mythology, an Earth and fertility goddess, the sister and wife of Osiris.

Kali in Hindu mythology, the great warrior goddess and enemy of demons; usually represented with symbols of life and death.

Khnum an Egyptian creator god said to have fashioned people and deities on a potter's wheel.

lintel a horizontal beam or stone over an opening, usually carrying the weight of the wall above it

mandala in Hinduism, Buddhism, and Jainism, a stylized diagram of the universe based on a circle and a square, used as a meditational device and as the ground-plan for temples.

manitou an Algonquian term describing the all-pervading divine spirit.

"medicine wheel" a prehistoric arrangement of stones and boulders found on the North American plains and prairies, with an outer "rim" and radiating "spokes."

megalith any prehistoric, massive, undressed block of stone of the kind widely erected in northwest Europe from c.3200–c.1500BCE, for building, or on its own as a monument.

menhir a single upright monumental stone, dating from prehistoric times.

Mesopotamia the region, largely in Iraq, between and adjacent to the rivers Tigris and Euphrates, where the Sumerian, Akkadian, Babylonian, and Assyrian civilizations developed.

mihrab a niche in the wall of a mosque or other Muslim building, facing Mecca and indicating the direction of prayer.

minaret the high narrow tower of a mosque used for calling the faithful to prayer.

Mount Meru in Hindu, Buddhist and Jain belief, the axis of the cosmos—a mountain at the center of the world, often believed to link different layers of the universe.

nave the main, longitudinal body of a Christian church from the western entrance to the transept.

Neolithic the last period of the Stone Age. It lasted in Europe from about 6,000 to 4,500 years ago and in southwest Asia from about 11,000 to 8,000 years ago. The earliest organized agriculture dates from this period.

pagoda a Far Eastern development of the Buddhist *stupa*, consisting of a tower with several stories usually diminishing in size as they ascend.

passage-grave a prehistoric tomb in the form of a roofed stone corridor buried under an earth mound.

Paleolithic Age literally "Old Stone Age." The period characterized by the use of rudimentary chipped stone tools, from 2.5 million years ago until the beginning of the Mesolithic period ("Middle Stone Age"), c.8,500BCE. The Middle Paleolithic began approximately 200,000 years ago; the Upper Paleolithic, 35,000 years ago.

pediment the triangular end of the pitched roof of a Greek temple or other building.

puja in Hinduism, Buddhism, and Jainism, the ritual of worship and offering.

pylon the massive gateway to an ancient Egyptian temple, comprising pairs of rectangular, truncated towers with sloping walls, on either side of the entrance.

reredos an ornamental screen of wood or stone behind a Christian altar, often used to display paintings or carvings.

sanctuary the sacred area around the main altar of a Christian church; see also chancel.

shaman a ritual specialist who contacts the spirits and communes with them in order to cure, divine, or send magical illness. An important figure in tribal society in Asia, the Americas, and parts of Africa.

shikhara a tower or spire of a Hindu temple, often tapering.

Shiva in Hindu mythology, a great god of nature and fertility who embodies the contrary forces of destruction and rebirth; his symbol is the *lingam*, or erect phallus.

step pyramid an early pyramid ascending in stepped terraces to a flat top.

stupa a domed or pointed structure containing relics or marking a holy site, as a Buddhist memorial.

Sumerians a non-Semitic people who established a civilization in southern Mesopotamia during the fourth millennium BCE and developed the first writing, cities and law codes; they were superseded by the Akkadians.

Tiamat in Akkadian mythology, the primal female monster who gave birth to the gods; she was slain by the god Marduk; one half of her became the sky and the other the Earth.

trabeate an early type of construction using upright posts and horizontal lintels rather than arches or vaults; used for example in Egyptian and Greek temples.

transept the transverse arms of a Latin-cross church, usually shorter than the main hall formed by the nave, sanctuary and apse.

triglyph in a Doric temple, a panel with three vertical grooves.

vault an arched ceiling or roof.

yin and *yang* in Chinese thought, the female-male principle of the balanced complementariness of opposites.

yurt a single-roomed dwelling of the native peoples of Central Asia, usually round or polygonal in shape, easily movable, and with a central smoke-hole in the roof.

ziggurat a pyramidal Babylonian temple-tower in the form of a step-pyramid.

Bibliography

Allen, J. and Griffiths, J. *The Book of the Dragon*, Charwell Books, Secaucus, New Jersey/Orbis Publishing, London: 1979

Ashe, G. *Mythology of the British Isles*, Methuen, London/Trafalgar Square Publishing, North Pomfret, Vermont: 1990

Aveni, A.F. *Skywatchers of Ancient Mexico*, University of Texas, Austin and London: 1980

Aveni, A.F. (ed.) *World Archaeoastronomy*, Cambridge University Press, Cambridge, England, and New York (NY): 1989

Bierhorst, J. *The Mythology of North America*, William Morrow, NY: 1985

Bierhorst, J. *The Mythology of South America*, William Morrow, NY: 1988

Bierhorst, J. *The Mythology of Mexico and Central America*, William Morrow, NY: 1990

Bloomer, K.C. and Moore C.W. *Body, Memory and Architecture*, Yale University Press, New Haven: 1977

Braunfels, W. *Monasteries of Western Europe: the architecture of the orders*, Princeton University Press, Princeton, and Thames and Hudson, London: 1972

Brown, P. *Indian Architecture*, (2 volumes), Taraporevala, Bombay: 1956

Burl, A. *The Stone Circles of the British Isles*, Yale University Press, New Haven, Connecticut, and London: 1976

Burl, A. *Prehistoric Avebury*, Yale University Press, New Haven: 1979

Burl, A. *From Carnac to Callanish*, Yale University Press, New Haven, Connecticut, and London: 1993

Carrasco, D. (ed.) *To Change Place, Aztec Ceremonial Landscapes*, University Press of Colorado, Niwot, Colorado: 1991

Chippindale, C. *Stonehenge Complete*, Cornell University Press, Ithaca, NY: 1983

Daniel, G.E. *The Megalith Builders of Western Europe*, Hutchinson, London: 1958

Davies, J.G. *Temples, Churches and Mosques: a guide to the appreciation of religious architecture*, Blackwell, Oxford: 1982

Davies, J.G. *The Secular Use of Church Buildings*, S.C.M., London: 1968

de Groot, J.J.M. *Chinese Geomancy*, Element, Shaftesbury, Dorset: 1989

Edwards, I.E.S. *The Pyramids of Egypt*, Penguin, Harmondsworth: 1947

Eliade, M. (ed.) *Encyclopedia of Religion*, (16 volumes), Macmillan: NY, 1986

Fakhry, A. *The Pyramids*, (2nd edn) University of Chicago Press, Chicago and London: 1969

Fontenrose, J. *The Delphic Oracle*, University of California Press, Berkeley, California, and London: 1978

Fox, M.V. (ed.) *Temple in Society*, Eisenbrauns, Winona Lake: 1988

Gasparini, G. and Margolies, L. *Inca Architecture*, (Lyon, P. trans.) Indiana University Press, Bloomington, Indiana, and London: 1980

Germann, G. *Gothic Revival in Europe and Britain*, Lund Humphries, London: 1972

Gimpel, J. *The Cathedral Builders*, Pimlico, London: 1993

Godwin, J. *Mystery Religions in the Ancient World*, Harper and Row, San Francisco/Thames and Hudson, London: 1981

Grant, C. *Canyon de Chelly, Its People and Rock Art*, University of Arizona Press, Tucson, Arizona:1978

Griffin-Pierce, T. *Earth is My Mother, Sky is My Father: Space, Time and Astronomy in Navajo Sandpainting*, University of New Mexico Press, Albuquerque: 1992

Gutmann, J. (ed.) *The Synagogue: studies in origins, archaeology and architecture*, Ktav, NY: 1975

Hadingham, E. *Lines to the Mountain Gods, Nazca and the Mysteries of Peru*, Harrap, London/Random House, NY: 1987

Haran, M. *Temples and Temple-service in Ancient Israel*, Clarendon, Oxford: 1978

Hastings, J. (ed.) *Encyclopedia of Religion and Ethics*, (13 volumes), Clark, Edinburgh: 1908–26

Hawkes, J. *Atlas of Ancient Archaeology*, McGraw Hill, NY

Heggie, D.C. *Megalithic Science*, Thames and Hudson, London: 1981

Hemming, J. and Ranney, E. *Monuments of the Incas*, Little, Brown & Co, Boston: 1982

Heyden, D. and Gendrop, P. *Pre-Columbian Architecture of Mesoamerica*, Abrams, NY: 1975

Heydenreich, L.H. and Lotz, W. *Architecture in Italy 1400–1600*, Penguin, Harmondsworth: 1974

Hultkrantz, A. *The Religions of the American Indians*, (Setterwall, M., trans.) University of California Press, Berkeley, California, and London: 1979

Huntley, H.E. *The Divine Proportion*, Dover, NY: 1970

Isaacs, J. *Arts of the Dreaming, Australia's Living Heritage*, Lansdowne, Sydney: 1984

James, E.O. *From Cave to Cathedral: temples and shrines of prehistoric, classical and early times*, Thames and Hudson, London: 1965

Joralemon, D. and Douglas, S. *Sorcery and Shamanism, Curanderos and Clients in Northern Peru*, University of Utah Press, Salt Lake City, Utah: 1993

Joussaume, R. *Dolmens for the Dead*, (Chippindale A. and C., trans.) Batsford, London, 1987/Cornell University Press, Ithaca, NY: 1988

Korp, M. *The Sacred Geography of the American Mound Builders*, Edwin Mellen Press, Lewiston, NY, and Lampeter, Wales: 1990

Kostof, S.A. *A History of Architecture: settings and rituals*, Oxford University Press, Oxford: 1995

Kramrisch, S. *The Hindu Temple*, (2 volumes), University of Calcutta, Calcutta: 1946

Krautheimer, R. *Early Christian and Byzantine Architecture*, Penguin, Harmondsworth: 1965

Kuban, D. *Muslim Religious Architecture: the mosque and its early development*, Brill, Leiden: 1974

Laude, J. *African Art of the Dogon, the Myths of the Cliff Dwellers*, (Neugroschel, J., trans.) The Brooklyn Museum and Viking Press, NY: 1973

Lawlor, R. *Sacred Geometry*, Thames and Hudson, London: 1992

Lawrence, A.W. *Greek Architecture*, Penguin, Harmondsworth: 1984

Layton, R. *Australian Rock Art*, Cambridge University Press, Cambridge and NY: 1992

Lethaby, W. *Architecture, Mysticism and Myth*, Architectural Press, London: 1974 (first edition 1891)

Lundquist, J.M. *The Temple: meeting place of heaven and earth*, Thames and Hudson, London: 1993

Lyle, E. (ed.) *Sacred Architecture in the Traditions of India, China, Judaism and Islam*, Edinburgh University Press, Edinburgh: 1992

McGaa, E. *Mother Earth Spirituality*, Harper and Row, San Francisco and London: 1990

Mann, A.T. *Sacred Architecture*, Element, Shaftesbury, England: 1993

Meletzis, S and Papadakis, H. *Delphi, Sanctuary and Museum* (Freeson, R.C. trans.) Schnell and Steiner, Munich /Argonaut, Chicago: 1967

Meyer, J.F. *Peking as a Sacred City*, Chinese Association for Folklore, Taipei: 1976

Michell, G. (ed.) *Architecture of the Islamic World*, Thames and Hudson, London: 1978

Mirsky, J. *Houses of God*, Constable, London, 1965

Moon, B. (ed.) *An Encyclopedia of Archetypal Symbolism Shambhala Publications*, Boston, Massachusetts and London: 1991

Morgan, L.H. *Houses and House Life of the American Aborigines*, Chicago University Press, Chicago: 1965 (first edition 1881)

Morphy, H. (ed.) *Animals Into Art*, Unwin Hyman, London and Boston: 1989

Mus, P. *Barabudur: esquisse d'une histoire du bouddhisme fondée sur la critique archéologique des textes*, (2 volumes), Arno Press, NY: 1978 (1st edition 1935)

Nabokov, P. and Easton, R. *Native American Architecture*, Oxford University Press, NY and Oxford: 1989

Nitschke, G. "Building the sacred mountain: Tsukuriyama in Shinto tradition", in John Einarsen (ed.) *The Sacred Mountains of Asia*, Shambhala, Boston and London: 1995

Norberg-Schultz, C. *Existence, Space and Architecture*, Praeger, NY: 1971

Nuttgens, P. *The Story of Architecture*, Phaidon, Oxford: 1983

O'Kelly, M.J. *Early Ireland*, Cambridge University Press, Cambridge and NY: 1989

Oliver, P. *Dwellings: the house across the world*, Oxford, Phaidon: 1987

Paine, R.T. and Soper, A. *The Art and Architecture of Japan*, Penguin, Harmondsworth: 1975

Parish, S.M. *Moral Knowing in a Hindu Sacred City*, Columbia University Press, NY: 1994

Pevsner, N. *An Outline of European Architecture*, Penguin, Harmondsworth: 1960

Piggott, S. *The Druids*, Thames and Hudson, London: 1985

Purce, J., *The Mystic Spiral: journey of the soul*, Thames and Hudson, London: 1974

Renfrew, C. (ed.) *The Megalithic Monuments of Western Europe*, Thames and Hudson, London: 1983

Ringis, R. *Thai Temples and Temple Murals*, Oxford University Press, Singapore: 1990

Roux, G. *Ancient Iraq*, Penguin, Harmondsworth: 1975

Ruspoli, M. *The Cave of Lascaux* (Wormell, S., trans.) Thames and Hudson, London/Harry N. Abrams, NY: 1987

Scully, V. *The Earth, the Temple and the Gods, Greek Sacred Architecture* (revised ed.), Yale University Press, New Haven, Connecticut, and London: 1979

Silverberg, R. *Mound Builders of Ancient America*, NY Graphic Society, Greenwich, Connecticut: 1968

Smith, B. *The Dome: a study in the history of ideas*, Princeton University Press, Princeton: 1978

Smith, W.S. *The Art and Architecture of Ancient Egypt*, Harmondsworth, Penguin: 1971

Soper, A. *The Evolution of Buddhist Architecture in Japan*, Princeton University Press, Princeton: 1942

Stein, B. (ed.) *The South Indian Temple*, Vikas, New Delhi: 1978

Stierlin, H. *Encyclopedia of World Architecture*, (2 volumes), Macmillan, London: 1977

Stierlin, H. *The Art of the Maya*, Macmillan, London: 1981

Stockel, H.H. *Survival of the Spirit, Chiricahua Apaches in Captivity*, University of Nevada Press, Reno, Nevada, and London: 1993

Sullivan, M. *The Cave Temples of Maichishan*, University of California Press, Berkeley, California: 1969

Thacker, C. *The History of Gardens*, Croom Helm, London/University of California Press, Berkeley, California: 1979

Tompkins, P. *Mysteries of the Mexican Pyramids*, Thames and Hudson, London: 1976

Tompkins, P. *Secrets of the Great Pyramid*, Harper and Row, NY, 1971

Townsend, R.F. (ed.) *The Ancient Americas, Art from Sacred Landscapes*, The Art Institute of Chicago, Chicago/Prestel Verlag, Munich: 1992

Tucci, G. *The Theory and Practice of the Mandala*, Rider, London: 1961

Turner, H.W. *From Temple to Meeting House: the phenomenology and theology of places of worship*, Mouton, The Hague, 1979

Ucko, P.J. and Rosenfeld, A. *Palaeolithic Cave Art*, Weidenfeld & Nicolson, London: 1987

Ucko, P.J., Hunter, M., Clark and A.J., David, A. *Avebury Reconsidered From the 1660s to the 1990s*, Unwin Hyman, London and Boston, Massachusetts: 1991

Vale, L.J. *Architecture, Power and National Identity*, Yale University Press, New Haven: 1992

Vitebsky, P. *Dialogues with the Dead: the discussion of mortality among the Sora of eastern India*, Cambridge University Press, Cambridge: 1993

von Simson, O. *The Gothic Cathedral: origins of Gothic architecture and the medieval concept of order*, Bollingen, Princeton: 1988

Wheeler, M. *Roman Art and Architecture*, Thames and Hudson, London, 1964

Whitehouse, R.D. (ed.) *Dictionary of Archaeology*, Macmillan, London/Facts on File Publications, NY: 1983

Willcox, A.R. *The Rock Art of Africa*, Croom Helm, London/Holmes and Meier, NY: 1984

Willis, R.G. (gen. ed.) *World Mythology*, Simon and Schuster, London/Holt, NY: 1993

Index

Picture Credits

The publisher would like to thank the following people, museums, and photographic libraries for permission to reproduce their material. Every care has been taken to trace copyright holders. However, if we have omitted anyone we apologize and will, if informed, make corrections in any future edition.

t = top
c = center
b = bottom
l = left
r = right

Archiv fur Kunst und Geschichte, London = AKG
Bridgeman Art Library, London/New York = BAL
British Library = BL
British Museum, London = BM
Images Colour Library, London = Images
Robert Harding Picture Library = RHPL
gettyone Stone = Stone
Science Photo Library = SPL
Victoria & Albert Museum, London = V&A
Werner Forman Archive, London = WFA

Page 1 John Cleare Mountain Camera; 2–3 Images; 4l RHPL/Adam Woolfitt; 4r Stone/Paul Wakefield; 5l Robert Estall Photo Agency/Bob Croxford; 5r Axiom/Chris Caldicott; 6–7 Stone/Kevin Schafer; 9 G. Dagli Orti.; 10–11 Stone/Tom Till; 13 The Stockmarket; 14 SPL/ESA/PLI; 15 SPL/ Keith Kent; 16–17 South American Pictures/ Kathy Jarvis; 18 Mick Sharp; 19 WFA/Private Collection; 20–21 Hutchison Library; 22 Corbis; 23 the art archive/San Zeno Cathedral, Verona; 24–25 SuperStock; 26 Images; 28 Hutchison Library/Mary Jelliffe; 29 Hutchison Library/Mary Jelliffe; 30 Ancient Art & Architecture/Lonne Sower; 32–33 Stone/Paul Chesley; 34 BAL/ Bibliotheque Nationale, Paris; 37 RHPL/Corrigan; 38–39 Michael Holford/BL; 40 Barnaby's Picture Library/D. McLaughlin; 41 RHPL/David Beatty; 43 Sonia Halliday Photographs; 44 Hutchison Library/Keith Job; 46 Hutchison Library/ Mary Jelliffe; 48 Images; 49 Robert Estall Photo Agency/ David Coulson; 50 Colorphoto Hinz/Allschwil-Basel; 51t Colorphoto Hinz; 51b Colorphoto Hinz; 53 Hutchison Library/Keith Job; 54–55 Images; 56 Jean-Loup Charmet; 57 Max Milligan; 59 RHPL/Adam Woolfitt; 60 Axiom/James Morris; 61l Hutchison Library/B.Regent; 61r Sonia Halliday Photographs; 63 RHPL/Tony Gervis; 64 RHPL/Michael Jenner; 66–67 RHPL/Adam

Woolfitt; 68 Hutchison Library/ Jon Burbank; 69t Images; 69b Mick Sharp; 70 Stone; 71 BAL/BL; 72 RHPL; 74–75 John Cleare Mountain Camera; 77 RHPL/Duncan Maxwell; 78 Images; 80–81 Images; 82 Hutchison Library/Juliet Highet; 84–85 The Stockmarket; 86 Michael Holford/BM; 87 Mick Sharp; 88 RHPL/Geoff Renner; 90–91 Mick Sharp/Jean Williamson; 92–93 V&A; 94 the art archive/Biblioteca Estense, Modena; 95 Mick Sharp; 96 Bath Archaeological Trust; 97t Mick Sharp/Roman Baths Museum; 97b Bath Archaeological Trust; 98 Michael Holford; 100 Stone/David Sutherland; 101t RHPL; 101b Axiom/Frances Bacon; 102–103 Stone/Paul Wakefield; 104–105 Bryan and Cherry Alexander; 106 South American Pictures/Tony Morrison; 109 Robert Estall Photo Agency/Bob Croxford; 110l McClung Museum, The University of Tennessee; 110r Network Photographers/Georg Gerster; 111t Ohio Historical Society; 111b BAL/Private Collection; 112–113 Fortean Picture Library/Klaus Aarsleff; 114 SPL/Bill Bachman; 115 SPL/Pekka Parviainen; 117 Wellcome Institute; 118 RHPL; 121 BAL/Louvre, Paris; 124–125 Tibet Images/Ian Cumming; 127 BAL/Oriental Museum, Durham University; 128l RHPL; 128r The Stockmarket; 129 RHPL; 130 RHPL/Adam Woolfitt; 133 RHPL/Adam Woolfitt; 134 Max Milligan; 135 Max Milligan; 138 RHPL/Adam Woolfitt; 139 Skyscan Balloon Photography; 140–141 Mick Sharp/Jean Williamson; 142 Spectrum Colour Library; 143t RHPL/Robert Frerck; 143b Spectrum Colour Library; 144–145 Stone/Jerry Alexander; 147 RHPL; 148–149 Graham Harrison; 150 AKG; 151t BAL; 151b The Stockmarket; 153 RHPL/AdinaTovey; 154 Royal Asiatic Society, London; 155t Axiom/Jim Holmes; 155b Spectrum Colour Library; 156 RHPL; 157 A. F. Kersting; 158 TRIP/F. Good; 159t TRIP/F. Good; 159b TRIP/F. Good; 160–161 Graham Harrison; 162 Spectrum Colour Library; 163t Spectrum ColourLibrary; 163b Spectrum Colour Library; 165 The Stockmarket; 166 Spectrum Colour Library; 167t Stone/ Richard A Cooke; 167b Chris Caldicott; 169 Sonia Halliday Photographs; 170 RHPL/ Roy Rainford; 171t RHPL/Roy Rainford; 171b Michael Holford/BM; 172 TRIP/H. Rogers; 174 The Stockmarket; 175 TRIP/Dinodia; 178 Spectrum Colour Library; 179t Spectrum Colour Library; 179b South American Pictures/ Robert Francis; 181 The Stockmarket; 182l South American Pictures/Tony Morrison; 182r South American Pictures/Tony Morrison; 183t RHPL/

Christopher Rennie; 183b South American Pictures/Tony Morrison; 184–185 RHPL/Robert Frerck; 186 Hutchison Library/Tim Beddow; 188 Stone/Nabeel Turner; 189t Stone/Nabeel Turner; 189b Ancient Art & Architecture/Ronald Sheridan; 191 A. F. Kersting; 192 The Stockmarket; 193t Panos Pictures/Jeremy Horner; 193b Axiom/Chris Coe; 194 Skyscan Balloon Photography/Edmund Naegele; 196–197 Tibet Images/Ian Cumming; 198–199 John Cleare Mountain Camera; 201 Hutchison Library/Mary Jelliffe; 202–203 Tibet Images/Ian Cumming; 204 Corbis/Raymond Gehman; 205t Corbis/Raymond Gehman; 205b Corbis/Gunter Marx; 206–207 Panos Pictures/Ray Wood; 208 Michael Holford; 209t Axiom/Dorian Shaw; 209b RHPL/Christina Gascoigne; 210 RHPL; 212–213 Axiom/Chris Caldicott; 215 Stone/Glen Allison; 216 Tibet Images/Ian Cumming; 218 RHPL/Robert Francis; 219 Angelo Hornak/Courtsey of the Dean and Chapter of Canterbury Cathedral, Canterbury, Kent; 222 RHPL/Jeremy Bright; 224–225 Angelo Hornak; 226–227 RHPL/Gavin Hellier; 228 RHPL/Robert Frerck; 230 Panos Pictures/Jean-Leo Dugast; 231t Bruce Coleman Collection/Gerald S. Cubitt; 231b The Stockmarket; 233 DBP/Private Collection; 234 RHPL/Adam Woolfitt; 235t RHPL/Adam Woolfitt; 235b RHPL/Adam Woolfitt; 237 Royal Geographical Society/Dr Stephen Coyne; 238–239 Stone/Olaf Soot; 240 RHPL/John Ross; 241t Chris Caldicott; 241b Chris Caldicott; 243 Stone/Richard Passmore

Prelim captions
Page 1: Inscribed prayer stones, Nepal.
Pages 2–3: Thor's Hammer, Bryce Canyon, Utah.
Pages 4–5: (left to right), caves and rock formations of Cappadocia, Anatolia; Lough Conn, Mayo, Ireland; the White Horse at Uffington, Oxfordshire, England; the Nabatean "monastery" at Petra, Jordan.